Ideas *Without* Boundaries

International Education Reform Through Reading and Writing for Critical Thinking

David J. Klooster
Hope College
Holland, Michigan, USA

Jeannie L. Steele
University of
Northern Iowa
Cedar Falls, Iowa, USA

Patricia L. Bloem
Grand Valley
State University
Allendale, Michigan, USA

Editors

INTERNATIONAL
Reading
Association

800 Barksdale Road, PO Box 8139
Newark, Delaware 19714-8139, USA
www.reading.org

T 40989

LA-P
Id23
2001

The International Reading Association attempts, through its publications, to provide a forum for a wide spectrum of opinions on reading. This policy permits divergent viewpoints without implying the endorsement of the Association.

Director of Publications   Joan M. Irwin
Editorial Director, Books and Special Projects   Matthew W. Baker
Special Projects Editor   Tori Mello Bachman
Permissions Editor   Janet S. Parrack
Associate Editor   Jeanine K. McGann
Production Editor   Shannon Benner
Editorial Assistant   Pamela McComas
Publications Coordinator   Beth Doughty
Production Department Manager   Iona Sauscermen
Art Director   Boni Nash
Senior Electronic Publishing Specialist   Anette Schütz-Ruff
Electronic Publishing Specialist   Cheryl J. Strum
Electronic Publishing Assistant   John W. Cain

Project Editor   Tori Mello Bachman

Photo Credits   David J. Klooster, p. 1; David Landis, p. 49; Hana Jandová, p. 129; Jill Lewis, p. 165

Library of Congress Cataloging-in-Publication Data
Ideas without boundaries : international education reform through reading and writing for critical thinking / David J. Klooster, Jeannie Steele, Patricia L. Bloem, editors.
    p.   cm.
    Collection of articles from participants in the Reading and Writing for Critical Thinking Project (RWCT); a long-term, multinational school-restructuring project.
    Includes bibliographical references and index.
    ISBN 0-87207-285-1
    1. Reading and Writing for Critical Thinking Project.   2. School improvement programs—Cross-cultural studies.   3. Educational change—Cross-cultural studies.   4. Educational exchanges.   5. Teacher exchange programs.   I. Title: International education reform through reading and writing for critical thinking.   II. Klooster, David J.   III. Steele, Jeannie L.   IV. Bloem, Patricia L.
LB2822.8.I34   2000
371.2—dc21   00-046132
Printed in Canada

DEDICATION

We dedicate this book to teachers everywhere who work to build open societies and democratic cultures, especially the extraordinary volunteers, host country leaders, and participating teachers of the Reading and Writing for Critical Thinking project.

CONTENTS

SECTION I: Goals and Contexts for Educational Reform

SECTION II: How Teachers and Students Change

SECTION III: How Practices and Paradigms Change

SECTION IV: Lessons for Educational Reform From the RWCT Project

Ideas Without Boundaries was conceived on a sweltering June day in 1997, on the verandah of a conference hotel overlooking Lake Balaton in Hungary. One hundred and twenty educators from nine former socialist countries, along with volunteers and project organizers from the United States and Canada, had gathered to launch a new school improvement project called Reading and Writing for Critical Thinking (RWCT). At the end of the second day of the meeting, energized by terrific workshops and inspired by our impressive new colleagues from countries that history had hidden from us, three or four participants were comparing notes about what had transpired. All of us felt we were on the verge of something big. The meeting rooms had crackled with energy and wit, and we had watched in awe as a framework for teaching and learning enriched and enlivened by a handful of progressive literacy teaching strategies—such as freewriting, clustering, dual-entry diaries, and small-group discussion—had caught the fancy of teachers from Kazakstan to California, from Albania to Albany, New York. As we experienced together the ways the framework and accompanying classroom strategies led not only to deeper engagement with ideas, but also to the development of critical thinking abilities and changed social relationships within the classroom, we began to catch the vision of the program organizers: "critical thinking," in the broad and flexible definition of this program, would become a powerful educational tool for the development of engaged citizens in democratic societies. The realization was thrilling. "You know," someone said, "this is going to be an amazing experience. We ought to write a book about it." Fortunately, a dozen educators from that first conference accepted the challenge, and now you hold in your hands the results of their experience and inquiry.

Background of the Reading and Writing for Critical Thinking Project

The foundational beliefs and practices of RWCT had successfully supported several school change efforts in the United States. However, it was not certain they could support school change processes elsewhere, though there was reason to believe that the collaborative nature of this model provided room for cultural differences, goal and outcome variations, as well as differing implementation processes. The generalizability of the professional development model across cultures was tested when, in the early 1990s, the Minister of Education for Slovakia came to the United States seeking assistance with school reform. Minister Pišut arrived at the University of Northern Iowa with one daunting question: "How do you teach democracy?" Jeannie Steele, Kurt Meredith, and other colleagues began to meet with educators in Slovakia to begin the process of answering Minister Pišut's question. From the beginning they worked with Slovak education leaders as equal partners. The ensuing collaboration resulted in the Orava Project, a systemic school restructuring effort grounded in literacy-based research on teaching and learning and the principles of school change described in Chapter One of this book.

In lengthy deliberations over Minister Pišut's question, the Orava Project educators concluded that the characteristics of students who are successfully engaged in lifelong learning as well as the applications of knowledge and understanding to their daily lives and work, parallel those characteristics and behaviors that sustain a civil and productive democratic community. These parallel characteristics include the capacity to listen with caring and respect to the perspectives and opinions of others; skill in constructive problem solving; ability to independently form opinions and reflect; the capacity to integrate multiple sources of information; the ability to work collaboratively; the skills to articulate alternative points of view; and the recognition of the essential importance of sharing opinions and participating in the communal construction of knowledge, understanding, and governance.

Fortuitously, in 1995, author and educator Charles Temple conducted an interim evaluation of the Orava Project. This work provided the codirectors of the project, Meredith and Steele, with the opportunity to work as colleagues with Temple. His interim evaluation found that the Orava Project model was effectively reaching across cultures and bringing about real school change.

This collaboration lead to extended discussions about school change in the region as other newly democratic nations were seeking assistance with school restructuring. At the same time Scott Walter, the International Reading Association's Director of International Development, was working with literacy educators throughout the Central European region, focusing on professional development and encouraging literacy educators in the region to rejoin their Western European colleagues in the ongoing dialogue about literacy and learning. As Charles Temple discusses in Chapter Three of this volume, he began to work in cooperation with Scott Walter and the International Reading Association (IRA) to respond to a call for assistance with educators in Romania. This cooperation was funded by the Open Society Foundation in Romania and led to the development of the Reading for Understanding Project. Meredith and Steele joined with Temple and Walter, and their collaboration began in earnest.

Under Temple's direction the Reading for Understanding Project was well-received and again confirmed that educators across vast cultural divides can collaborate to bring about relevant education reform at the classroom level. With examples of successful, collaborative school change in two different countries with different languages and histories, the Soros Foundation took a broader interest in implementing a regional program. Under the guidance of Liz Lorant, who had 17 years of experience in the Open Society Institute's regional programs and working with educators in the region, the RWCT codirectors developed a collaborative multinational school change proposal. Liz Lorant presented the proposal to philanthropist George Soros, understanding critical thinking to be a central concern of Mr. Soros's philanthropic interests in Central Europe. Mr. Soros agreed that indeed critical thinking and independent opinion formation and decision making were key to regional development of open societies, and he gave the project his support.

From this endorsement for critical thinking, the codirectors—Kurt Meredith, Jeannie Steele, Charles Temple, and Scott Walter—along with Liz Lorant discussed what to call this collaborative effort. Drawing from the theme of critical inquiry and the school reform model for effecting cross-curricular and cross-grade level change, it was decided that "reading and writing for critical thinking" best characterized the primary elements and intent of the project. It was also believed, though the word "critical" would later prove to be a troublesome word to translate, especially in Russian, that the "reading and writing for critical thinking" title would resonate with education colleagues in the participating countries.

With funding from Soros's Open Society Institute and continued leadership of Liz Lorant, sponsorship of the International Reading Association in collaboration with the University of Northern Iowa's Office of Education for Democracy, the dream of RWCT became a reality in early summer of 1997 when 120 educators gathered at Lake Balaton to make concrete plans for implementing the program.

Overview of This Volume

The chapters in this book report on the first 3 years of the RWCT project, which has grown markedly in these years—expanding from the original 9 countries to 24, from a first group of 43 U.S. and Canadian volunteers to more than 80, and from a bold dream in the minds of the four codirectors into a major international school reform movement that will affect the lives of hundreds of thousands of school children. Volunteers in the program were recruited from the membership of the International Reading Association (IRA), and thus the majority are professors in schools and departments of education in many of the leading colleges and universities in the United States and Canada. The volunteer ranks also include professors of philosophy and English and a number of elementary classroom teachers. In the second and third years of the program, volunteers from Great Britain and Australia joined as well.

The authors of the chapters in this volume participated in the project from its beginnings in 1997, and thus their writing is based on at least 3 years of observation, conversation, and research. Several of the authors have more extensive experience in school reform projects and progressive teaching methods in Central and Eastern Europe (CEE) and Central Asia (CA), and a sizable number of the chapters included here benefit from coauthorship between the RWCT volunteers and their host country colleagues.

In an attempt to portray the rich human experience of the RWCT project, the chapters employ a wide variety of methodological and structural approaches. Several chapters are mainly descriptive, providing readers with the necessary background and overview to understand what we have done and why. Some chapters examine the historical contexts of various elements of the program. Other chapters employ conventional research methods in posing a researchable question and gathering data for analysis and speculation. Some chapters seek to acquaint readers with a sense of the human dimensions of the project, and these pieces read more like personal essays than research reports. In every case, we have tried to keep the varied needs of our audience of classroom educators in mind, and we hope we have anticipated your interests and questions.

The first three chapters of this book, written by three of the codirectors of the Reading and Writing for Critical Thinking Project, provide a comprehensive overview of the content, approach, and historical setting of the project. Chapter One describes the foundational beliefs and operating principles of the project, and provides a clear description of the content and methods of RWCT workshops. It also summarizes the elements of a model for professional development that has proven to be extraordinarily adaptable and successful in many countries around the world. Chapter Two examines the historical and political contexts of our work with RWCT. This chapter provides readers with an overview of the remarkable events that have led to social, political, and educational reform on a scale unprecedented in human history. The third chapter in this introductory section aims to present a ground-level view of the program—the people, the workshops, the classrooms, the teachers who have transformed RWCT from dream to reality. Together these first three chapters tell the story of how, when, and why RWCT came to be.

The main body of the book examines what RWCT has accomplished by describing changes in teachers and students, and changes in practices and paradigms. Because many of the chapters were written between the second and third years of program operation—a time when authors had sufficient time to observe participating teachers carefully for an extended period but before large-scale studies of student learning were possible—the attention to teacher change is most remarkable. Drawing from the rich data of written records, classroom observations, and interviews, the chapters in Section II describe in detail the ways RWCT has encouraged teachers to reexamine their pedagogical practices and their professional identities. These chapters also investigate some of the challenges inherent in working across cultures. The authors in this section further extend the inquiry by asking how the program has influenced students. As the authors of Chapter Seven remark, educational reforms have seldom bothered to ask students what they think of new programs, and these chapters remedy that oversight by offering abundant commentary through student voices of the ways RWCT has influenced classroom life and has altered student-teacher relationships.

The third section of the book examines the effects of the program on practices and paradigms of education. Two Czech educators who participated in the beginnings of the RWCT program in their country describe how their work in the classroom and school library have changed as a result of the program. Both of these chapters provide a sense of how

RWCT is part of larger influences in education reform in their country. A final chapter in this section explores a conundrum that has been a constant source of productive tension in the program: the American emphasis on pragmatic classroom strategies versus the Eastern European commitment to theory. In a chapter coauthored by U.S. and Russian colleagues, this tension is examined especially as it relates to teacher training programs.

Ideas Without Boundaries closes with two chapters that explore the lessons RWCT volunteers have brought home with them from abroad. Chapter Twelve describes four concrete lessons for educators gleaned from the author's observations in Eastern Europe, and Chapter Thirteen assesses the accomplishments and challenges of the program in its first 3 years, emphasizing the lessons to be learned for large-scale professional development projects.

The RWCT project has become a wellspring of human tales about teaching and changing, about reaching across cultural and language divides to find deep conceptual and interpersonal harmonies. The RWCT project has come to represent a vast and far-reaching network of people whose professional and personal lives have been irreversibly altered by their involvement. For the volunteers who deliver the program to the education leaders of the various participating countries, involvement in RWCT has led to profound changes in how they think about their students, about teaching and learning, and about working with others. The project has changed how they interact with others outside the education community and how they view themselves as educators. These volunteers report that RWCT involvement has contributed enormously to their further professional development. Many also report that their participation has changed their understanding of where they place themselves in the world, their understanding about the critical relationship between literacy and the broader human experience, how they think about problems, and what they now set as priorities for their own lives. For them, RWCT has become a beacon of light in their personal and professional lives, and readers will sense their enthusiasm in the chapters that follow.

We hope this volume will convey that the RWCT project has become a story about teachers and teaching and about the human capacity for joy, risk-taking, and success when cultures meet to bring about positive change. RWCT is about caring and respect—even love—between people who never imagined they would encounter one another.

RWCT PARTICIPANT COUNTRIES

Countries Joining RWCT in 1997:

Albania
Czech Republic
Estonia (Estonian and Russian
  language teams)
Kazakstan (Russian language
  team)
Kyrgyzstan
Lithuania
Macedonia
Romania
Russia

Countries Joining RWCT in 1998:

Bulgaria
Croatia
Georgia
Hungary
Kazakstan (Kazak language team)
Latvia
Moldova
Mongolia
Ukraine

Countries Joining RWCT in 1999:
Armenia
Azerbaijan
Uzbekistan

Countries Joining RWCT in 2000:
Kosovo
Belarus
Bosnia
Slovenia

Further information about RWCT and the participant countries can be found at www.uni.edu/coe/rwct.

(Maps adapted from Relief Web and *Webster's New World College Dictionary*, Fourth Edition.)

ACKNOWLEDGMENTS

The editors of this volume wish to thank the following people for their assistance:

George Soros, for his unprecedented generosity and unwavering support for education and for the teachers and children of Central and Eastern Europe and Central Asia.

Liz Lorant of the Open Society Institute, for her wisdom, guidance, and partnership in leading the Reading and Writing for Critical Thinking project, and for her years of support for education programs throughout the region.

The RWCT codirectors—Scott Walter, Charles Temple, Kurt Meredith, and Jeannie Steele—for attending to both the big picture and the small details of this ambitious program.

The colleagues and family members of the program volunteers, who generously covered the homefront for weeks at a time in our absence.

Ondřej Hausenblas and Hana Koštálová, for their kind assistance in language and logistics with several chapters of this book.

Mark Christel and David O'Brien of the Hope College Library, for their assistance in locating maps.

Joan Irwin, Matt Baker, and Tori Bachman of the International Reading Association, for expert help in producing this volume.

The Reading and Writing for Critical Thinking (RWCT) Project is cosponsored by the Open Society Institute, the International Reading Association, and the University of Northern Iowa. Further information about the project can be found at www.uni.edu/coe/rwct and at www.reading.org/international.

CONTRIBUTORS

Elena Ackovska-Leskovska
Institute of Psychology
Skopje, Macedonia

Shamen Ahimbekova
High School #1 after Abai
Taldykorgan, Kazakstan

Hiie Asser
Tartu University
Tartu, Estonia

Carol S. Beers
Williamsburg-James City County
    Schools
Williamsburg, Virginia, USA

James W. Beers
School of Education
College of William and Mary
Williamsburg, Virginia, USA

Elena Beliaeva
High School #23
Petropavlovsk, Kazakstan

Božena Blazková
Zakladni Skola-Knihovna
Pardubice, Czech Republic

Patricia L. Bloem
Grand Valley State University
Allendale, Michigan, USA

Natalia Evseeva
High School #5
Lisakovsk, Kazakstan

Tatiana Galaktionova
St. Petersburg, Russia

Daniel R. Hittleman
City University of New York/
    Queens College
Queens, New York, USA

Jodi Patrick Holschuh
University of Georgia
Athens, Georgia, USA

Cynthia Hynd
University of Georgia
Athens, Georgia, USA

Rysaldy Kalieva
High School #6
Semipalatinsk, Kazakstan

David J. Klooster
Hope College
Holland, Michigan, USA

David Landis
University of Northern Iowa
Cedar Falls, Iowa, USA

Jill Lewis
New Jersey City University
Jersey City, New Jersey, USA

Ruth F. Longman
Athens, Georgia, USA

Peter C. McDermott
The Sage Colleges
Troy, New York, USA

Maureen McLaughlin
East Stroudsburg State University
   of Pennsylvania
East Stroudsburg, Pennsylvania,
   USA

Kurtis S. Meredith
University of Northern Iowa
Cedar Falls, Iowa, USA

Suzana Miovska
Institute of Pedagogy
Skopje, Macedonia

Anna Mirnaya
High School #1 after Abai
Taldykorgan, Kazakstan

Bud Ogle
Good News Partners
Chicago, Illinois, USA

Donna M. Ogle
National-Louis University
Evanston, Illinois, USA

Penny Oldfather
College of Education
University of Georgia
Athens, Georgia, USA

Meeli Pandis
Tallinn Pedagogical University
Tallinn, Estonia

Marina Pastuhova
High School STIKS
Pavlodar, Kazakstan

Katrin Poom-Valickis
The Center of Excellence in
   School Improvement
Tallinn, Estonia

Alison Preece
University of Victoria
Victoria, British Columbia,
   Canada

Janet C. Richards
University of Southern Mississippi
Long Beach, Mississippi, USA

Maria Sadikova
High School #5
Lisakovsk, Kazakstan

Zuzana Šaffková
Technical University Liberec
Liberec, Czech Republic

Galina Seleznyova
Kazakstan

Jeannie L. Steele
University of Northern Iowa
Cedar Falls, Iowa, USA

Larisa Stepanets
High School #1 after Abai
Taldykorgan, Kazakstan

Tamara Sushina
High School #17
Atyrau, Kazakstan

Charles Temple
Hobart and William Smith
  Colleges
Geneva, New York, USA

Sirje Tikk
"Veritas" University of the Social
  Sciences
Tallinn, Estonia

Rick Traw
University of Northern Iowa
Cedar Falls, Iowa, USA

Neva Viise
University of Virginia
Charlottesville, Virgina, USA

SECTION I

◯◯

Goals and Contexts for Educational Reform

CHAPTER ONE

The Reading and Writing for Critical Thinking Project: A Framework for School Change

Jeannie L. Steele

The Reading and Writing for Critical Thinking project (RWCT) is unique because it is a long-term, multinational school-restructuring project being implemented simultaneously in 24 different and extraordinary formerly communist countries in Central and Eastern Europe (CEE) and Central Asia (CA). It has brought together teachers of all content areas and grade levels along with university teacher-preparation faculty to speak about and implement genuine school change. RWCT is also worthy of attention because the model for change embodied in the project has proven to be a powerful force for genuine and lasting change in literally thousands of classrooms across a vast array of cultures and contexts. At a time when school improvement has been stymied by the absence of effective models for change, RWCT provides a blueprint for change through an affirming professional development process that acknowledges the values of teachers and the role of students in their own learning.

This chapter will describe the RWCT school-change model and the beliefs about teachers, students, schools, thinking, and learning that form its foundation. The model is not described easily because it is, at its core, experiential: A teacher cannot simply read about the process and implement change. The model represents both the content of change and a change process experienced simultaneously with that content. It is organized this way so teachers will understand not only how to implement differing instructional practices, but they also will know firsthand how those instructional practices impact learners and learning. One task for this chapter is to communicate the feel and effect of that process, to place the reader for a moment inside an RWCT workshop.

The foundational beliefs underpinning the change process embodied in RWCT will be presented. The chapter will also detail the RWCT model, explaining how the project is delivered and who the in-country project participants and volunteer educators are. The chapter also will present the in-service and implementation model that has made RWCT so successful. Understanding the change model and implementation process, both for the RWCT project as a whole and for classroom implementation as well, will provide the reader with the context necessary for understanding the stories of change retold later in this volume.

School Change

Because hindsight is a powerful teacher, the lessons learned from previous school reform efforts are instructive. A review of school restructuring literature in North American schools tells the story of missed opportunities, prematurely truncated efforts, disappointing outcomes, and frustrated teachers and students (Darling-Hammond, 1990; Fullan & Stiegelbauer, 1991; Glickman, 1990; Lewis, 1990; Orlich, 1989; Shannon, 1989). School-change efforts in U.S. schools often failed to take into account the complexity of school culture, failed to recognize the time required for change to occur, and failed to acknowledge the successes and strengths of the existing system in which reform was introduced (Meredith & Steele, 2000a). Foremost, however, many school-change efforts failed because they did not establish a co-equal relationship between those facilitating reform and those implementing reform (Fullan & Stiegelbauer, 1991). It has become clear that reform occurs when the relations among all parties in the change process are defined by a high level of trust, respect, collaboration, and commitment.

The record of school change efforts does include, of course, successes at many levels. For example, this author along with many colleagues began working with educators more than 25 years ago in Virginia and Louisiana to bring about reforms in instructional practices meant to effect lasting change at the classroom level (Estes, Vaughn, Steele, & Vaughn, 1983). These early efforts successfully introduced innovative instructional practices that enhanced student learning while increasing independent thinking and learning. Later, this work evolved into a model for implementing school change that was tested successfully in numerous school districts across the United States (Steele & Meredith, 1991). These U.S. school-change efforts were based on well-grounded beliefs about teaching and learning and the change process. These beliefs serve as the foundation for the RWCT project today.

Foundational Beliefs of the RWCT Project

School change requires tremendous human resources and time. It requires an extensive time commitment by a school or district. Consequently, to be successful, school change at the classroom and whole-school level will occur when the impetus for change comes from within the school or district. Imposed change has rarely been effective without damaging the school culture in ways that negatively affect school functioning. Lasting change cannot be imposed without paying too high a price in terms of loss of teacher ownership of the instructional process and teachers' sense of professional empowerment.

RWCT is built on six foundational beliefs:

1. Teachers must have primary ownership of the entire change process, yet change must be a collaborative process involving school administrators, university colleagues, students, and parents.

2. Change is manifest in classrooms in the relationships between teachers and students and among students.

3. The change process must be coherent, well-articulated, theoretically defensible, practical, and applied.

4. It is essential to recognize that change involves risk and that teachers engaged in the change process are at risk (a) professionally, by stepping outside their original professional training; (b) socially, by placing new expectations on both the school culture and teachers' relations with students; and (c) emotionally, by risking failure when trying new, unfamiliar approaches to teaching. Consequently, teachers engaged in the change process must be networked with their peers and provided formal ongoing support.

5. The change process must be given sufficient time. Time is required to design models, implement them incrementally, develop expertise, and measure impact.

6. Implementation, content, and outcomes cannot be entirely fixed if the process is to be collaborative. Rather, final outcomes and the steps to reach them must remain flexible to respond to the changing landscape created by the change process itself. Project leaders affectionately refer to this element as the "Principle of Unfolding

Design." (This term was originally coined by Brian Shirley, a curriculum coordinator in Augusta County, Virginia, USA, with whom I worked in the 1970s and 1980s.)

These fundamental beliefs are intended to respect the power and importance of school culture and the varying cultural contexts in which schools are immersed. However, the vast number and enormous breadth of the cultures represented by the RWCT participating countries originally seemed daunting. As we considered this reality, we began to realize that the vast range of cultural variations is unique and should serve as a source of strength and inspiration—something not available to other school-change efforts (Meredith & Steele, 2000b). Cultural diversity offers differing realities, alternative viewpoints on what is important, varying perspectives on relationships, and unique constructions of meaning. In short, RWCT began celebrating its enormous multicultural base and worked from the inherent strength derived from such a contextually rich foundation to develop a plan that would weave these cultural similarities and differences into the fabric of school change.

RWCT is unique because it relies on the vast professional knowledge and skills base of a corps of professional volunteers associated with the International Reading Association (IRA), working in partnership with highly skilled educators from our host countries. To succeed, this project had to rely on the skills, expertise, and intellectual and professional integrity of a large number of people within the region and beyond. There is no doubt that the success of the RWCT project and the professionalism of the volunteers and in-country leaders are measures demarcated on the same beaker.

RWCT Participants

It is helpful to understand the participants to some degree because the change process is a difficult and often lonely experience. RWCT participants are teachers of uncommon dedication for many reasons. First they have volunteered to participate. They receive no compensation for their involvement despite the burden of expectations this change model places on them. Often, especially in the larger countries such as Ukraine, Russia, Kazakstan and others, the participants must travel for hours by train to reach inservice sites. They are under enormous pressure to minimize time away from school, as most countries involved do not have a system of substitute teachers available to cover absences. The participants represent all grade levels and content areas. In addition to classroom teachers, there are university faculty and a few participants from pedagogical inservice centers. All of them are similar in their belief in the importance of meaningful education experiences for their students, their desire to give their students the best instruction possible, and their willingness to risk their own credibility, if necessary, to bring about school change. They are an exceptional group of educators.

Assembling a group of teachers of this quality and commitment does not occur accidentally. The program requires specific criteria regarding teacher characteristics for participant selection, including:

- openness to changes and readiness to change the traditional methods of work;
- capacity to be a leader and work in a team;
- the wish to study and use the acquired knowledge in everyday work;
- capacity to deliver the course to other teachers; and
- willingness to commit to the project for 3 years.

The volunteers are similar in many ways to their in-country counterparts. The volunteers all applied to participate in RWCT and underwent considerable scrutiny. The scrutiny was not to check their professional credentials, because the entire volunteer applicant pool represented a remarkable collection of people with excellent skills, extensive professional experiences, and well-earned professional reputations. The scrutiny was in regard to their capacity to commit to the project and to the people with whom they would work. The commitment of the in-country people was uncompromising. The RWCT project volunteers had the obligation to match that commitment. The volunteers selected and the in-country leaders have become the backbone and driving force of the project. We have already discussed the incredible commitment of the in-country leaders. In the case of the volunteers, their dedication is nothing short of astonishing, committing a month of each year to this volunteer work, taking days and weeks out of already full professional lives to teach and mentor new colleagues in places far from home. It is because of the partnership between the volunteers and their in-country leaders that the project has succeeded.

RWCT Framework

Drawing from the work of Alvermann, Smith, and Readence (1985); Anderson, Hiebert, Scott, and Wilkinson (1985); Pearson and Fielding (1991); Rosenblatt (1978); Temple and Gillette (1996); Vaughan and Estes (1986); and many others, we have articulated the primary structure of the RWCT model as a three-phase framework for teaching. The model was developed in Slovakia (Steele & Meredith, 1995) for the Orava Project (Meredith & Steele, 2000a), a *systemic* school-change initiative that preceded RWCT and serves as the model for the RWCT program. (The Orava Project is funded by a grant from the United States Agency for International Development [USAID], which administers the U.S. foreign assistance program that provides economic and humanitarian assistance in more than 80 countries worldwide.)

The three phases of the model are named for their specific functions and are referred to as *Evocation, Realization of Meaning*, and *Reflection*, or ERR. The framework serves as a working instructional guide and is demonstrated at the outset of the program to give substance and coherence to all subsequent instructional practices. A brief description of these phases of the learning process may provide a sense of the structure and its impact on the teaching process. The initial phase, Evocation, is intended to help students evoke prior knowledge, sentiment, or impressions; create a context for new learning; provide stimulus for future exploration; and generate individual and/or collective understandings about the tasks to be studied. It is in this phase that students first begin to speculate, make predictions, and set purposes for exploring newly introduced topics or themes. Evocation is also the initial point of engagement for students. It is here that students decide if they will go forward willingly and knowledgeably or be pulled into the content to be studied. It is also at this early point in the learning process that students begin to decide whether they will be intrinsically or extrinsically motivated to learn new ideas and information and blend them with their existing knowledge base.

Too often in traditional teaching the Evocation phase is overlooked. Teachers may assume that students will arrive in school prepared to learn. For some this is true, but many others must first build expectations, evoke interest, create awareness of prior knowledge and prior constructs, and create an atmosphere of inquisitiveness that will drive student learning. Even for those who come to school prepared to learn, the Evocation phase enhances learning by creating the necessary psychological set for meaningful, long-lasting learning. The first phase in the ERR framework is intended to drive the learning process forward.

The Realization of Meaning phase embodies that point in the instructional process when students are exposed to new information or ideas, to new content, or to new deliberations. Whether the instructional medium is a discussion, guided lecture, textbook reading, videotape, artistic performance, or other event, this second phase marks the students' encounter with that medium and its content. The task of the student during this phase is to remain engaged with the content, remain cognizant of the mix of new ideas with already held knowledge and beliefs. To learn effectively, students need to be engaged purposefully and thoughtfully, monitoring their comprehension, reacting to their encounters with information and actively managing the information. Students in the Realization of Meaning phase should make decisions about the relative importance of the information and ideas being presented by filtering out the incidental from the essential, integrating new knowledge with existing knowledge, and considering the utility and applicability of the information to new settings and opportunities.

Reflection is the final phase of the learning process and marks the time when students begin to express new knowledge and understandings in their own words. The intent of this phase is to provide students the time, structure, and means to actively integrate information with previously held beliefs and ideas so that their learning will be contextualized and, consequently, real and more lasting. This phase is typified by robust discussions, practical applications of knowledge, the generation of new ideas and concepts, open speculation about implications, or a call for further investigations. It is the time when learning becomes personal.

It is in the Reflection phase that the learner takes ownership of new knowledge. Through the reflective process students articulate their thoughts, receive peer and teacher feedback, and test their integration of information and their construction of meaning. Until students engage in this process, their learning is of someone else's ideas or beliefs. Only by removing the information from the realm of the idea of "other" does it become one's own. In fact, for many learners new information can be profoundly contradictory to previous learning. Yet without reflection, mutually exclusive ideas can be held without overt awareness by the learner.

The ERR framework provides a model for understanding teaching processes and serves as a mechanism for organizing instruction that corresponds to what is known about how students learn best. It stands alone as an inclusive model under which teachers can incorporate those strategies that they already employ in their teaching and that meet the goals and purposes of the various framework phases.

Guidebooks

In addition to the strategies good teachers already implement in their classrooms, there exists within the global teaching literature a storehouse of effective strategies that engage students in meaningful learning experiences. The RWCT project has assembled many instructional strategies that reflect the project's philosophy and purposes into eight guidebooks, which are presented through a series of inservice seminars to practicing teachers and university teacher-preparation faculty. The guidebooks begin with a presentation of the ERR framework so that all subsequent strategies can be placed within the framework. The eight guidebook titles are

1. *A Framework for Critical Thinking Across the Curriculum* (Steele, Meredith, & Temple, 1998);
2. *Methods for Promoting Critical Thinking* (Steele, Meredith, & Temple, 1998);
3. *Reading, Writing, and Discussion in Every Discipline* (Temple, Steele, & Meredith, 1998);
4. *Further Strategies for Promoting Critical Thinking* (Temple, Steele, & Meredith, 1998);
5. *Cooperative Learning* (Meredith, Steele, & Temple, 1998);
6. *Lesson Planning and Assessment* (Temple, Steele, & Meredith, 1998);
7. *Writing Workshop: From Self-Expression to Written Arguments* (Temple, Steele, & Meredith, 1998); and
8. *Creating Thoughtful Readers* (Meredith, Steele, & Temple, 1998).

The instructional strategies offered in the guidebooks are dependent on the ERR framework. ERR forms the umbrella under which all teaching strategies aggregate, and those strategies, like the framework itself, must in some way oblige students to

- activate thinking,
- engage in rich discussion,

- integrate ideas and information,
- consider consequences for thought and take responsibility for those consequences,
- become a constructively motivated learner,
- stimulate personal change,
- reflect on previously held beliefs as well as new information,
- respond respectfully to varied opinions,
- ask their own questions,
- form and express their own opinions, and
- think critically and flexibly.

The guidebooks are organized into the various general themes ascribed by their titles but the key to their utility is that they are constructed to guide participants through each strategy within the context of an authentic learning experience. In this way participants first experience the strategies as learners. Then they are guided through a reflective process that first directs participants to consider their experiences with the strategies as a learner. Only after this are they asked to reflect on their experiences from a pedagogical point of view.

A critical feature of the guidebooks is that they are not considered finished products. We know that teachers are already doing wonderful work in their classrooms engaging students in active learning processes. These teachers are encouraged to add their own strategies to those presented and to organize them according to the guidebook themes and the ERR framework. As they implement the RWCT program in their classrooms, they are also expected to add to the literature and study material in the guidebooks, textbooks, and curriculum materials they use in their own classrooms. In each of the 24 countries, we expect participants to revise the guidebooks to include authentic literature from local cultures, to work with passages of prose from their own textbooks, and in a myriad of ways make the books their own by infusing the flavors and texts of their local culture.

Experience-Based Inservice

As mentioned earlier, the core of the inservice program is its experience-based delivery. The instructional model for delivery of presentations is organized to provide participants with first-hand experiences with the framework and the strategies presented. This means that nothing in the guidebooks is taught directly as content, nor is it discussed in terms of pedagogical relevance until the participants have gone through an authentic learning experience that has employed the strategy as the method of instruction. In other words, the program is arranged so that there is minimal distinction between content and process or between medium and message. Whether the actual content of the lesson is to learn a strategy or the framework itself, any discussion about practice takes place only after participants have engaged in a comprehensive learning experience. Through this approach, participants first encounter a strategy within a genuine learning experience on which they can reflect to examine what happened, analyze their reactions to the strategy as they worked through the content of the lesson, and look at how the strategy affected them as learners and whether or not it enhanced their learning. After this reflection is complete the pedagogical implications of strategy are discussed. This discussion concludes by determining where the strategy fits within the framework. This consideration is based on the type of actions in which the students are engaged and the specific learning outcomes anticipated from that particular strategy.

It may be useful to outline a brief interactive learning experience from a guidebook to understand the process and power of the model. In Guidebook I, participants are told that today they will be studying about marine life and that they will be reading a short piece about sea turtles. Participants are told that throughout the program they will be operating on two levels: They will be engaged in a content lesson learning experience, and they should attend to that content as if they were students. But they also should be cognizant of process and what is happening to them as learners so they can reflect on this as teachers after the lesson and discuss the pedagogical practices they experienced.

In the beginning of the lesson, participants are asked first to write their own list of what they know or think they know about sea turtles. Then, they are asked to form pairs by turning to the person sitting next to them. Their task is to share what they wrote with their partners. They are encouraged to write down everything that comes to mind and not worry about whether the items on the list are right or wrong.

This process takes only 5 minutes, and then participants are asked to share their thoughts with the entire group. Participants are encouraged to recite just one or two thoughts at a time from their list so everyone has a chance to respond. The group responses are listed on chart paper or overhead transparency. As the list forms, the teacher is aware of the content of the article participants will soon read. Because comprehension is, according to Pearson and Fielding (1991), a matter of having your own questions answered, the teacher might prompt an inquiry related to the article. For example the teacher might ask, "Did anyone say anything about turtles laying eggs? About how many do they lay and how big are they?" or "What do you suppose turtles eat?"

There may be some disagreements in the group. This is acknowledged, even encouraged, and the differences of opinion are reflected on the chart paper. No effort is made to resolve these differences at this time. If they will be resolved in the reading, then the teacher may say that the article will speak about this issue.

Once this group brainstorm is completed, participants are given the short article to read. Before reading, however, participants are taught the brief instructions for the INSERT method so they can apply it to their reading. INSERT (Vaughn & Estes, 1986), which stands for Interactive Notating System for Effective Reading and Thinking, asks readers to make specific notations in the text as they read:

a (✔) when encountering something they already know;

a (-) when reading something that contradicts what they already know;

a (+) when reading new information; and

a (?) if they are unsure or want to know more.

Participants are asked to read the article employing the INSERT method and to recall some of their own thoughts and questions about the topic. When they are finished reading, participants are asked to share with the group some of the outcomes of their application of INSERT, and a chart like the one in Figure 1 is created. While this chart is incomplete, it illustrates the type of ideas normally recorded.

This part of the lesson concludes by looking back at the chart paper with notes from the group brainstorm to see if participants' thoughts were consistent with the article, to determine if some differences of opinion were resolved, and to determine what questions for further study remain. Participants are then guided back to their original listing of what they knew or thought they knew to modify their own INSERT chart in order to reflect on their own learning.

Figure 1
Sample Group INSERT Chart

✔	-	+	?
young left to survive on their own	lays 50 to 100 leathery eggs	eats plants and fish	where do the young go
lays eggs on same beach every year		travels thousands of kilometers	how do they find the same beach again
		sheds tears	

After this authentic learning experience is complete, participants are asked to begin reflecting on their learning experience. They are asked to think back through the lesson and to recall their experiences as a learner: What did they think and feel, how engaged were they, and when did they become engaged in the process? Following this reflection participants are prepared to discuss pedagogical implications. They have experienced the lesson as they will teach it (or a similar one based on the content of their own curriculum), and they are ready to deconstruct the lesson and rephrase it in pedagogical terms.

The next task of the participants is to develop specific implementation plans for using the presented framework and strategies in their own classrooms, integrating their own curricular content and materials. They are asked to develop lesson plans that incorporate the strategies and are built on the ERR framework. They are then expected to implement these plans in their classrooms as early and often as possible between the inservice sessions. They are reminded that a single attempt is not sufficient to be able to master the strategies. The teachers are expected to engage in ongoing implementation, making appropriate modifications to meet the needs of their particular content and setting. They are also asked to observe and note several outcomes—to be aware of their students' responses to the strategies in terms of motivation, participation, interest level, and learning performance. They are also asked to observe classroom interaction patterns and assess their own comfort with the instructional practice. It is important to note that all participants, whether they are university faculty, classroom teachers, school administrators, or Ministry of Education personnel, are expected to be in classrooms applying the strategies.

We have shared here only one experience from the vast array of strategies that are part of the RWCT project. As participants progress through the program, their repertoire of strategies grows along with their understanding of where strategies fit in the teaching and learning framework.

RWCT's Dynamic Change Process

RWCT unfolds through a considered sequence of events designed to develop expertise in the teacher participants so that they are ultimately prepared to teach others without loss of program integrity. It is also sequenced to provide teachers maximum opportunity for trial and error in the kind of risk-free and supportive environment necessary for lasting change to occur. As indicated earlier, RWCT content is presented through eight guidebooks, which are delivered approximately two at a time in four 4-day intensive inservice programs over the course of 1 academic year. Typically this requires one inservice session every 2 months. A team of two volunteers delivers the inservice and, ideally, the volunteer teams alternate delivery so both teams travel to their respective countries twice each year over the 3-year program.

The interim period between inservice presentations is quite active. Each inservice concludes with the development of explicit implementation plans for the content from the guidebook, plans that will apply the new instructional strategy to the teacher's own curriculum. Participants are expected to introduce those plans into their classroom instruction as soon as possible and to continue incorporating them into their daily teaching practice. Also during this interim period, monthly meetings are held for participants to gather and work on classroom implementation, which is critical to sustaining momentum and providing support.

Though participating teachers are aware that they will eventually become trainers of others, during the first year they are encouraged to concentrate on developing their own level of expertise, and they have no obligations to provide trainings or inservice programs. During this time they concentrate on incorporating their curricular content into the strategies and the framework while gathering student materials to use for demonstration purposes once they begin their inservice delivery. The first year of the program is intense as participants work to develop expertise. It is a time of risk-taking accompanied by successes and failures, all of which occur under the scrutiny of colleagues and foreign volunteers. Trust and respect are necessary parts of the climate and these qualities emerge among participants as they work together to create new classrooms.

During the first year, volunteers have other roles in addition to presenting content. It is crucial that they gain an appreciation for the settings in which their participants teach and live, and therefore they meet with students, administrators, and university teacher-preparation faculty. It is also important that participating teachers be observed implementing the program strategies in their classrooms and given honest and supportive feedback. Therefore, each volunteer team visit lasts 2 weeks. During that time the 4-day inservice is delivered and, in addition, the team travels to schools and communities throughout the country to observe RWCT program implementation and to gain first-hand experience of life in their assigned country.

Monthly Meetings

The momentum of the change process must be sustained, and therefore teachers engaged in the process are asked to gather together to renew their energy and their commitment for their work. Between inservices the participants come together in monthly meetings. These meetings are either in small regional groups, where country size prohibits bringing everyone together so frequently, or large central meetings that include all the participants. In some countries, participants meet in groups organized by discipline or type of school. More important than the configuration of the group, however, is the simple act of their coming together to discuss progress. One intent of these meetings is to discuss implementation effectiveness in general and implementation of the framework and strategies in particular. Teachers are encouraged to share their successes and failures with equal candor. Successes are noted, and clear descriptions of how implementation was handled are sought so others can duplicate these successes. The group responds to failures by working to identify potential remedies and by offering encouragement to renew implementation efforts.

Through repeated implementation trials and continuing deliberations, new teaching practices begin to become a natural part of a teacher's routine. During these monthly meetings teachers also share the modifications they have made to particular strategies. These modifications are carefully examined to determine if they have maintained the intent and integrity of the instructional practice, or if the practice has been compromised by the alteration. It is also intended in these meetings that participants sustain and build on their sense of camaraderie, shared professional development, empowerment, and belief in their own capacity to contribute to the growing global fund of innovative instructional practices. The latter is an essential belief if the participants are ultimately to take responsibility for delivery and dissemination of the project.

This process of first experiencing new instructional practices, responding to them, deconstructing them, and then implementing, modifying, and re-implementing is repeated throughout the inservice sequence. As new strategies are presented, they are continuously placed within the larger context of the ERR framework and a coherent instructional philosophy. As the teachers become more expert, they increasingly share their own experiences and become more valuable and valued resources for their colleagues within the participant group and within their schools.

The Power of Change

It is difficult to fully articulate the dynamic change process set in motion by the program. It is palpable, observable, and exciting. Participating educators become consumed by it. They come to believe in the process and its power of renewal for them as professional educators and human beings. Later chapters in this volume offer rich evidence, usually in quotations from teachers and students themselves, of the depth and breadth of the changes participants experience. Perhaps a story retold by Hana Košť'álová (2000) from the Czech Republic in the journal *Thinking Classroom* captures this. She writes,

> I have an interesting story about a teacher who joined the program at the beginning of the last academic year. At that time she had many objections. She was especially angry when we did the part on evaluation and assessment. She couldn't stand the idea of student self-evaluation, and was against rubrics and against portfolio. After nearly 20 years of teaching, she strongly believed in the motivating role of grading—both good and bad grades. Fortunately, she was too fair not to try something new. Slowly, she found herself encouraging students to express their own opinions. Instead of standing in front of the classroom, she was among her students—and she was happy and full of enthusiasm. "How could I give a grade four or five for an independent essay by a student who had never written more than five boring lines on an assigned topic—without many mistakes—and who now produced four pages of deep and original text on his problems with his older brother? The text was full of misspellings, the handwriting was ugly, and I felt a vague inclination to give it a worse grade, but I couldn't. Since then, I think

about last year's session on evaluation and I know I will never be so strongly convinced about my own ideas, and I will become very careful in evaluating my students' work."

Participant Preparation for Inservice Delivery

As stated earlier, participants know from the beginning that they will become the core RWCT trainers in their country. Thus, they understand that in the second year their role is to become the local RWCT experts. The second year usually frightens participants more than the first, because they know they will have to begin delivering their own inservice programs. Though they are assured that they will only deliver inservice programs when they are fully prepared and supported, many are concerned that their colleagues will not accept them as trainers: "It's one thing for international experts to fly in to conduct a workshop," they say. "It's quite another for a local school teacher to be in charge." Despite their concerns, during Year 2 they draw comfort from the group and begin the process of developing inservice programs.

The second year is dedicated to preparing participants for their training role, but expectations for continued classroom implementation remain. Preparation for their new role as workshop leaders begins with participation in a workshop that focuses on how to design and deliver inservice programs and how to work with adults. It is often assumed that because the participants are teachers they already know how to deliver workshops to adults, but this is not the case. Working with first, fifth, or eleventh graders is far different from working with adult colleagues. Special preparation is necessary before teachers will feel comfortable working effectively with adults. During this inservice, participants are paired, and each pair is assigned to prepare in great detail a 2- to 3-hour workshop based on a coherent segment of project content to be delivered to their colleagues. The participants always work in pairs. They are never asked to work alone, nor are the groups made larger as someone could get lost in the crowd. It is vital that each participant be fully engaged in planning and delivering the workshops.

These short workshops will be the participants' initial inservice delivery experience. They do not deliver the workshops, however, until they have planned them precisely and rehearsed them before their participant colleagues. When they feel fully prepared, and only then, the workshops are delivered. This has turned out to be a successful formula, and typically after these workshops have been presented the nervousness disappears, and most participants are eager to deliver more inservice programs. Most participants feel as Maria, a third-grade teacher from the Czech Republic, did: "I was so nervous I did not sleep the night before, but once we started I loved it, and now I want to do it again. My colleagues were so nice, and we were a great team!" The in-country participants do learn that their colleagues are quite manageable, even appreciative of their efforts, and the response to these workshops is usually an overwhelming call for more. Once they are comfortable with their training role, participants are then asked to work in larger groups, usually two or three pairs working together, to deliver the entire RWCT program as they experienced it through the guidebooks and under the guidance of the volunteers.

The workshop delivery component of the model is interesting because of its impact on project success. This component actually serves two valuable functions. Obviously the participant inservice programs provide a powerful mechanism for project dissemination. Less apparent is that by asking participants to prepare to deliver training to others, the stakes are raised in terms of their own level of expertise. For participants to become credible presenters, they soon understand that they must be able to speak with the weight of genuine classroom experience. Their motivation to become experts increases, and consequently their inservice presentations become more credible. In the process of teaching others, participants take on ownership of the content.

As the second year progresses, volunteers and participants work to fulfill the goals of the country plans that have been developed over the previous summer at a large project reunion meeting. Those plans address issues of *dissemination* and *institutionalization* of project content and method. These two terms are linked strategically and become the focus of the project for the second half of Year 2 and for Year 3 and beyond. The model for dissemination varies from country to country, but in all cases the participants become the vital resources for dissemination among their colleagues at various levels of the education community. In all cases the initial participants become the preparers of teachers and the primary force for dissemination of the RWCT program.

Summary

With the collapse of the Soviet Union, the seeds for school change across the vast region of Central and Eastern Europe and Central Asia were sown in the latter part of the 1980s and early 1990s. The historically unprecedented period of transition for so many peoples and cultures presented an unparalleled opportunity for cross-cultural collaboration. The keys to successful collaboration turned out to be simple, though not easy. Participants were expected to work as equal partners, to base all collaboration on respect and trust, to understand the power of diversity, to apply a flexible and tested model for change, to empower great people to do great things, and to recognize up front the enormous amount of work required.

RWCT begins with a set of foundational beliefs about the school change process. These beliefs acknowledge the teacher's role in the change process, the complexities of school culture, and the culture that surrounds schooling. They also respect the needs of students and their wisdom and capacity to think and take responsibility for their own learning. From these foundational beliefs a coherent and theoretically defensible framework for teaching and learning is offered that enables participants to contextualize their experiences and their subsequent instructional practices.

Despite the rigor of the program implementation, the key to RWCT success is the people involved. The in-country leaders and participants are extraordinary. They have dedicated themselves to the change process without compromise and have steadfastly adhered to the program model and implementation. The volunteers have formed powerful bonds with their volunteer partners and their in-country participants. They have applied their knowledge, wisdom, and years of experience to RWCT in ways never imagined and have added immeasurably to both content and process.

The content of the inservice program is found in the eight guidebooks, which are crafted to provide direct experience with the strategies before examining them pedagogically. The guidebooks do not stand alone but accompany interactive workshops. They are open ended and amendable to meet country, school, and specific classroom needs yet have an immutable core that is preserved in all settings. The guidebooks become a resource for classroom change and an invitation to carry on a continuous dialogue about best practices in teaching and learning.

Finally, participants become the experts. They go through a rigorous, 2-year preparation process to learn the content and process and how to deliver it to their colleagues. This preparation serves as both a continuation of the initial learning of the program and as a mechanism for moving to more advanced levels of professional development.

Reading and Writing for Critical Thinking has been received by teachers throughout Central and Eastern Europe and Central Asia with overwhelming support, and its future is bright. The changes that have occurred are secure and positive, and the prospects for continued implementation are also excellent. However, in keeping with the Principle of Unfolding Design, it is not known exactly how RWCT will proceed after the third year. With each year it is increasingly important that the in-country leaders and participants take responsibility for the project and carry it forward. The volunteers have been steadily working their way out of their role, leaving in their place a large corps of exceptionally well-prepared teachers ready to deliver the program in the future through the institutional structures of the respective countries.

At a recent RWCT reunion meeting attended by people from 29 countries, a participant reflected on what has been accomplished. She said, "Borders have been crossed, boundaries no longer matter, language differences have been lost in the joy that fills the room because of the connections among everyone working toward this important common goal."

REFERENCES

Alvermann, D.E., Smith, L.C., & Readence, J.E. (1985). Prior knowledge activation and the comprehension of compatible and incompatible text. *Reading Research Quarterly, 20,* 420–436.

Anderson, R.C., Hiebert, E.H., Scott, J.A., & Wilkinson, I.A.G. (1985). *Becoming a nation of readers: The report of the Commission on Reading.* Urbana, IL: University of Illinois, Center for the Study on Reading.

Darling-Hammond, L. (1990). Achieving our goals: Superficial or structural reforms. *Phi Delta Kappan, 72,* 286–295.

Estes, T.H., Vaughn, J., Steele, J.L., & Vaughn, N. (1983). *Reading in the content areas: Institute guidebook.* Belmont, CA: Learning Institute.

Fullan, M., & Stiegelbauer, S. (1991). *The new meaning of educational change* (2nd ed.). New York: Teachers College Press.

Glickman, C.D. (1990). Pushing school reform to a new edge: The seven ironies of school empowerment. *Phi Delta Kappan, 72,* 68–75.

Košťálová, H. (2000). Look who's talking. *Thinking Classroom: An International Journal of Reading, Writing and Critical Reflection,* inaugural issue, 10.

Lewis, A.C. (1990). Getting unstuck: Curriculum as a tool for reform. *Phi Delta Kappan, 71,* 534–538.

Meredith, K.S., & Steele, J.L. (1993). *Reading, writing and learning curriculum.* Moline, IL: Moline Public Schools.

Meredith, K.S., & Steele, J.L. (2000a). *Orava Project 1994–1999: Educational collaboration for the 21st century.* Bratislava, Slovakia: Orava Association for Democratic Education.

Meredith, K.S., & Steele, J.L. (2000b). Education in transition: Trends in Central and Eastern Europe. In M.L. Kamil, P. Mosenthal, P.D. Pearson, & R. Barr (Eds.), *Handbook of reading research: Volume III*. Mahwah, NJ: Erlbaum.

Meredith, K.S., Steele, J.L., & Temple, C. (1998). *Cooperative learning* (English version). Newark, DE: International Reading Association.

Meredith, K.S., Steele, J.L., & Temple, C. (1998). *Creating thoughtful readers* (English version). Newark, DE: International Reading Association.

Orlich, D.C. (1989). Education reforms: Mistakes, misconceptions, miscues. *Phi Delta Kappan, 70,* 512–517.

Pearson, P.D., & Fielding, L. (1991). Comprehension instruction. In R. Barr, M.L. Kamil, P. Mosenthal & P.D. Pearson (Eds.) *Handbook of reading research: Volume II*. White Plains, NY: Longman.

Rosenblatt, L.M. (1978). *The reader, the text, the poem: The transactional theory of literary work.* Carbondale, IL: Southern Illinois University Press.

Shannon, P. (1989). *Broken promises: Reading instruction in twentieth century America.* New York: Bergin & Garvey.

Steele, J.L., & Meredith, K.S. (1991). *Working together—growing together: Constructive evaluation of language learning.* Moline, IL: Moline Public Schools.

Steele, J.L., & Meredith, K.S. (1995). *Democratic pedagogy national staff development manual.* Bratislava, Slovakia: Orava Foundation for Democratic Education.

Steele, J.L., Meredith, K.S., & Temple, C. (1998). *A framework for critical thinking across the curriculum* (English version). Newark, DE: International Reading Association.

Steele, J.L., Meredith, K.S., & Temple, C. (1998). *Methods for promoting critical thinking* (English version). Newark, DE: International Reading Association.

Temple, C., & Gillete, J.W. (1996). *Language and literacy: A lively approach.* New York: HarperCollins.

Temple, C., Steele, J.L., & Meredith, K.S. (1998). *Further strategies for promoting critical thinking* (English version). Newark, DE: International Reading Association.

Temple, C., Steele, J.L., & Meredith, K.S. (1998). *Reading, writing, and discussion in every discipline* (English version). Newark, DE: International Reading Association.

Temple, C., Steele, J.L., & Meredith, K.S. (1998). *Lesson planning and assessment* (English version). Newark, DE: International Reading Association.

Temple, C., Steele, J.L., & Meredith, K.S. (1998). *Writing workshop: Self-expression to written arguments* (English version). Newark, DE: International Reading Association.

Vaughn, J.L., & Estes, T.H. (1986). *Reading and reasoning beyond the primary grades.* Newton, MA: Allyn and Bacon.

CHAPTER TWO

⊂⊃⊂⊃

The Political and Historical Context for Educational Reform in Central and Eastern Europe and Central Asia

Kurtis S. Meredith

When Maria, a sixth-grade teacher from the Czech Republic, speaks about her teaching experience before the "Velvet Revolution," a quiet revolution that lifted her country (once part of Czechoslovakia) out from under totalitarianism, she exposes a wide range of emotions. She alternately recalled the sadness, anger, cynicism, humor, anguish, joy, and concern she once felt during her years of teaching under the Soviet regime. "We lived two lives always," she whispered, as if the walls still had ears. "We had to make sense of it all. We were required to say and do things that supported the actions of the state. We had to recite the propaganda. We were tools for spreading the communist doctrines. It was terrible." Lifting her head, her blue eyes still and clear, a faint half-smile–half-grimace flashed across her face. "Of course some teachers signed on to the whole program and taught it as truth. Most of us knew it for what it was, pure dogma—'red painting' we called it—and most of us devised ways to get over it, under it, around it in any way we could without causing us or our students trouble. We couldn't speak about it much with each other, but we knew. In some ways it made us be more clever." Then her eyes welled with tears, and Maria lowered her gaze. "Teachers were not respected then," she said. "Everyone knew we were the ones to teach the dogma to their children." Then, almost defiantly, "What could we do? We wanted to teach, but giving lip service to that state propaganda was required of us as teachers. Not everyone saw it that way. It is how it was. Today we still have problems, but it is better. We got rid of the dogma and now we can teach, we can do what we are supposed to

22

do. It won't be so easy though. We need to find new ways to teach our children. The old ways won't work for our students. Their world is different from ours; we can only guess what their lives will be like."

The Czech Republic is one of more than two dozen countries in Central and Eastern Europe (CEE) and Central Asia (CA) struggling to define themselves in the postcommunist era (Rutland, 1999). In the early 1990s, 27 countries emerged out of what were 8 nations. Each of these new nations, whether new or reemergent, are now engaged in a great transition, a transition taking place on a scale unprecedented in history. Within each country, every institution, every aspect of culture, and every habit is undergoing some form of transformation. From media access to employment opportunities and job expectations; from food choices and daily diet to the rules of commerce, community services, and basic housing availability; from political context to social constructs and mores— in all of these areas people and institutions are under enormous pressure to change, to adapt, to be invented anew, or to become marginalized. Schools are no exception. The demands for school change are enormous, complex, and compelling. Schools are not only caught up in the process of change, they also are being called on to lead the change process by preparing young people to live, work, and become leaders of a tomorrow no one can legitimately anticipate from past experience (Dobert & Manning, 1994). There are few traditions to guide, and looking back to the wisdom of preceding generations offers little insight about the future of this region.

To understand what happened to many of these societies it might be useful to imagine a society in a canoe paddling on a spoiled but familiar lake. Everyone was carefully avoiding the outlet stream and its terrible waterfall. Then one day, compelled by forces not fully understood (Rutland, 1999), the canoe suddenly veered into the outlet stream and plunged over the falls. Fortunately, most everyone survived the falls, but now they are in completely uncharted waters. There is no way back up the falls, and worse yet, most of the paddles were lost during the sudden descent. The river is moving swiftly now; there are eddies, cross-currents, dead-end channels, and dangerous rapids ahead. In the midst of all this, while the boat is moving, young people must become navigators. In other words, schools are caught in the cross-current of having to simultaneously recover from the sudden collapse of socialism and the resultant vacuum left behind, yet they are expected to lead the way into the future without navigational aids (Štech, 1994). Wolfgang Mitter (1996) adds, "At this moment the whole region is involved in the transition process, whereby education must be seen in close relation with the overarching socioeconomic, cultural and political transformation processes" (p. 150). The evolving societies of CEE and CA are contending simultaneously with assembling civil, democratic societies and restructuring schools in ways that will sustain and nurture a new social order. Any consideration of trends in education during this transitory period must be linked to considerations of this aqueous cultural, social, economic, and political context.

The Soviet Legacy

There is ample evidence that the historical, sociological, linguistic, political, economic, and moral character of any society is inseparable from its cultural context. This is perhaps nowhere more apparent than in CEE and CA, where history, politics, culture, and economics lie at the vortex of all issues, especially education, literacy, and learning (Mitter, 1996). It is not possible to understand education in the region or the need for reform without first becoming aware of some of the historically significant realities that impinge on current educational practices and constructs (Karsten & Majoor, 1994).

It may be helpful to begin by defining the geographic boundaries of CEE and the newly independent states of the former Soviet Union in Central Asia. Although there is debate as to just who may lay claim to European identity, the most inclusive definition of Europe, beyond the borders of "Western" Europe, is proposed by Mitter (1996) and incorporates all the former Soviet empire satellite nations cut off from "Western Europe" after World War II, plus the newly independent states (NIS) of the former Soviet Union that lie between the Central European corridor and Russia. These would include the Baltic nations, Belarus, Ukraine, and Moldova. To this is added Russia and the new nations to her south, ranging from the huge far Eastern countries of Mongolia and Kazakstan to Armenia, Azerbaijan, and Georgia. As indicated previously, 27 nations grew out of the 8 that existed before 1989. The division of the Soviet Union alone resulted in the creation of 15 separate countries. The once single nation of Yugoslavia fragmented into five countries, and the Czechoslovak Federation has split into the separate Czech and Slovak Republics.

This vast array of cultures, languages, and peoples had often been seen as a largely homogeneous group. Under Soviet domination this was superficially true (Rust, Knost, & Wichmann, 1994). However, as tensions and nationalist tendencies of the post-1989 collapse of Soviet domination have revealed, the region is a mosaic of peoples as various in culture, habit, and language as anywhere on earth. Perhaps the two most distinctive features these nations now share are (1) a recent past during which the imposition of Soviet rule and Marxist ideology nearly crushed their respective economic, cultural, and social infrastructures (Revel, 1993), and (2) since approximately 1989 (or for the former Soviet nations, since 1992) they have been attempting to make a transition to a different, mostly more democratic, social order—revitalizing or recreating their cultural, social, economic, and political foundations (Rust, Knost, & Wichmann, 1994). For many, the re-creation of their culture includes such basic issues as returning their native language to the status of an official language. Such is the case, for example, in Kazakstan. Even more basic in Mongolia is the present effort for Mongols to rediscover their family names, which they were forced to drop in an effort by Soviet officials to marginalize the Mongol culture and replace it with a "Russified" one.

It is helpful to remember that within the Soviet legacy there are distinctions of time and intensity of influence of the central system. Some countries, such as Armenia and Mongolia, were incorporated into the Soviet Union early in the 20th century and were dominated by Russian language and culture for more than 80 years. Others, such as Poland, Czechoslovakia, and Hungary, were brought under Soviet domination after World War II. These latter countries managed to maintain a greater sense of identity and self-determination.

During the period of Soviet domination, a universal Soviet system of education was imposed. The hallmark of the Soviet system was centralized control: All relevant administrative decisions were made within the Ministries of Education (Szebenyi, 1992; Döbert & Manning, 1994; OECD, 1996). The school system model, in general, included extensive kindergartens (preschool programs for children ages 2–6), an 8-year basic school, and vocationally focused secondary programs with enrollments determined by national employment needs. Consequently, some students were directed toward the academically elite gymnasia for eventual university training. Others were steered toward technical schools for later work in technically oriented industries or toward attendance at technical universities. Service schools such as restaurant and hotel high schools and, in countries such as Romania, elementary teacher training high schools, as well as other vocational schools, were established in accordance with centrally determined needs. Curriculum was centrally controlled, intermixing general content with Marxist ideology. Educational research was removed from universities and placed in research academies. Research questions were typically formulated by state authorities and were intended to show support for the imposed political system. University faculty did not experience academic freedoms in the same sense Western faculties do, and they were not allowed to establish and pursue independent research agendas.

Karsten and Majoor (1994) describe the impact of the Soviet model more starkly, and there is considerable agreement among other sources with their description (see Kaufman, 1996; Read, 1989; Revel, 1993). Suggesting that communism is its own culture, Karsten and Majoor observed that substantial damage was done to education systems in four fundamental ways. Damage was done to *knowledge* through neglect, oppression, controlled access, and pervasive censorship; to *thinking* through limitation in experimentation with new ideas; to the *teaching profession* through loss of prestige, lack of respect for roles, and by requiring schools to transfer ideology; and to *values* by imposing a pseudo-value structure. Stanislav Štech (1994), decrying the Czech experience with the Soviet model writes, "The past school system model brought us not only pain, but it became anchored deeply in our consciousness and can be linked to some [prescribed] values accepted by people in everyday life" (p. 71).

This quandary over values and ideological manipulation is something the region struggles with today. It is an issue about which the poet, former dissident, and current President of the Czech Republic, Václav Havel (1992), has thoughtfully considered. He writes that, "the former regime systematically mobilized the worst human qualities, like selfishness, envy, and hatred. The regime was far more than something we deserved; it was also responsible for what we became" (p. 4). But Havel is optimistic. He states that, "Time and again I have been persuaded that a huge potential of goodwill is slumbering within our society. It's just that it's incoherent, suppressed, confused, crippled and perplexed—as though it does not know what to rely on, where to begin, where or how to find meaningful outlets" (p. 3). He concludes, "There is no simple set of instructions on how to proceed. A moral and intellectual state cannot be established through a constitution, or through laws, or through directives, but only through complex, long-term, and never-ending work involving education and self-education" (p. 20). These issues of values, and especially of overcoming decades of the manipulation of values by the state, are issues schools in these countries are confronting today.

The Context of Reform

Just what instructional practices were promoted, and why are changes needed? There are many educators throughout the region—throughout the world for that matter—who would say the educational systems of Central Europe have enjoyed enormous success. Students from the Czech, Slovak, and Baltic nations, along with students from other Central European countries, consistently score near the top percentile on international tests in science and math. Literacy rates throughout the region are typically among the highest in the world—often 85% to 90% of the population or better are literate. These rates exceed many Western countries, including most of CEE's Western European neighbors. So just what is it Central European and Central Asian educators can learn from Western reform efforts?

The answer is complicated but speaks to the heart of education in two important respects. Most nations of the region are struggling simultaneously to create democratic societies and to convert to free market economies. As recent history has shown with the struggles in Albania, Slovakia, Belarus, Russia, and Romania, establishing democratic societies is a complex and difficult process that requires a relatively sophisticated population able to make decisions that dramatically affect the quality of daily life in the near and long term (Meredith & Steele, 1998). Young democracies are fragile. It takes diligence, acceptance, consistency, reconciliation, and reconsideration to sustain genuinely democratic societies. People must be open, flexible, and willing to take responsibility for themselves and others (Meredith, 1997). Open markets require another set of sophisticated behaviors. They rely on entrepreneurship, risk taking, creativity, market sensitivity, understanding of capital markets, carefully coordinated economic sectors, relinquishing of centralized governmental controls, and creation of a system for rewarding initiative. The grand transition underway in the region requires educators to look at the end game of schooling. Great performance on a standardized test is not sufficient. The successful creation of lasting democratic institutions and robust economies depends on people capable of manifesting the behaviors, attitudes, and other prerequisite skills and abilities that undergird these institutions (Meredith & Steele, 2000a).

Consequently, the success of schooling in the region is measured more directly by the evolution of the social and economic community than by a series of tests and other artificial measures. In effect, the dynamic environment in which schools are imbedded demands that educators be reality-based. They do not have the luxury of declaring success when students score 100% on exams while their economic productivity plummets or their social institutions become ineffectual or collapse in disarray.

Toward Educational Reform

So how ready were schools in the region to accept this challenge to prepare young people for this vastly different and unpredictable future? It is helpful to know what schools and instructional practices were like, how the school day unfolded, and what the curriculum contained. As mentioned, curriculum was centrally controlled. Control was not general but specific. Significant deviations from the curriculum were not permitted. The curricular content and pace of instruction was dictated. For example, a fifth-grade science teacher would have a textbook to follow for the year. The content was to be thoroughly and meticulously taught with a series of exams conducted to monitor student success. The content was parceled out into daily instructional doses, with every fifth-grade science teacher in the country teaching from the same page on the same day. In other words, a student could leave one school in one community, cross the country to another school, and pick up exactly where he or she left off. This was true for all grades and all subjects.

In 1997, education leaders from nine nations of the region gathered for the Reading and Writing for Critical Thinking Institute in Balatonfured, Hungary (Temple, Meredith, Steele, & Walter, 1997). These educators were asked to form groups by country and to identify the strengths and weaknesses of their present education system. Within the countries present some school reform efforts had been initiated, but the school systems still largely represented pre-1989 conditions. What was most remarkable in their presentation was the similarity of both the strengths they acknowledged and their concerns.

A strength expressed unanimously by participants was the high level of expectations schools, teachers, and parents have for their young people. Students are expected to work hard, to complete assigned tasks on time, to work quietly and respectfully, to come to school prepared to learn, and to show respect for their school and their teachers. Another universal strength was that students were well-disciplined and attentive: "no extra movements" in the words of one Russian educator.

The lists of school system weaknesses of the various nations were lengthy and nearly universal. Issues of overcrowded classrooms, poor teacher salaries (teachers in Moldova, for example earn approximately US$20.00 per month and have gone as long as 7 months without being paid), insufficient supplies and materials (one of the relatively well-to-do nations of the region had a supplies and materials budget of approximately US$2.00 per pupil per year), and impoverished physical environments. This latter point varies greatly throughout the region. Schools in Estonia, Lithuania, Slovakia, Croatia, Hungary, and some other countries are clean, warm, cheerful, inviting environments where children's writings and drawings decorate hallways. Children eat in family-style cafeterias daily with soup served in large serving bowls as a first course at each table. In other countries, however, conditions are difficult to imagine. In Albania, for example, schools have suffered egregious injuries as a result of civil unrest (Meredith & Steele, 1998). Buildings typically have broken windows, limited numbers of desks and chairs or benches, no heat in the winter, and few, if any, textbooks. The same is true in Moldova. In Romania, the flow of people to Bucharest from the more rural regions resulted in triple scheduling of elementary schools, where three consecutive 3-hour school day sessions with three distinct pupil populations occurred daily in each elementary school (that is, one group of students attended in the morning, a second group in the afternoon, and a third in the early evening) to accommodate increasing enrollments, leaving already desperate buildings and staff overtaxed.

These are serious structural issues that will take time and money to resolve. Yet these were not the issues about which educators of the region were most concerned. Issues causing most concern included content taught, instructional practice, and the outcomes or consequences of schooling. Educator after educator—whether elementary, high school, or university—complained of the density of the curriculum. "Volumes of unrelated facts," complained a Kyrgy educator. "Totally teacher dominated," was the Albanian view; and from Macedonia, "full frontal teaching!" The Czechs decried the teaching atmosphere, acknowledging that the "teacher is boss and good student behavior means silence" and "truth is only one—the teacher's!" Finally, the Romanian teachers agreed that in their schools, "to learn means to eat and swallow the teacher's answers to questions...."

It is well-documented (see Gusseinov, 1996; Mitter, 1996; Meredith & Steele, 2000; Švecová, 1994) that in schools throughout the region, students' primary task is to memorize an enormous volume of factual information—"factology" as it is sometimes called. Students complete school able to recite facts across a broad array of topics and fields. What is typically absent, though, is any attention to application of the information to real situations, or integration of knowledge across fields, or the ability to decide what knowledge is useful, helpful, or important and what is not. Jana Švecová (1994) notes that there is a broad understanding that the remains of the Soviet education system cannot adequately support students in the new, market-driven, civil societies now emerging.

Educators looking toward the future believe, as the Romanians did at the Balaton institute, that the "lack of active methodology, the reliance on the simple transmission of information [is] not fostering student abilities." There is fear that students leave schooling unprepared for the challenges they will face and that they will not be prepared to integrate, initiate, create, form individual opinions, negotiate, or build consensus. There is concern, too, that students will not have had genuine experiences developing these skills and will not have a sense of their own minds. In short, they will enter a fledgling democratic community having spent their school life in a relatively voiceless, autocratic setting where dialogue, problem solving, collaborative work, the sharing of ideas and the formation of ideals, and beliefs has been discouraged.

When describing the present situation in his country, the Russian author and philosopher Abdusadan Gusseinov (1996) posits that "three tendencies characterize the recent system of education in Russia: (1) democratization, (2) a material and financial slump, and (3) loss of prestige of higher education and education in general." Vanora Bennett (1996), writing about present-day Russian schools, could have been describing the entire former sphere of Soviet influence when she said, "Today the old monolith, in which every Soviet pupil turned the same page on the same textbook on the same day in every school across eleven time zones, has been pulled apart." The question confronting educators is no longer, "Should there be reform?" Rather the question being asked is, "What form should reform take and how quickly can it be accomplished?"

What many educators in the region are calling for is a careful protection of what is good about their system coupled with a curriculum and instructional approach that will prepare young people to engage actively and productively in the reformation of their social order and the reinvention of their economic community. Balaton institute participants' wish lists included the call for more individual and group learning experiences, more active learning and teaching, greater teacher autonomy, more thoughtful and less packed curriculum, more choices for students, more practical content, more integrated curriculum, more democratically oriented classrooms, and an environment that acknowledges more than one right answer.

History and Content of Reform

Cracks began to appear in the uniform educational model prior to 1989. In the early 1980s Hungary began moving toward a decentralized system (Harangi & Toth, 1996; Németh & Pukánský, 1994; Szebenyi, 1992). This was done more on paper than in practice, but it was a benchmark in education reform that had a ripple effect throughout the region. These reforms were inspired by the belief that schools needed to become more humane. As indicated earlier, instructional practices under the Soviet model emphasized a teacher-dominated classroom where students were passive learners and teachers were repositories of knowledge. Another issue was the question of for whom the curriculum and instruction were intended. That is, without any flexibility, was instruction targeting the middle student, upper level student, or the less able students? Gusseinov (1996) answered emphatically, "The Soviet curricula...always were characterized by a comprehensive inclusiveness. The volume of information, as a rule, was beyond the student's ability to learn...every teacher faced a hard problem: To whom should the teacher orient instruction....[T]he Soviet curricula were unconditionally aimed at the strongest students" (p. 159).

As a result of these concerns about the Soviet model, five basic understandings have driven the original reform movements and continue to drive some reform efforts today (Meredith & Steele, 2000):

1. Rewriting the curriculum by removing Marxist ideology and rewriting historical accounts, broadening the literature base, and increasing textbook choices.

2. Restructuring schools to better serve newly established democratic institutions, initially targeting changes in the civic education curriculum.

3. Humanizing schools so students will have more opportunity for active learning.

4. Preparing schools for Western evaluations to bring schools up to "Western European" standards and the countries' eventual membership in the European Union.

5. Decentralizing school management by giving local authorities greater decision-making powers.

Restructuring schools so they can better support a civil society[1] and humanizing schools by introducing alternative instructional practices has proven difficult. A number of innovative school reform programs have been introduced throughout the region. Most CEE nations have adopted independent reform agendas. New education legislation is passed annually. Most legislation, in fact, focuses on restructuring the education community in one way or another. In addition, many Western organizations have supported the change processes. Such diverse groups as the World Bank, the Open Society Institute and its Soros Foundations, the European Union, the United States Agency for International Development, the United States Information Service, UNICEF, several individual nations of the European Union, as well as numerous smaller foundations and independent universities have contributed substantially to school restructuring. New civic education curricula have been developed in most nations with varying degrees of implementation success. For some nations the push for entry into the European Union intensifies the need, especially for universities, to have in place systems and standards consistent with Western European standards. This push has prompted calls for even more rapid change.

Decentralization of schools has found only limited success. Many countries have struggled with issues of local school control. Resistance is appearing, however, from many quarters. Many believe in the necessity of a national curriculum to maintain standards and a cohesive national culture. Those opposed to decentralization of schools point out that there is little expertise in rural communities to run schools. Often localities resist because control is handed over without any financial resources (UNICEF, 1998). Schools also continue to be seen as political mechanisms. Keeping school administrator positions as political appointments gives central governments a large number of political patronage jobs.

---

[1] Readers might find useful a definition of the phrase civil society. This phrase is often used synonymously with democratic society, but it is not an interchangeable term. What is implied in the term civil society is the notion that society grants what Revel (1993) refers to as "private freedoms" (p. 30). These freedoms permit individuals to act, again in Revel's words, "on their own initiative, outside the rules of the state and not in response to a rule made by the state" (p. 30). Thus a civil society is not necessarily a democratic one, while a democratic society, if it is truly democratic—that is acting on behalf of individuals and self correcting—must necessarily be civil.

Giving schools up to local control would mean letting go of this productive political asset of national governments. Finally, schools have been centrally controlled since their inception. There is no historical basis for decentralization, and thus no strong call to move in that direction (Stech, 1994).

What is clear is that schools and universities are presently defined as institutions in need of fundamental change and that school reform is inexorably linked to economic, political, and social reform (Havel, 1992; Meredith, 1998). The reforms now underway are, to some extent, meeting resistance within the schools and universities. One reason is that under the previous Soviet regime school reform was regarded with antipathy (Kaufman, 1997; Mejstřik, 1999) because it usually led to increasing bureaucracy without genuine change or measurable improvement. Most educators in the region recognize that substantive and extensive reform is critical. As one Hungarian teacher told Kaufman, "[T]raditional reform is not the answer. The only reform that stands a chance is one that will aid in overcoming crisis. Any new education policy must help as well, to reform the economy. Students may need both more education and a different education" (p. 91). In fact, reform is not simply important, it is paramount. The rejection of the Soviet model has left a void. After the 45-year imposition of a single model, few instructional alternatives are readily available. This was due to the rigid and effective control of the flow of ideas across the iron curtain. New ideas and discussions in the West about pedagogy and practice did not reach, to any significant degree, educators in the East, and the resulting isolation led to an absence of awareness of coherent alternative instructional practice models. What is needed to fill this void is not a series of piecemeal interventions but long-term, systemic school restructuring programs intended to provide a coherent education restructuring process that is open to all stakeholders and responsive to the compelling academic, social, and economic imperatives (Meredith & Steele, 1994).

Final Thoughts

The case for school reforms over the vast region of Central and Eastern Europe and Central Asia is compelling. As these nations vie for their share of the global economy, it becomes increasingly evident that the former instructional model is inadequate. The nations engaged in the great transition recognize that their young people must be equipped with far greater skills than the capacity to recite information. At a conference attended by Pedagogical University faculty and administrators from Vilnius Pedagogical University in Palanga, Lithuania, in January 1999, participants were asked what they wanted their students to be able to do as a result of their university training 10 years after graduation. Their responses are instructive. Among the most frequently cited opinions were these: students should be open to innovation; independent, responsible, critically thinking, life-long learners; eager to use new research or new tools; able to learn from failure; competent in communications; open to information but aware of its temporality; open to change; and competent in their field.

The demographic data for the countries included in the RWCT project is disturbing. These societies are aging rapidly. UNICEF (1998) presents the picture rather starkly. Since 1989 most total populations have either stagnated or declined. The population of Ukraine has declined by almost 1 million people in 8 years. More troublesome is the declining child population. Due in part to exit migration, declining child birthrate, and the increasing tendency for women to marry later, most nations of the region are experiencing precipitous declines in the school-age population. In 1997 the Czech Republic had 1.5 million fewer children between the ages of birth and 17 than in 1980. Poland had 1.2 million less, and in Bulgaria this population has been cut nearly in half from 3.3 million in 1980 to 1.8 million in 1997. These statistics mean that for these societies to function, young people will have to be far more productive, clever, flexible, resourceful, and have greater initiative than their parents or grandparents ever imagined. The kind of education they receive will determine how able they will be to overcome the enormous challenges they will face.

For those watching from a distance or contributing in some way to the transition process there are valuable lessons to be learned. The urgency of reform in the regions has given a richness to the process of change that is often lost when Western institutions, especially schools, engage in change. There is a tremendous amount at stake for the people of the region. The success of school reform will, to a large degree, predict the level of success nations will have making the transition from socialism to democracy and open-market economies. Because the stakes are so high— because the outcome is so visible in the community beyond the school walls—educators are able to link their efforts to genuine outcomes. There is a direct link to reality and schooling loses its abstract quality. Students do not wonder if education is relevant to their future, because they can clearly see what is relevant and what is not. In this context, the school reform discussion has become more focused. Questions of "whether or not" become questions of "how and when." Issues of type of reform become imperatives to develop models of reforms that work, that reach the most classrooms in the shortest time with the greatest level of integrity.

Education reform is taking longer than most thought it would. The transition has not gone quietly or smoothly. Mejstřik (1999), writing of the Czech experience since 1989, laments, "Another great disillusion of Czechs is the realization that the process of transformation from Socialism into normal open society won't last 2 or 3 years, but two or three generations. In a best-case scenario, it will be our children who will live to see a normal, naturally structured society" (p. 41). It is clear that the degree of success of the transition begun at the close of the 20th century will not be known until well into the 21st century. Therefore, it is the young people of today and tomorrow who will determine the final outcome.

Teachers like Maria quoted at the beginning of this chapter, who are engaged in the hard work of reform at the classroom level, are encouraged, even hopeful about what they see. Iveta, a young Slovak first-grade teacher enthusiastically describing how her school now works more democratically, announced, "Now we [teachers] are solving school problems through teamwork, and when we come to a solution we *have* to carry it out. We must; it's our solution." Luba, having opened her fourth-grade class to allow students to share their knowledge and opinions freely, declared in an inservice meeting of core teacher leaders in Dolny Kubin, Slovakia, "I never knew my students knew so much, thought about so many things. I feel I know them now as people." Meeli, in a monthly meeting of participating teachers, describing student responses to the RWCT reform activities in Estonia that are bringing to classrooms instructional methods that engage students in dialogue, inquiry, and active exploration of ideas and knowledge, observed that, "Students are happier, their learning is more real, it is more useful to them in their life. They are so much more involved now." Her colleague Katrin, at the same gathering of teachers, added, "Yes, they are taking responsibility now—it's not just the teacher anymore. Students are responsible."

This latter observation may be the most profound. Attempting to make sense of the 10 years of transition since 1989, Mejstřik concludes, "[O]ne of the biggest tasks ahead...is to learn responsibility. The second pole of freedom, that gift of God, is responsibility. Responsibility for every word I utter, responsibility for every child I raise. Responsibility for family, community, for the planet on which we live" (p. 41).

The peoples of this vast region are committed to the transition. The young people of the region have demonstrated over the years on the academic measures available to them that they can compete with their peers on a global level and come out on top. They represent a population of bright, industrious, serious people. Many of them are on a mission to thrive in their new 21st-century world. If school reforms are successful, the industry, discipline, and intellectual intensity of these young people will present a formidable challenge to the established Western community. Then, perhaps, school reforms in the West will take on the same kind of reality-based urgency.

REFERENCES

Bennett, V. (1996, October 24). Old-world educators preparing a generation of new Russians, *Star Tribune*, p. A22.

Döbert, H., & Manning, S. (1994). The transformation of the East German school and its relation to international developments in education. In V.D. Rust, P. Knost, & J. Wichmann (Eds.), *Education and the values crisis in central and eastern Europe*. Frankfurt, Germany: Peter Lang.

Gusseinov, A. (1996). Education for democracy in Russia. In A. Oldenquist (Ed.), *Can democracy be taught?* Bloomington, IN: Phi Delta Kappa Educational Foundation.

Harangi, L., & Toth, J. Sz., (1996). Hungary. In S. Haddad (Ed.), *International Review of Education*, 42(1–3), 59–74. Hamburg, Germany: UNESCO Institute for Education.

Havel, V. (1992). *Summer meditations*. New York: Vintage.

Karsten, S., & Majoor, D. (1994). Differences and similarities in Hungary, Czechoslovakia and Poland. In S. Karsten & D. Majoor (Eds.), *Education in East Central Europe: Education changes after the fall of Communism*. Munster, Germany: Waxman Verlag.

Kaufman, C.C. (1997, February). Transformation education in Hungary. *Social Education*. pp. 89–92.

Mejstřik, M. (1999, January). Czech Republic: The revolution's fading velvet. *Transitions*, pp. 38–41.

Meredith, K.S., & Steele, J.L. (1994). *The Orava Project: A Slovak Republic/University of Northern Iowa collaborative national education restructuring program*. Grant proposal funded by the United States Agency for International Development, Washington, DC.

Meredith, K.S. (1997a). *Education in Albania: The status of education and education reform*. A report prepared for United States Agency for International Development, Orava Foundation for Democratic Education, Bratislava, Slovakia.

Meredith, K.S. (1997b, April 17). Albania adrift. *Des Moines Sunday Register*, p. C1.

Meredith, K.S. (1998). What does democracy and education mean anyway? In *Ways of democracy in instruction and education*. Bratislava, Slovakia: Iunenta.

Meredith, K.S., & Steele, J.L. (1998). *Multilevel reform of the Albania education system: Obstacles and opportunities*. A comprehensive evaluation of Albanian education submitted to the United States Agency for International Development, Washington, DC.

Meredith, K.S., & Steele, J.L. (2000). Education in transition: Trends in Central and Eastern Europe. In M.L. Kamil, P.B. Mosenthal, P.D. Pearson, & R. Barr (Eds.), *Handbook of reading research*, Vol. III. Mahwah, NJ: Erlbaum.

Meredith, K.S., Steele, J.L., & Shannon, P. (1994, December). *Critical literacy as a foundation for critical democracy*. Paper presented at the National Reading Conference, San Diego, CA.

Mitter, W. (1996). Democracy and education in Central and Eastern Europe. In A. Oldenquist (Ed.), *Can democracy be taught?* Bloomington, IN: Phi Delta Kappa Educational Foundation.

Németh, A., & Pukánský, B. (1994). Tendencies and reforms in the Hungarian school system in historical perspective. In V.D. Rust, P. Knost, & J. Wichmann (Eds.), *Education and the values crisis in central and eastern Europe*. Frankfurt, Germany: Peter Lang.

Organization for Economic Cooperation and Development (OECD). (1996). *Reviews of national policies for education—Czech Republic*. Paris: Commission of the European Communities, OECD.

Read, G.H. (1989, April). Education in the Soviet Union: Has Perestroika met its match? *Phi Delta Kappan, 70*(8), 606–613.

Revel, J.F. (1993). *Democracy against itself*. New York: The Free Press, Macmillan.

Rust, V.D., Knost, P., & Wichmann, J. (Eds.). (1994). *Education and the values crisis in central and eastern Europe*. Frankfurt, Germany: Peter Lang.

Rutland, P. (1999, January). The Meaning of 1989. *Transitions*, pp. 23–28.

Štech, S. (1994). Values changes in the Czech school system: Looking beyond the ideological bias. In V.D. Rust, P. Knost, & J. Wichmann (Eds.), *Education and the values crisis in central and eastern Europe*. Frankfurt, Germany: Peter Lang.

Švecová, J. (1994). Czechoslovakia. In S. Karsten & D. Majoor (Eds.), *Education in east central Europe: Educational changes after the fall of communism*. Munster, Germany: Waxman Verlag.

Szebenyi, P. (1992). State centralization and school autonomy: Processes of educational change in Hungary. In D. Phillips & M. Kaser (Eds.), *Education and economic change in eastern Europe and the Soviet Union*. Wallingford, UK: Triangle Books.

Temple, C., Meredith, K.S., Steele, J.L., & Walter, S. (1997). *Report on the Reading and Writing for Critical Thinking Institute*. Cedar Falls, IA: Consortium for Democratic Education, University of Northern Iowa, Department of Education.

UNICEF. (1998). *Education for all? The Monee Project CEE/CIS/Baltics Regional Monitoring Report No. 5*. Florence, Italy: United Nation's Children's Fund International Child Development Center.

CHAPTER THREE

Interactive Literacy Education, Engaged Citizenship, and Open Societies

Charles Temple

At first glance, it may seem odd that institutions interested in promoting the construction of open societies would recruit a group of literacy educators to work the front lines. It may seem odder still that the literacy educators, once recruited, have rarely spoken of "open societies," or "democracy" or "citizenship." Once in-country the RWCT volunteers have done what we always do in North Carolina, Iowa, New York, Ohio, British Columbia, Queensland, Virginia, Texas, or the Midlands of England. We ask open questions. We encourage diverse opinions. We ask the participants to decide. We invite the participants to write what they think and what they feel. We show them structures for working in groups to solve problems. We urge them to be respectful of differences and show them what we mean by that. Now, after 3 years in the 24 countries in Central and Eastern Europe and Central Asia in which we work, Reading and Writing for Critical Thinking is listed among the most successful projects in the region's efforts to reform education and promote engaged citizenship.

The relationship between classroom practices and the construction of open societies is not obvious to everyone. Before making my first trip to Romania in 1996, I reviewed five books written since 1989 on political transformation in that country. Four made no mention of education. The fifth said education would be of no consequence in political transformation because the teachers in Romania were conservative and supported the old regime (one wonders how the author got this information).

Those who have read John Dewey, Celestin Freinet, Paolo Freire, and other progressive educators see a direct connection between the practice of schooling and students' participation in society. In 1915 John and Evelyn Dewey wrote in *The Schools of Tomorrow*:

> If we train children to take orders, to do things because they are told to, and fail to give them confidence to act and think for themselves, we are putting an almost insurmountable obstacle in the way of overcoming the present defects of our system, and of establishing the truth of democratic ideals. Our state is founded on freedom but when we train the state of tomorrow, we allow it just as little freedom as possible. Children in school must be allowed freedom so that they will know what its use means when they become the controlling body, and they must be allowed to develop active qualities of initiative, independence, resourcefulness, before the abuses and failures of democracy will disappear. (p. 304)

Those who do not see this connection perhaps have a static view of education or democracy or both. Brophy, Temple, and Meredith (in press) put the problem this way:

> When many people think of education, the concept that comes to mind is one of imparting knowledge; and knowledge of democracy evokes the mechanics of voting or the contents of political treatises. If "democracy" is merely associated with the pantheon of heroic democrats, or a body of treatises on democracy, or even the mechanisms of voting and government, then the study of democracy is not likely to go very far toward achieving the societal transformations for which democratic institutions are themselves means.

> If "education" is thought to be the accumulation of facts for passing examinations, then education in that sense will not change behavior in any appreciable way. But when democracy is understood dynamically, as daily habits of communication and behavior, then the outlines of a democracy-enabling approach to education become perceptible: It is one that links educational practice to specific behaviors associated with democracy.

In designing the Orava Project in Slovakia, Jeannie Steele and Kurt Meredith forged a connection between a dynamic definition of democratic citizenship and student-centered classroom practices. For their definition of democracy, they drew from James Revel (1993), who suggested that for democratic societies to flourish, citizens must practice behaviors in their daily lives that support and promote democratic ideals, including self-reflection, responsibility for self, social responsibility, tolerance, power sharing, opinion formation, critical thinking, and decision making. It is fairly easy to see how the classroom practices of journal writing, writing-to-learn, interpretive discussions, debates, workshop-based instruction, cooperative learning, and problem solving contribute directly to the formation of these behaviors and the habits of the heart and mind that support them. In fact, it is difficult to imagine any other institutional approach that has nearly the potential to influence these behaviors and attitudes as schooling does.

Having said all that, I need to remind the reader that the Reading and Writing for Critical Thinking Project is not, never was, and never will be an exercise in politics. That will be clear if one considers the origins of the project.

Reka Demeter was a young mother who worked as assistant librarian at the Soros Foundation office in Cluj, Romania. Her daughter, Czengi, was 9 years old and attending a school so heavy with academics that the joy of reading and the pleasures of sharing ideas were being lost. Reka happened to attend a conference of the International Reading Association (IRA), where she met Attila Nagy, then president of the Hungarian Reading Association. She told him of her wish to form reading groups for children Czengi's age, and Attila suggested she contact the International Reading Association's headquarters in Delaware, USA. Reka wrote an e-mail to IRA Headquarters and asked if someone might be willing to come to Transylvania to give workshops to show teachers and librarians how to form book clubs and manage discussions, so children would get more enjoyment out of reading. Later the invitation was expanded to include workshops in Bucharest, as well. I conducted the workshop in Cluj, Transylvania, and Jeannie Steele and Kurt Meredith led the one in Bucharest.

I will never forget that first workshop. The teachers were polite but skeptical. Other local education experts led off with speeches about reading theory. When my turn came, because the trip was partly sponsored by the Open Society Institute, I thought it appropriate to speak on the relationship between progressive reading methods and the process of democratization. Bad idea—arms folded even more tightly across chests, and neutral expressions turned to frowns. Then we got into what I had actually come to do. During a whole week, I demonstrated a range of interactive teaching methods: a Directed Reading-Thinking Activity (DRTA), a Shared Inquiry Discussion, a Dual-Entry Diary, and a writing workshop. One by one, people were drawn into the activities.

But there were still doubts. Vasile Fleurasch asked, "How do we know this isn't Walt Disney education you're offering?" I explained that I wrote books for children, and that he could count on me as an ally in the struggle to keep the purveyors of commercial culture from taking over the world. I told him, "Critical thinking is the best defense we have of our independence and originality." He unfolded his arms, and has since become a tireless advocate of RWCT, conducting as many as four workshops a week.

By the time we reached the writing workshop, people were enjoying themselves. Iuliu Parvu, a highly respected member of the group, shared his writing from the author's chair. In my office at the university I keep a cherished photograph of his beaming face.

At the end of the week, I asked people which of the demonstrated approaches appealed to them. They wanted comprehension-building strategies, discussion strategies, writing-to-learn strategies, and the writing process. And they wanted more workshops. A forerunner project to RWCT was born: Reka named it "Reading for Understanding." What turned out to be democratic about the workshop was the way in which the participants were invited to choose the contents and the methods themselves. We never mentioned open societies or democratic citizenship again.

What value do participants see in interactive methods? The teachers we meet are well-trained, intelligent, well-read, and dedicated to children. For an example of dedication, consider the teachers of Moldova, who taught through most of the 1998–1999 school year in unheated buildings, with sporadic electricity, no running water, and no paychecks. The schools of Central and Eastern Europe and Central Asia have high standards. For an example of the level of rigor the schools maintain, a Romanian couple told me about moving with their two children to the suburbs of Washington, DC. By the end of September, their seventh-grade son was at the top of his class in the school. Their sixth-grade son, who did not know any English when they arrived in August, was at the top of his class by March.

But there are problems with the schools. When we begin a series of workshops in the region, we always begin with a needs assessment activity, and here we learn interesting things. On the positive side we hear that the students and teachers are both serious, and that they teach and learn plenty of information. Among the criticisms, though, are that students are disengaged, that they do not express original opinions or go beyond the information that is provided them. Teachers lecture too often, it is said, and reduce students to passive listening and giving back what was told to them. As a participant in an RWCT workshop in Albania demonstrated, "We have teachers who look like this:" [He drew a face with a big mouth and small ears]. "We need teachers who look like this:" [He drew a face with a small mouth and big ears]. (See Chapter Two in this volume for further discussion of the issues faced by educators and schools in the region.)

We also hear that the curriculum is jammed full of facts—"factology," is how one educator describes the phenomenon—but with too few connections to the students' lives. Students absorb prodigious amounts of information, yet their teachers complain that they are unable to do very much with it. This latter problem was recently reflected in the comments by Czech Minister of Education, Jan Sokol:

> Quite simply, our students hate most of our schools, and they have reason to do so. [Our] education is performance-oriented, designed to increase the absorption of facts and produce good results on exams. What about the other roles that schools must serve? What about personal development? (quoted in Viviano, 1998)

Thirteen-year-olds in his country had just registered the highest science achievement test scores in the world. A Czech physicist complained, "The top scientists, the imaginative thinkers, don't come from our country. They come from America and Asia. Somewhere around the age of 20 here [when, the physicist says, elsewhere critical thinking and not factual knowledge alone becomes the criterion of success], the edge is lost."

The teaching strategies RWCT volunteers brought to this setting involve prediction and hypothesis testing, eliciting prior knowledge, encouraging debate among students, writing to learn, response techniques, and cooperative learning. From the very beginning, the methods struck a responsive chord. As a Russian participant put it, "We have the big ideas [the theories behind active learning and critical thinking and why they are good things]; what we need are the small ideas [how you actually teach critical thinking]."

Success did not always come all at once, however. For example, evoking personal responses lies at the heart of several of our strategies, yet at the start of a workshop, willingness to share personal responses could not be taken for granted. When we first asked for a personal response, we often got flourishes of intellectual brilliance instead. I recall a workshop I gave with another volunteer to a group of university pedagogical specialists. After we told a sad and provocative story, I broke the silence by asking, "What is on your mind right now? How did the story make you *feel?*" One professor raised his hand and said, "What is on my mind is the binary oppositional theory of Claude Levi-Strauss applied to the duality between the first and second elements in the story...."

Another troublesome issue for many participants was the authority of knowledge. At one workshop we were discussing the poem, "As Best She Could" by Donald Jones, a poem that invites competing interpretations. Although over the course of 30 minutes the participants heatedly set out and supported three sound interpretations, at the end of the session they turned to us and said, "All right, this is an American poem, so you please tell us, what does the poem really mean?" It seemed that our lecture on the "interpretive community" was first taken as an evasion, and it was only after several sessions that people grew comfortable with the idea that a group of people might have the power, and the right, to make interpretations without relying on an outside authority. (See Beers et al., Chapter Eleven in this volume, for an investigation of the theoretical issues associated with literary interpretation in Russia.)

The authority of knowledge and the nature of the truth, of course, should not be taken lightly. At a workshop in Albania, I shared one of my favorite stories, a tale of the selchie who has a family on land after her eventual husband steals her seal skin, but is then forever separated from that family when she recovers the skin and slips back into the sea. At the story's end I posed this question: "Would it have been better if her husband had never taken the seal skin?" In the course of the ensuing debate, the group divided into two groups. One group thought the husband was right to take the skin, because man should assume power over nature, and man must satisfy his curiosity regardless of the consequences. The other thought the husband was wrong because he violated the rights of the seal-woman. Not surprisingly, those in the first group were mostly men and those in the latter mostly women. This time, when asked which side was right, I had an answer ready. I reminded them that the argument they had raised was as old as the Book of Genesis. It was the theme of the Greek tragedian Euripides's *The Bacchae*. And it was the basis of fascinating debates today between scientists and environmentalists, between traditional scholars in many fields and feminists. Dignifying disagreements by relating positions to philosophical traditions has become a strategy we use when the interpretive community shakes down to more than one interpretation.

We have had other challenges, too: people extending a teaching strategy beyond its natural reach (such as using a prediction strategy to teach impressionistic literature), or using an inquiry strategy in a didactic way and turning it into something more like an inquisition. In some settings, the idea of an open discussion, with everyone contributing to everyone's understanding, has not come naturally. In the beginning, instead of the give-and-take of discussion we sometimes hear a series of speeches, even by children. (In one classroom, when it came his turn to speak, an 11-year-old boy stood, folded his arms behind his back, stared over the heads of his classmates, and shouted out his ideas, like a politician giving an oration.) And everywhere teachers are challenged to find time in a packed national curriculum to build a lesson around the students' inquiry.

But the problems have been surprisingly few. For one thing, the participants are excellent teachers. For another, the volunteer workshop leaders are excellent trainers. Third, in most countries, RWCT is moving education in a direction many leaders want it to go—ministers of education, for example, are now certifying people who have participated in RWCT to be national trainers in school reform efforts. Then, the implementation blueprint of the project calls for an intelligent pattern of activities: demonstration lessons, open discussion and critique, explanation of the procedures, guided practice, classroom practice, observation and feedback, and modification of the strategy or the teacher's use of it. In the process we use, people have ample opportunities to learn when and how to use the teaching methods. If problems arise, they are dealt with before they become entrenched.

The communication among all of us is another advantage built into this project that goes a long way toward ensuring its success. For example, in one of my workshops I had been semi-conscious of the difficulty of having truly participatory discussions, but it was not until another volunteer named the problem in an e-mailed note that many of us became fully conscious of it. Within the week, helpful suggestions began to roll in, spelling out strategies for dealing with this problem. We have used communication proactively, too. When RWCT was about to expand into a country that had recently experienced a fratricidal war, I worried what the effect of doing writing workshops there might be. After all, our volunteers would go in, show people how to do writing workshops, then go away for 6 weeks. How might the students react to the invitation to write freely about their experiences, when they had experienced unspeakably terrible events? I put this question to an incoming volunteer who had long conducted writing workshops in inner-city neighborhoods and was used to working with students who were surrounded by violence. She wrote a well-reasoned and reassuring set of suggestions, and we circulated it to all the volunteers.

How has the project been received by the participants? We have been told in several countries that RWCT is far and away the most professionally delivered and most useful teacher training available. Teachers note changes in their students and in themselves. For example, after a year-long series of workshops in Kyrgyzstan, the participants wrote these comments about changes they had observed in the students:

Students are taking more risks in learning and communicating.

The classroom is a psychologically safer and more comfortable learning environment.

Students are assuming more responsibility for learning in the classroom.

Students appear to feel more comfortable using creative and higher order thinking.

When asked what changes they had noted in their own teaching, the teachers noted the following:

They spend more time planning their lessons.

Before teaching the material, they examine it for opportunities to promote critical thinking.

They allow students more opportunities to work alone and in groups.

They look for additional materials to help students learn on their own.

They wait longer to listen to what students are going to say.

They ask more open-ended questions.

They encourage more (varied) responses to their questions.

They look for ways for the students to relate what they are learning to their own experiences and prior knowledge.

They think of ways for students to "mine" their own knowledge, instead of thinking of students only as places to "deposit" more knowledge.

They have become more like what they want their students to become: patient, flexible, takers of risks, analytic.

It was noted at the beginning of this chapter that although the sponsors of RWCT are committed to preparing young people to participate as active and engaged citizens in open societies, those of us directly involved in the project do not talk politics in our workshops. In fact, in their orientation, we deliberately ask volunteers to avoid political discussions. In this light, it is interesting to note the political language in which these Romanian participants recount the benefits of using RWCT methods:

> These methods promise to free the child's thinking from the dictatorship of the teacher's belief that "I know everything and I want you to know the truth that I have."

> These methods suggest that we should forget about pedagogical theories and free ourselves from the censorship each of us has been equipped with. The methods imply knowing our material and knowing our children.

> This is a different method of transmitting knowledge that brings you closer to your students and makes you feel forever young, forever capable of learning new things.

> This is more dynamic activity, based on constructive contradiction. The student is forced to find arguments on both sides, which means they will think critically and reach a conclusion that they will have to support. This means they will have to confront their own beliefs, and entertain arguments against them.

And what have *we* gotten out of this experience? (One source of surprise and delight is that the pronoun *we* now embraces Mongolians, Kazaks, Kyrgyzs, Russians, Latvians, Albanians, Australians, Slovaks, Romanians, Macedonians, Americans, Canadians, one priceless Englishman, and many, many more). As a volunteer in Romania and Albania and as one of the founding directors and authors of this project, I identify with much of what the Kyrgyzs and Romanians said. I understand what the person meant by feeling "forever young," having gone to places I never thought I would go, made new friends, and put my shoulder to the wheel alongside some of the most interesting people one could ever meet. Other volunteers report the same sentiments: After her first workshop, one volunteer said, "I am 50 years old. I never expected to be this excited again."

In being careful to practice what we preach, I suspect many of us have become more engaged and responsive teachers. In seeing the teaching methods we have long used applied in new settings, we have certainly become aware of their potential contribution to the building of more participatory and more humane societies. All of us need to work for such societies, wherever we live. Teachers, as John Dewey (1916) told us, are at the front line of that work. In order to do it well, Dewey suggested that we use methods that we now call constructivist, cooperative, and student-centered. After the experience of working in the Reading and Writing for Critical Thinking Project, we have a better appreciation for the transformative power of those methods.

REFERENCES

Brophy, S., Temple, C., & Meredith, K. (in press). Can civic virtue be taught? In D. Gordon & D. Durst (Eds.), *Civil society in uncivil times*. Amsterdam: Rodopi Press.

Dewey, J. (1916). *Democracy and education*. New York: Macmillan.

Dewey, J., & Dewey, E. (1915). *The schools of tomorrow*. New York: Dutton.

Revel, J.F. (1993). *Democracy against itself*. New York: Free Press, Macmillan.

Viviano, F. (1998, April 21). World's top test scores not enough for Czechs; Top thinkers seem to belong to west. *San Francisco Chronicle*, p. A1.

How Teachers and Students Change

CHAPTER FOUR

In Their Own Voices:
Reflection as an Agent of Teacher
Change in Estonia

Maureen McLaughlin and MaryEllen Vogt
with Katrin Poom-Valickis, Meeli Pandis, and Sirje Tikk

I have risen to a new stage of thinking. My approach to problems is more creative, more open, and more positive. I am much more confident and my
lessons are more diversified and interesting than 2 years ago. The main value of these 2 years is the discovery that it is so simple, refreshing, and enrapturing to learn.

Katrin Kalamees

The quotation that opens this chapter mirrors our experience in the
Reading and Writing for Critical Thinking (RWCT) project in
Estonia. Whether volunteer, host country project director, team
member, or interpreter, we have each experienced a personal metamor-
phosis that compels us to heartily endorse the thought that "it is so simple, refreshing, and enrapturing to learn."

Beyond our individual experiences, as a team we have witnessed another remarkable transition. Workshop participants have transformed
themselves from traditional teachers into multidimensional educators focused on student-centered learning. Their efforts have been validated not
only by their peers, but also by their students' development from passive
observers to active learners.

In this chapter, we examine our participants' reflections as they experienced a paradigm shift from traditionally structured, factology-driven,
lecture-based instruction to active, cooperative, student-centered teaching. We begin by offering background information about the participants
and by introducing a theoretical framework for reflectivity. Next, we focus on our participants' use of reflection at three different phases of the
project: while learning about critical thinking, when applying the strate-

gies in teaching their students, and after having taught the strategies in their classrooms and in their workshops. The chapter concludes by presenting the outcomes of RWCT in Estonia and participants' hopes for the future. Examples of participants' reflective thinking and their students' reactions to using the critical thinking strategies appear throughout the chapter, and themes emerging from these reflections are identified and discussed.

Background of RWCT in Estonia

In the initial stages, participants in the RWCT project in Estonia described themselves as focused on "teaching facts through lecture, covering the text, and testing." The contexts in which they taught were often teacher-centered, and the students' roles focused on activities such as reading, listening to lectures, notetaking, and test taking. Essentially, the learning experiences were driven by the acquisition of facts, and elements of student-centered learning, such as response-centered classrooms, critical thinking, cooperative learning, strategy use, and integration of language arts, were markedly absent. It is important to note, however, that education in Estonia was not always characterized in this manner. Active learning strategies were promoted even before World War II, but they were suppressed while the country was under Soviet rule.

The 35 Estonian educators who first participated in the RWCT project were selected from 100 applicants. According to their application essays, teachers, professors, doctoral candidates, and representatives from the Ministry of Education engaged in the program for a variety of reasons: motivation, interest in the topic, new knowledge, new methods of teaching, and reformation of an outdated educational system. They came searching for methods to put into practice, to gain self-confidence, to experience cooperation and to develop better relationships with their students. They believed that critical thinkers desire knowledge, ask questions, use resources, revise their thinking, express themselves logically, seek alternatives, build connections, and remain open-minded.

Theoretical Framework

The role of reflection in the educational process can be traced to Dewey (1933). He believed that engaging in reflection enhanced the thinking process, and he encouraged teachers to abandon prescribed routines and become thoughtful students of their own practice. Current thinking about reflection is underpinned by Dewey's work. King and Kitchner (1994) reported that thinking reflectively includes an "ongoing evaluation of one's fundamental assumptions about knowledge and about the process of learning" (p. 230). Freire (1985) observed that "reflectivity is rightfully active. It calls for personal and professional transformation" (p. 5).

Self-reflection is a critical component of the teaching and learning process (Darling-Hammond, Ancess, & Falk, 1995; McLaughlin & Vogt, 1998, 2000; Schon, 1987). It encourages educators "to ask better questions, break out of fruitless routines, make unexpected connections, and experiment with fresh ideas" (Brandt, 1991, p. 3). As educators engage in instruction, they reflect on their teaching and the effectiveness of the lesson. The same can be true for students. When they are learning, they can reflect on the effectiveness of the experience. Such reflections offer insights into various dimensions of the teaching and learning process that can lead to better understanding (Schon, 1987).

Reflectivity in RWCT Estonia

Reflection has been an integral part of our RWCT experience in Estonia. From the outset, participants regularly engaged in reflective activities during the workshops, maintained self-reflective journals when workshops were not in session, and shared reflections at monthly meetings. They also wrote detailed reflective essays titled, "The Teacher I Was...The Teacher I've Become" at the end of the first year. Examples of reflective activities that occurred during the workshops included quickwrites, responding to prompts, Think-Pair-Share interactions, Gallery Walks, and monitoring techniques such as "Tickets Out." The journals, which were maintained outside the workshops, were initiated at the start of the program in September 1997 and continued through June 1998. Entries focused on teachers' learning experiences, planning sessions, and personal, as well as student, reactions to changes in teaching and learning. The monthly meetings incorporated reflectivity that focused on implementing the critical thinking strategies and other innovations in the classroom. On these occasions, participants were able to take an in-depth look at their teaching and share their successes and challenges with colleagues in a supportive environment. Later in the project, participants maintained "trainer journals" as they began to offer their own RWCT workshops.

The integration of reflection throughout the RWCT process offered opportunities for participants to experience *reflection-on-action* as they contemplated how to use the strategies with their students; *reflection-in-action* as they integrated their new knowledge into their teaching; and *reflection-for-action* as they analyzed their performance as teachers and workshop presenters (Killion & Todnem, 1991; Schon, 1987). As suggested by Reagan, Case, Case, and Freiberg (1993), the reflection functioned as a spiral activity in which the result of one type of reflection led to another.

Reflection-On-Action

Reflection-on-action was a natural component of our RWCT workshops. It occurred in multiple formats, including individual, paired, and small-group activities; discussion; writing; and strategy use.

While learning the critical thinking strategies, one of the reflective activities in which our RWCT participants engaged was a monitoring technique called "Tickets Out." At the end of each workshop, we gave participants index cards and asked them to write something important they had learned that day on one side of the card and a question they had about what they had learned on the other. This offered the participants an opportunity to reflect on what they had learned. They were not required to write their names on the cards. The activity is called "Tickets Out" because we collected the cards from the participants as they left the workshop session.

Once all the cards were collected, we could use the information for two valuable purposes: to monitor participants' understanding and to give direction to future teaching. The information on side one afforded us insights into the accuracy of the participants' learning. The student-generated questions on side two helped us understand what topics needed to be clarified or expanded on. After reading side one of all the cards, we noted what the participants had learned, as well as any misinterpretations of information. While reading side two of the cards, we set aside those questions that needed to be addressed. We then responded to the questions at the start of the next workshop session. This provided a wonderful sense of continuity for both teaching and learning. In addition, the participants quickly understood how they could use "Tickets Out" in their own classrooms.

Participants first engaged in "Tickets Out" at the conclusion of our initial workshop. As we reviewed their questions, the first query raised was, "How do you make students active without giving orders?" We were surprised when we read the question, but we knew it arose from the factology-based view of education that existed in Estonia at that time. We also knew that a meaningful answer would become evident only over the course of the training sessions. However, we did respond to the question at the start of the next class. It was an interesting experience because it involved further development of a climate of trust among our small educational community. What we told participants was that the answer would become clear to them as the workshops progressed. Several workshops later, we revisited this question and our initial response. Our students smiled. They knew from their own experience that we were not making them active; they were becoming active on their own. A prime example of this transition can be seen in our participants' reflective responses to a small-group activity during the first workshop and a planning activity completed in the final workshop of Year One. During the first workshop participants discussed how they assessed their students, and the collective response was, "We give tests." When this same issue was revisited after our assessment workshop, participants' responses varied considerably and included that they would have their students write, analyze, create, design, synthesize, maintain journals, quickwrite, use graphic organizers, experiment, illustrate, question, or solve.

Other activities that we used to encourage reflection-on-action included quickwrites and cooperative activities such as "Think-Pair-Share" and "Gallery Walk." The "Think-Pair-Share" cooperative strategy (McTighe & Lyman, 1988) incorporates wait time and promotes interaction and reflection. Participants listen to a question, think about their individual response, talk with a partner, and then share with the class. The "Gallery Walk" was used to promote the sharing of ideas. When participants met in small groups to brainstorm responses, they recorded their ideas on chart paper. These were pasted around the room, like paintings in a gallery. Then each group visited all of the charts, discussing the ideas set forth and raising related questions. The activity concluded with a whole-class discussion of responses. These reflective monitoring techniques encouraged both the participants and us to think critically. The outcome was improved teaching and learning.

Reflection-In-Action

Reflection-in-action occurred in a variety of contexts, including the workshops, the participants' classrooms, and sessions the participants directed as RWCT trainers. In all three settings, participants developed plans, taught lessons, and engaged in reflection-in-action. They also sought the reactions of their peers, their students, and those who participated in their workshops. The participants then used this information to analyze personal growth, to promote discussion with fellow participants during workshops and monthly meetings, to plan the workshops they conducted as RWCT trainers, to add a reflective dimension to their portfolios, and in several cases, to develop theses for their master's degrees.

Journals were the primary means of recording these reflections. Entries included lesson plans with marginal notes on successes and failures, students' reactions to lessons, goals for future teaching, and thoughts about achieving goals for individual lessons and for the entire year. In the following excerpt, Kadri-Ly Trahv, an educator for more than 30 years, who currently teaches physics to grades 10 and 12 in the Rakvere Gymnasium, delineates the role her journal played in her RWCT training:

> I have used my journal to jot down a preliminary vision of a lesson or myself as a teacher or trainer. After each lesson or workshop, I have recorded an objective analysis of the work, finding the pluses and minuses. I have found this to be an excellent means of critical reflection. Because I am a teacher using critical thinking strategies, I must myself be a critical thinker. This is an important step in helping my students become critical, lifelong learners, which is characteristic of a democratic society.
>
> When I analyze the journal after some time, it's good to perceive how my own way of thinking has changed and whether I have reached the next level of development. When I have been confused or uncertain about something, I can say that the journal has helped me to clarify my ideas and create a kind of inner order of thought. A kind of new certainty forms which encourages me to take new steps.

Examples of reflection-in-action concerning strategy use, time allocation, and classroom organization can be seen in the following excerpts from the journals of three project participants. Information about the author precedes each entry.

Mari Karm teaches Estonian language and literature in the Tartu Music School and public performance in the Audentes Business High School. She joined RWCT to get new ideas about how to get her students to think, learn, and do research. Mari believes that the project has changed her attitude toward teaching and learning. She trusts her students more now and expects more of them. She has also started to think about teaching and learning in greater depth. Mari's journal entry focuses on teaching poetry to fourth-year students. This lesson had positive aspects and a moment of self-discovery:

> The strategy, "Save the Last Word for Me," was used with the poem "The Snake's Movement on a Stone Leaves a Mark" by Karl Ristikivi. A special atmosphere was created and I managed to have the students look into themselves to reflect on the poem. The students respected the ideas of their classmates.
>
> In the beginning, I was afraid there would be no responses to what was read out, so I interfered too early by expressing my opinion. Through this lesson I came to understand that students need to be given more time for thinking and I should be more patient and wait to express my opinion. Conclusion: I should observe myself and not hurry to express my own ideas.

Siri Jehe and Tiina Nurm are project participants who have been teaching for about 20 years. They are currently faculty members at Rapla Vesiroosi Gymnasium. Siri teaches the Estonian language and Tiina teaches English. Siri and Tiina's papers were based on the use of critical thinking strategies in Estonian literature and foreign languages, respectively. Siri and Tiina participated in RWCT because they wanted to find a new approach to their teaching. Since completing the program, they have conducted workshops for the teachers and headmasters at their school. Participants, students, parents, and colleagues have acknowledged the positive impact of the program.

In one of her journal entries, Siri reflected on using the concept of definition map with her eleventh-grade students. The topic was literary realism:

> I began the lesson by having students brainstorm what they already knew about realism. I put the graphic organizer on the chalkboard and asked students to complete it in pairs. This took more time than I had allotted.
>
> The good aspects of this concept map lesson were that the students found it challenging, the discussion worked well, the questions were meaningful, and students felt they could use the strategy in multiple subject areas. The negative aspects were that it took a lot of time to complete the strategy and that the text in the book was too long and too complicated. Next time, I would organize differently and perhaps have the students complete the map independently and then compare it with a peer's.

Tiina's entry was taken from the journal she maintained as an RWCT trainer. In this excerpt, she reflects on what Siri, her training partner, and she experienced while conducting a workshop:

In the third session of our workshops, we planned too little time for participants to discuss the achievements and challenges they had experienced since our last meeting. We did it through the Gallery Walk and that was good, but it did take time. Because of this we were not able to explain the strategy until the next morning and this caused some misunderstandings. We must remember never to economize on time while unpacking a strategy. It wastes a lot of time later on. I must remember to give instructions in a really clear way and not over explain.

We also introduced the idea of maintaining portfolios for certification and realized that in the future we should explain this concept at the very start of the course. One solution might be to have a contract stating our tasks and participants' obligations. This may just be a problem connected with having the course in our own school.

On the whole, our goals for the session were achieved. The ERR framework has become clearer and the strategies have become more essential for everybody. We have shown our achievements, helped each other to overcome problems, and started planning concrete lessons. For the next session participants will analyze lesson plans they have created.

Because the journals contained information about successes, failures, and new goals, they served as valuable resources in workshop sessions and monthly meetings. Writing their reflections helped participants remember details of their experiences and provided a rich, real-life record of what they thought and felt as they were teaching the strategies for the first time. These served as powerful teaching examples when the participants themselves became RWCT trainers. The journals also encouraged a wonderful sense of camaraderie, because participants freely shared what worked well and what did not. This, in turn, promoted small- and large-group discussion, which fostered further change.

The full text of participants' journals indicates that redefining the relationship between teachers and students was a recurring theme. In a culture in which the teacher has traditionally been viewed as an authority responsible for knowledge and evaluation, these newly defined relationships, describing teachers and students as members of the same team, were a major indicator that a positive transition had begun to take place. Other themes that emerged from the journal entries included the importance of goal-setting, the value of response-centered classrooms, and the collegial atmosphere promoted by cooperative work. When one of the participants described her journal as her "coteacher," the others heartily agreed, adding that their journals had become wonderful resources and that they could clearly see their own development by looking at the entries.

Reflection-For-Action

Our participants also used reflection to seek direction for their future teaching. Evidence of reflection-for-action can be found in the reflective essay "The Teacher I Was…The Teacher I've Become," which participants wrote at the end of the first year, their students' reflections on the impact of RWCT on their learning, and participants' responses to prompts about being RWCT trainers. In their own voices, the participants and their students spoke about their personal growth, the impact of their teaching and learning experiences, and their hopes for the future.

Participants' reflections on the teachers they have become. When participants reflected and wrote about the teachers they had become, every essay described attributes of positive change. Their writing focused on changes in themselves (self-knowledge, self-esteem), changes in their students (openness, sense of trust), and changes in their teaching (more courage, greater dedication). They also focused on changing one's way of thinking and putting theory into practice. Katrin Poom-Valickis, a project participant and director, incorporated many of these themes in her essay:

> For me, participating in RWCT has meant learning to think in a different way, reconsidering and evaluating certain things, quite often discovering the old in an integral context. I agree with the participants who have said that before the course they had some knowledge and acquired different methods. But those seemed to be separate pieces of a puzzle that found their right spot in the picture just this year, as they formed a system and a meaningful whole.

> Our teachers have helped us to understand this new way of thinking. I especially appreciate the practical examples they have been able to give from their own experiences, how they have used a strategy, what has worked well, what not, how to overcome difficulties. Being close to schools, knowing what is going on in schools, what students' reactions can be, etc.—this is something many university professors cannot do. It has also been very important that the last word and decision making have been given to the participants of the course. We as personalities and teachers are different, so it is not possible to have only one right solution or absolute truth. In our work, everyone has found that truth for him or herself first by experiencing it, then analyzing it, and then sharing it in the course or in monthly meetings. This openness has contributed to our development as a team. We have all become quite close and this has given us new energy to continue to make efforts.

> Thinking about the past year and drawing conclusions for myself, I can say that my understanding about teaching and learning has broadened and my

thinking has changed. When preparing my lessons I keep in mind the three phases of Evocation, Realization of Meaning, and Reflection, and try to think about how to encourage students to be active and involve them in the learning process, and how to increase their responsibility. My hope is that my students will be life-long learners who are not afraid to ask, to think, to doubt, who will enjoy experimenting and new challenges, who will experience the joys of discoveries and success just as we have experienced them in the first year of the RWCT Project.

Katrin's essay was strikingly similar to those written by her peers. All the essays captured a spirit of progress, moments of self-realization, and evidence of significant change.

Students' reflections on their learning experiences. The participants' students also engaged in reflection-for-action. The students contemplated how the critical thinking strategies affected their learning. The majority of the students found the influence to be extremely positive. They cited as the primary benefits their ability to think for themselves, the more creative and interesting learning experiences, and improved social interactions. On the negative side, a few students noted that sometimes the strategy received more attention than the content. They also reported that the effects of group work were not positive when all group members did not contribute with the same levels of enthusiasm and knowledge.

Figure 1 on page 60 features reflections from twelfth-grade students from the Water Lily Gymnasium in Rapla, Estonia. They wrote in response to how their learning had changed due to the innovations in instruction.

When offering more detailed ideas about their learning, tenth-grade students from Water Lily Gymnasium in Rapla and the second year of Tartu Music School wrote the following:

In 10th grade I was lazy, but I didn't realize it. I also thought all the teachers were boring. By this year I realized I was lazy (I still am), and that the teachers have a new way of teaching. It's quite interesting and more educating. It makes learning more fun, to me at least.

I think that the use of new strategies and methods is the best innovation in our school. The learner can think and express his or her own opinions— this is the main thing. All groupwork activities develop communication skills and make the learner more confident. The learners now have courage to think and be more open. The widening of thinking helps us to understand ourselves and find solutions to problems.

Figure 1
Students' Reflections on School Before and Since RWCT

Before RWCT	Since RWCT
We couldn't speak at all in lessons.	We are able to explain our thinking in our own words.
Lessons used to be boring.	Strategies arouse interest in learning.
Lessons were confusing.	Teachers teach according to a system. This makes learning easier.
We passively learned the facts.	We think critically and creatively. Now we understand.
We were receivers of knowledge.	Teachers make us feel useful and smart.
We did not interact with others.	If we do not understand on our own, others can help to explain it.
Teachers provided information.	We search for information, think, and analyze.
Learning the subjects ended when we left school.	We have the strategies in our heads and can use them in school and in our lives outside of school.

Of course I like the strategies because they make lessons interesting. The strategies help me to understand the topic of the lesson because all the teaching and learning in this school is conducted in Estonian but I am a Russian girl. At first it was difficult for me to learn here, but now it is easier because the different group work activities enable us to speak a lot and they also make me feel comfortable.

A small number of students also reflected on what they perceived to be negative aspects of using the critical thinking techniques:

Sometimes learning seems to be too superficial.

In group work where the responsibilities and tasks are shared, if other group members besides me do not bother to work thoroughly, my *learning too becomes incomplete* and later it is difficult to fill in the gaps in my knowledge by myself.

Sometimes the playful part of the task takes more energy and attention than its purpose.

Participants' reflections on their experiences as RWCT trainers. In another example of reflection-for-action, participants wrote reflective responses to four prompts about their roles as RWCT trainers. Questions focused on how it felt to be a trainer, what they have learned from the experience, how training impacted their teaching and vice versa. Themes that permeated the responses included the increased value of knowledge, broadened perceptions of the roles of teachers, teaching adult learners, enriched relationships with students, and excitement about being actively involved in the promotion of critical thinking. For example, when explaining how it feels to be a trainer in the RWCT project, responses included the following:

> It is a good, pleasant feeling that requires also responsibility. I have become used to thinking in two roles: what I give as a teacher and what I as a student get from the teaching.

> Fantastic! Only positive experiences dominate, although sometimes my feet were shivering in the beginning. Exciting! Everlasting enrichment!

> It is a good feeling because I am not alone; I can turn to my colleagues for help. It is good to know I have colleagues who think in the same way, who love their work with students, and who are ready to share their experience with others.

When asked what they have learned from being an RWCT trainer, responses addressed personal growth and included the following:

> I have learned that the formation of a learner, of a life-long learner, is important for the new era. I have understood that it is possible to form such a learner by helping the teacher become a critical thinker. The teacher's work is creative, but in order to be able to fly you need not always invent the plane by yourself—these strategies and teaching them have given me a possibility to create something new.

> I have learned cooperation—teaching with a partner, flexibility in every sense (as regards time, plans, and people). I have learned to reflect, to analyze others and myself and learn from experience.

> I have learned that teaching means learning and vice versa. I have learned not to be afraid of failing; everything can be solved and improved.

When participants reflected on how their experiences as trainers enhanced their classroom teaching, they concluded that it improved their teaching in several ways. Specifically, they noted that they had become more patient; had developed greater understanding of their students—both in the workshops and in their classrooms; had learned how to communicate better with parents; and had gained a greater understanding of the role context plays in teaching.

Participants also commented on how teaching their elementary and secondary school students impacted their teaching of the adults. Their reflective responses indicated that having classroom experience teaching the critical thinking strategies provided them with meaningful examples with which to model the strategies. This garnered the respect of the adult learners. Further, they concluded that many factors influenced learning and that learning was a personal, constructivist experience.

Outcomes and Hopes for the Future

RWCT in Estonia supports current thinking that teachers who engage in reflection become better thinkers and, consequently, better practitioners. They "develop problem-solving skills in examining their experiences, generating their alternatives, and evaluating their actions. These skills allow them to model risk-taking, open-mindedness, and continuous learning for their students" (Blake et al., 1995, p. 39).

Results of the RWCT project in Estonia indicate that the participants have made the transition to active, cooperative, student-centered teaching. Further, participants have reported that not only has their teaching changed, but that both they and their students have also changed significantly in the process. Particular areas of transformation for the participants and their students have included integration of theory and practice, redesign of the learning environment, practical experiences with critical and creative thinking, integration of cooperative learning, and ongoing self-analysis. They also have reported increases in self-esteem, risk-taking, effort, respect for others, understanding of the educational process, and enthusiasm for teaching and learning.

In addition, participants have noted that self-reflection has become a valuable source of information for them. It has helped them to document their thinking, provided bases for discussion with peers and instructors, offered direction to their planning, and encouraged them to take time to analyze their teaching and learning.

Irene Artma, one of the project participants, may have summarized the impact of RWCT in Estonia best when she wrote the following in her journal:

> Earlier I expected my students to learn what I had offered them, now I want to teach them to think. My role has changed—students are not passive in the classes, but they can creatively and actively express themselves, they learn more about themselves and others, and they also develop social skills. I believe that they will be better prepared for their future life than ever before.

REFERENCES

Blake, J., Blachman, J., Frys, M.K., Holbert, P., Ivan, T., & Sellitto, P. (1995). A portfolio-based assessment model for teachers: Encouraging professional growth. *National Association of Secondary School Principals Bulletin, 79*(573), 37–46.

Brandt, R. (1991). Time for reflection. *Educational Leadership, 48*(6), 3.

Darling-Hammond, L., Ancess, J., & Falk, B. (1995). *Authentic assessment in action: Studies of schools and students at work.* New York: Teachers College Press.

Dewey, J. (1933). *How we think: A restatement of reflective thinking to the educative process.* Lexington, MA: D.C. Heath.

Freire, P. (1985). *The politics of education.* Amherst, MA: Bergin and Garvey.

Killion, J., & Todnem, G. (1991). A process for personal theory-building. *Educational Leadership, 48*(6), 14–16.

King, P.M., & Kitchner, K.S. (1994). *Developing reflective judgment: Understanding and promoting intellectual growth and critical thinking in adolescents and adults.* San Francisco: Jossey-Bass.

McLaughlin, M., & Vogt, M.E. (1998). Portfolio assessment for inservice teachers: A collaborative model. In M. McLaughlin, M.E. Vogt, J. Anderson, J. DuMez, M.G. Peter, & A. Hunter, *Professional portfolio models: Applications in education* (pp. 3–74). Norwood, MA: Christopher-Gordon.

McLaughlin, M., & Vogt, M.E. (Eds.). (2000). *Creativity and innovation in content area teaching.* Norwood, MA: Christopher-Gordon.

McTighe, J., & Lyman, F.T. (1988). Cueing thinking in the classroom: The promise of theory-embedded tools. *Educational Leadership, 45*(7), 18–24.

Reagan, T., Case, K., Case, C.W., & Freiberg, J.A. (1993). Reflecting on "reflective practice": Implications for teacher evaluation. *Journal of Personnel Evaluation in Education, 6,* 263–277.

Schon, D. (1987). *Educating the reflective practitioner.* San Francisco: Jossey-Bass.

Smyth, J. (1989). Developing and sustaining critical reflection in teacher education. *Journal of Teacher Education, 40*(2), 2–9.

CHAPTER FIVE

Multiple Traditions and Open Lessons: Kazakstani and American Educators Consider Teacher Reflection

David Landis, Peter McDermott, Rick Traw, and Bud Ogle
with Shamen Ahimbekova, Elena Beliaeva, Natalia Evseeva,
Rysaldy Kalieva, Anna Mirnaya, Marina Pastuhova,
Maria Sadikova, Galina Seleznyova, Larisa Stepanets,
and Tamara Sushina

We are not able to foresee
What reflections our words will bring.

Larisa Stepanets, 1999

During the past 2 years, American and Kazakstani[1] educators in the Reading and Writing for Critical Thinking (RWCT) project have encountered differing notions of what constitutes teacher reflection. American educators expected that teacher reflection would consider ways to "open" lessons in order to encourage students' inquiries, incorporate students' interests, and consider students' real questions and perspectives. However, many Kazakstani educators prefer reflecting on ways to organize knowledge that students "should know"; teacher reflection in this case means "open lessons" for the purpose of demonstrating to observers how to systematize classroom instruction.

---

[1] In this volume, spelling the country name *Kazakstan* represents the correct transliteration in English of the spelling in the Kazak language; adding the *h* as in *Kazakhstan* represents a Russian language transliteration. *Kazak* refers to cultural, traditional practices of the Kazak people and to the language they speak. The term *American* refers to a citizen of the United States, while the term *Kazakstani* refers to a citizen of Kazakstan.

According to this view, strategies that encourage student participation appear useful for covering specified lesson content and accomplishing the teaching tasks mandated by the national curriculum—not because such strategies facilitate exploration of a topic from varying perspectives or because they promote thoughtful responses to a diversity of ideas. Cross-cultural communication is always challenging. When expectations, languages, and educational experiences are as diverse as those between teachers in the United States and in Kazakstan, it is no wonder that differences and difficulties arise in building trust and relationships that will support common understandings about teacher reflection. Such differences raise a number of possible avenues of inquiry.

In this chapter, we explore teacher reflections associated with implementing the RWCT project. We have two purposes: (1) to describe historical contexts that shape moments of teacher reflection in order to (2) provide additional insights into how American and Kazakstani participants have adapted and adopted practices for teacher reflection. Our review includes excerpts from our journal writing, essays about the project, conversations and interviews, as well as lesson plans. Because the purpose of our review is to understand the diversity of teacher reflections, several authors contributed to this chapter. Our discussion of teacher reflection proceeds in the following manner. First, we offer a brief historical perspective of educational philosophy and practice in Kazakstan in order to situate and describe two types of interactions that appear to have substantially influenced our teacher reflections. Next, we discuss differences in expectations about the whats, hows, and whys of teacher reflection. Finally, we examine hybrid practices of teacher reflection evolving from our collaboration as well as implications for our future teaching and future work with RWCT.

Kazakstani Educational Practices in Historical Context

In order to build trust and common understandings about teacher reflection, Kazakstani and American educators have had to confront questions of difference, character, motive, and action. For American educators, this has meant developing some understanding of life and education in Kazakstan. Kazakstan, a large country of more than 1 million square miles, lies between Russia on the north and China on the southeast, with Kyrgyzstan, Uzbekistan, and Turkmenistan sharing its southern border. The estimated population in 2000 is over 18 million (Olcott, 1997).

What follows is a brief history for the purpose of building understanding about current educational practices.

Ethnic Kazaks, reknowned as skilled horse riders, lived a nomadic life, caring for their sheep and horses throughout the great steppes of Eurasia. In the 13th century Genghis Khan conquered much of eastern Kazakstan; present day Kazaks are descendants of his empire. Later, merchants would travel "the Great Silk Road" to and from China. Traditional Kazak clothing, food, and shelter reflect a nomadic past; traditional songs, for example, are played on a "dombra," a stringed instrument shaped like a mandolin. The Kazak national poet Abai (Ibrahim) Kunanbaev (1845–1904) is revered for his philosophy, writing, and music about human virtue and character:

> Three great sources nurtured the ocean of Abai's knowledge: ancient Kazak culture, preserved in oral and written folklore; the best samples of Oriental culture; and last, but not least, Russian, and through it, world culture.... His encyclopedic knowledge...bestowed on us his unwithering poetry, wise precepts, subtle poetic translations. (Orazalinov, 1994, p. 39)

Abai's influence represents a long-established tradition of literature, the arts, science, and scholarship in Kazak education. Numerous educators and artists, such as the medieval scholar Abu Nasr al-Farabi and more recently Ibray Altynsarin (1841–1889), contributed a considerable body of scholarly writing on a wide range of topics including astronomy, orthography, calligraphy, folk art, rhetoric, arithmetic and geometry, history, philosophy, linguistics, sociology, music, logic, pedagogy, ethnography, folklore, languages, natural history, medicine, and geography. Skillful uses of oratory, storytelling, and poetry nurtured by life on the steppes fostered a considerable body of literature. Over time, Kazak educators and scholars produced many outstanding cultural and scientific achievements, rich libraries such as the renowned Otrar Library, and important educational institutions (DeYoung & Suzhikova, 1997; Serikbaeva, 1995). Thus, educators in Kazakstan today draw from an extensive and richly significant cultural history. Their current efforts in educational reform look not only to the future, as they prepare students for global culture in the 21st century, but also to the past, as they work to honor and to reinvigorate their own traditions.

Kazakstan became part of the Soviet Union in the early 1920s. As in the other RWCT countries, the Soviets imposed a centralized educational system on Kazakstan, a system that repressed national language, culture, and tradition. (See Meredith, Chapter Two in this volume, for further discussion of political and historical influences in other RWCT countries.) Kazak educators and intellectuals who resisted Soviet policies, primarily through the efforts of the Alash Orda[2], were hunted down and removed by the Stalin regime in particular (DeYoung & Suzhikova, 1997; Olcott, 1997):

> Stalin's Great Terror...cost the educational program.... Once the purge began anyone who had direct or even indirect contact with the Alash Orda...became suspect. How many of those arrested in the 1930s were teachers it is impossible to know.... Millions of Kazaks either were killed, starved to death, or fled the country during forced collectivization and Stalin's later purges.... The teaching of national culture and native language was also both formally and informally discouraged from the 1930s until independence [December 16, 1991]. (DeYoung & Suzhikova, 1997, pp. 443, 446)

The Stalin era produced education policies for the purpose of implementing industrial and agricultural projects initiated by central planners in Moscow—projects that carry enormous consequences to this day for Kazakstan. Premier Khrushchev, for example, instituted the "Virgin Lands Campaign" designed to transform the dry, grassy steppes into crop yielding lands for the Soviet Union. Further south, desert regions were irrigated by diverting rivers flowing into the Aral Sea, thereby depriving the sea of its supply of fresh water, which led to an environmental nightmare—vast amounts of airborne dust from the drying sea beds mixed with pesticides resulting in widespread pollution of water and land. Geographically remote cities of several hundred thousand people were built in Northern Kazakstan and sustained by developing military-industrial complexes. People from throughout the Soviet Union were assigned to work in these cities, forced to leave their homes at the command of the state. Northeastern Kazakstan became a site of Soviet nuclear test-

---

[2] The name of the Alash Orda party means "the Horde of Alash" and refers to a group of nationalists who tried to break away from Russian political control in 1917 to set up an independent national government. They invoked the name of the legendary Kazak, Alash, who established the Kazak people. By 1920, the Alash Orda party surrendered to Communist authorities (Olcott, 1997).

ing, and tragically, a neighboring city, Semipalatinsk, today contains deadly levels of radioactivity. Baikonur, the site of the Sputnik launch, is located in central Kazakstan and is still used for space exploration, most recently for launching the Mir space station.

Education curriculum and materials reflected similar kinds of political processes—top-down plans and projects implemented by the Communist Party in the years after Stalin. A principal goal of education was to supply the specialists, the new Soviet citizen needed to make the Soviet system work, not to encourage liberal, intellectually broad thinking and views (Kaiser, 1984). Autonomous efforts and special educational programs were discouraged; minimal concern was expressed for individual differences of children; and Western literature, philosophy, and social science were considered unacceptable because they promoted comparative, relative understandings instead of productive labor. The job of teachers was to support policies and institutions for maintaining the Soviet system (DeYoung & Suzhikova, 1997). Educational planning and curriculum were organized to conform clearly to scientific, ideological, and industrial policies and the need for manual labor. So, for example, it was common for elementary, secondary, and university students living in agricultural areas to miss 3 to 4 weeks of school during October and November in order to help harvest crops such as cotton and potatoes (Kaiser, 1984). Over time, the various demands from central planners in Moscow consumed any remaining flexibility in educational policies and little change could be introduced into the system. Curriculum overloading in educational programs reflected the overall ill health of the Soviet economy during the latter years of the USSR (DeYoung & Suzhikova, 1997).

Since the restructuring (Perestroika) and collapse of the official Soviet bureaucracy in the late 1980s, education reforms in Kazakstan have focused on how to deal with the legacy of decades of centrally planned education policies. Earnest debates about the organization and direction of schooling, grass-roots changes introduced by parents and teachers in various public and private schools, and a unique set of economic and national issues continue to influence teachers in Kazakstan today (DeYoung & Suzhikova, 1997). Cultural and national identities are being revised to re-create (and in some instances create) historical Kazak traditions. Kazaks in exile in China and Mongolia have been encouraged to return to Kazakstan; the national government promotes Kazak as the official language; parent groups increasingly work with teachers to organize new opportunities for learning about Kazak traditions, art, crafts, legends, and music; and widespread interest exists for how to introduce comparative studies and reflective thinking to replace Soviet ideology in education (DeYoung & Nadirbekyzy, 1996).

In addition to debates about goals for schooling, education funding has developed into a major problem in need of reform. There is no viable system to finance schools in Kazakstan. Teachers often go unpaid for months—earning less than US$100 per month—although many teachers tutor individual students after school in order to earn additional income. Many schools have closed, and basic resources for schools (such as heat, water, textbooks, and other supplies) are in very limited supply. Multiple groups within regional (Oblast) government, as well as the national Ministry of Education, among others, all claim authority over programs and budgets, and school directors must report to multiple officials. Parents, communities, and professional education organizations have yet to effectively influence public school policy:

> In the former Soviet Union, there were few non-government organizations which championed [causes] of citizens. Those objecting to the status quo or politically organizing for change were often jailed. Kazakstan shares the contemporary problem of a serious lack of citizen's advocacy groups or civic organizations to lobby for social or economic improvement and the fact that schools are in serious disrepair and understaffed is "explained" by the government as a logical outcome of fiscal difficulties rather than a choice made by leaders of the nation. (DeYoung & Suzhikova, 1997, p. 451)

Teacher Reflection in the Current Situation

Within this historical context, American and Kazakstani educators seek to establish relationships and identities, build trust, and clarify goals and common understandings about teacher reflection. So, for example, skeptical questions continue to be raised such as, "Who are these Americans and what do they want? Can they really teach us anything new?" Such questions have typically been encountered in two types of in-school events that influence teacher reflection: (1) conversations about education today compared with "the Soviet times," and (2) a distinctive kind of public meeting that the American educators dubbed "the press conference." Each of these events or situations is described in the following sections and their relevance to teacher reflection is discussed.

Looking Back to "the Soviet Times"

One way that Kazakstani educators reflect on teaching is to compare classroom and school life today with classrooms and schools in "the Soviet times"—an era that in some senses still continues today. Although well versed in pedagogical theories formulated by Soviet psychologists including Vygotsky, most elementary and secondary teachers continue to use formal, practical methods of instruction, which feature memorization and recitation of what was memorized. Instruction is typically text-driven, and most textbooks are outdated products of Soviet publishing firms. (A notable exception is found in Kazak language texts; Kazak language is now emphasized in the national curriculum, and certain publishers such as Soros Foundation–Kazakstan have published new texts for Kazak language study.)

During focus-group interviews conducted in December 1997 by American educators, the widespread impact of "Soviet-style" teaching was evident in the responses of many of the participants when asked to reflect on their teaching. (Responses from different teachers are separated by ellipsis points.)

Question: How did you teach before participating in the RWCT project?

Responses: I asked rather easy questions [with explicit answers]. I was not interested in the [thoughts] of the children; my children knew what kinds of questions I would ask of them, they could predict them; our textbooks contained the questions.... When I asked questions, my students answered them and I said, "Excellent." But when they answered incorrectly, I told them to "Think more deeply...." In literature methods, there are some standard questions and one of them is "What do you think the author wanted to say?" The answers are already written in the teacher [manuals] and we felt we needed to follow them. Now I understand the importance of accepting students' answers and not rigidly following the textbooks.... Before [RWCT] I used prepared teaching programs a great deal, and there was less of my own work in lesson planning. I believed the text was the one source of information.

Question: You were selected for this project because you were interested in teacher change, but what did you like best about the Soviet methods that is worth preserving?

Responses: There were interesting Soviet methods; one was group work. I used groups for years before this. But I felt there was something missing in the group work because I asked the questions for the groups and never required them to form questions or opinions....

My students liked group work best. They liked role-playing. I gave them a text and each group would be asked to develop a dialogue for each text. After discussion we would write an essay on the topic. Students liked to give their own lessons. They liked to work independently of the teacher when in their small groups.... Our old method gave us a global education, but we did not use that knowledge in our everyday life.... There were elements of critical teaching in the Soviet schools, but we used [the elements] to analyze texts.... I see critical thinking as similar to analytic thinking. For example, when analyzing *War and Peace* I always established my goals for the students. But I never thought much about the democratizing of the teaching process....

These responses from teachers as they discuss the influences of "Soviet-style" teaching provide important historical context for the RWCT project. The teachers mention the use of particular strategies such as role-playing, group work, or posing questions for the author (for example, "What do you think the author wanted to say?"), which sound very similar to strategies proposed by the RWCT guidebooks. What has been new and significant for teachers, as they consider RWCT, is realizing how such strategies support students' answers and opinion formation in and out of school—encouraging teachers and students alike to examine the implications of various ideas. Project participants realize that the guidebook strategies by themselves are not the end—the Soviets proposed somewhat similar strategies years ago. Rather the strategies are a means to the end of establishing the type of critical thinking (such as exploring a topic from varying perspectives, understanding circumstances, and reaching thoughtful informed decisions in order to solve problems), that supports a more open and democratic society.

The Press Conference

Another typical means of reflecting on teaching and lesson activities results in what is called "the press conference"—a type of meeting where official visitors to the school are seated facing the teaching staff. Such meetings remind us of similar kinds of question-and-answer sessions between reporters and politicians. These interactions typically begin with general statements from the visitors, and then the teachers and administrators pose questions about the impressions the visitors have of the school, the teachers, and the students, as well as questions about RWCT.

Typically, local school faculty views the press conference as way to discuss observations about teaching and lessons with newcomers. At one site, for example, the visiting American educators observed the use of strategies such as cubing and cooperative group discussion and reporting of group discussions to the rest of the class. Afterward, the visitors attempted to talk with the teacher about the lesson; however, the school administrator quickly escorted the visitors to a press conference. The press conference seemed to be the preferred venue for reflecting on the classroom observations.

One possible reason that Kazakstani educators may rely on situations such as the press conference involves their educational past. They have lived in a society in which critique is expected to come from outside, not from within. The visiting educators find that in a top-down culture encouraging teachers to view themselves as knowledgeable researchers of their own teaching is problematic. The Kazakstani educators took to the strategies espoused by RWCT as eagerly as Americans hoped for, but they seemed hesitant to discuss their teaching in any substantial way with outside observers.

Whats, Whys, and Hows of Teacher Reflection: Social, Cultural Norms and Expectations

Understanding discussions about teaching and learning during "the Soviet times" and the social situation that characterizes the press conference is important, because such interactions represent social, and cultural norms and preferences about the roles, rights, and responsibilities that are expected to accompany discussion and reflection about teaching. The following conversation about teacher reflection was constructed from written comments by several RWCT participants over the course of the project and reconstructed during the spring and summer of 1999. The comments probe underlying social and cultural expectations for American and Kazakstani teachers and make visible ways in which the expectations influence teacher reflection. (In each exchange, the first speaker is a Kazakstani educator, and the second is an American educator.)

Teacher Reflection: Fear of Disapproving Reactions

> Marina: My middle-school students became very still when I addressed a question to them. They were afraid to give a wrong answer, to become a joke for their peers, to hear my disapproving reactions.

Peter: I wonder if this reaction by students is similar to the reactions that our teachers have when they meet with observers to discuss a lesson. It's not that Kazak teachers aren't interested in reviewing their teaching, but they are unsure about how the review will go and whether there will be disapproval from those who observe.

Teachers and students often must confront fears of being vulnerable. Their speech and actions thrust them into what seem like glaring spotlights—students experience openness to criticism from peers or the teacher each time they respond publicly, and teachers confront fears of vulnerability when they open the classroom door for observers to enter and watch. Collaborating with students, teachers, parents, administrators, and other people with an interest in education "requires that we confront our own fears of difference and open our classrooms to discussions of topics that may raise tensions among the values of different individuals, groups, and institutions" (Wilson-Keenan, Willett, & Solsken, 1993, p. 212).

Teacher Reflection: Evaluating Students' Academic Progress

Rysaldy (first-grade teacher): My teaching was "Categorical," even authoritarian at times. I was pleased to hear the students' opinions when they were very similar to mine. I even continued asking questions until I received the answer I was looking for.

David: It seems convenient for us as teachers to "measure" our students' progress in terms of how cooperative they are with our teacher questions and with our ways of doing things. Even though we as teachers may believe that we evaluate students based upon their abilities for displaying certain reading and writing skills, for example, we still encounter limits to the certainty of knowing for sure that a student has displayed a particular skill or ability.

Limits to our understandings of students' progress could be represented by three particular questions: (1) Did the students use only the resources provided by the teacher for completing a task? (2) Did the organization of the task by the teacher present any barriers to students completing the task? (3) Did the students understand the task in similar ways compared to the ways the teacher understood it? (Heap, 1981). It may be that we adopt a set of social criteria for answering such questions, which reflects students' conformity to our views and our practices in order to measure academic progress and achievement (see Gilmore, 1987).

Teacher Reflection: Having Necessary Lesson Components

> Maria (school administrator): Many teachers [when observing an RWCT teacher and students] are impressed by a collaborative atmosphere of trust, by the fact that all students wanted to share and that they wanted to be heard; that students in fact have their own life experiences, personal opinions, and their own reasoning.... Some teachers were suspicious of the lack of discipline, an expected component of traditional lessons; some were suspicious of students receiving knowledge seemingly without any mental efforts, and of the secondary role of the teacher.

> Rick: Language like "suspicious" and "expected component" suggests an implicit assumption that there is one right way to teach. Some teachers may measure RWCT methodology against the assumed standards, and this in fact, represents a form of teacher reflection. But there is a rigidity in thinking here that may be socially embedded. We have witnessed teachers experimenting with RWCT methods who cling as tenaciously to the Evocation–Realization of Meaning –Reflection (ERR) framework as they previously clung to their traditional methods, even when the academic and social demands of a particular lesson indicate a need to abandon the framework and pursue a teachable moment. Many North American educators are also suspicious when they do not see the "expected components" during a lesson. The critical thinking we hope to foster in Kazak schools, with their flexibility and openness to dialogue and alternative ways of knowing, is the same critical perspective which must be fostered in American schools and teacher education institutions.

"With any new approach to the teaching of anything, there is a constant danger that sensitive edges to [students' opinions, discussions, writing, interests, thinking] will be lopped off in the guise of making the approach to teaching...more simplified" (Graves, 1984, p. 184). For RWCT participants, maxims can develop from procedures and practices set in place for observing lessons, for certifying teachers and trainers, and for carrying out other responsibilities associated with the project. Over time, attitudes can begin to harden towards expected components of an RWCT lesson—attitudes that abandon a priority for students' critical thinking and substitute teacher procedures instead. Some procedures are necessary for coping with teaching, but Graves reminds us of two ways to protect ourselves against establishing maxims and orthodoxies that hide students' interests and thinking. One way to deflect orthodoxy is to find out what our students know—to allow them to tell us their stories, their successes, their needs, their hopes and visions, their ways (Graves, 1994). A second way to halt hardening attitudes toward teaching is to read and write ourselves—to continually discover through our reading and writing new stories and fresh evidence about ourselves, our students, and about the world around us (Graves, 1994).

Teacher Reflection: Shouldering Accountability

> Anna (middle school teacher): After I left the walls of my university, I knew very clearly that it was my responsibility to the country, which educated me, to share my knowledge effectively. So, here I am now—a teacher who feels tremendous responsibility.... I used to be extremely satisfied when my students would flawlessly report to me what we had done during the previous lesson. I was terribly afraid if someone would not remember or understand everything. After I became acquainted with RWCT, I asked, "What is the point in stuffing my students with all this information? Instead, I should just teach them how to find this information." More often students are the ones talking now.... Even the shyest students whom I did not even count on participating, spoke up.... I became more tolerant of the students' mistakes. I stopped pushing them towards a conclusion, which I felt was necessary to make at the end of the lesson.

> Bud: Teachers in the U.S. feel similar pressures. The present focus on accountability, for example, forces teachers to measure success and failure in terms of whether students absorb information and can recall it on state proficiency tests. Such a focus on simply repeating information as the goal of education leads teachers to repeat mistakes in judgment and evaluation of their students (e.g., relying on misreading of student participation, becoming intolerant of students' mistakes, forcing conclusions about texts which students do not understand).

When policy makers push for "accountability" and children's performance on standardized tests becomes the measure of the children's learning and of the teacher's teaching, there is often pressure on teachers to ignore what children tell them about their learning. As Lindfors (1991) states, however, "Too often it is assumed that adults, not children, know about learning: about what children should learn, about how they should do it, about the contexts that are helpful.... But evidence from children developing language tells us that children follow their own course and employ their own processes in this complex learning" (pp. 281–219).

Unpacking Lessons: Taking Teacher Talk for Granted?

Reflecting and probing conversations, interviews, and comments about teaching and learning such as those in the preceding sections requires time and effort in order to build trust and common understandings. American educators early in the project dubbed such a process of probing as "unpacking." Yet, in the midst of unpacking, it seems that they assumed too much familiarity about teaching and learning, and devoted too little effort toward understanding social and cultural norms and expectations for teachers and students, appropriate communicative preferences and cultural norms for interaction, and ways of building relationships accepted by their Kazakstani colleagues. In particular, American notions of unpacking as a means of teacher reflection have not been broad enough to include substantial differences in (a) presentation of self (e.g., ways to get to know others and status or social relations expected between speakers); (b) distribution of talk (e.g., who gets to speak first, ways to establish control of a topic, and how to take turns); (c) ways to structure what is said (e.g., ways to signal information through intonation, stress, and other prosodic elements); and (d) ways to conceptually organize what is said (e.g., how and when to be explicit, how to organize information through themes or other units of organization) (Scollon & Scollon, 1981). The following journal entry describes how David tried to encourage teacher reflection by unpacking a lesson and attempting to be sensitive to the Kazakstani educator's topics of discussion, yet still fell short of the goal of building trust and common understandings:

> I thought the pattern of lesson observation—we encouraged teachers to state goals early during the lesson as an aid for students and observers—followed by discussion of the lesson with the teacher and other observers, was helpful for review and reflection. I tried to begin my comments by asking the teacher to discuss goals of the lesson and how successfully the teacher thought they were achieved. Sometimes I began by describing something I liked about the lesson. How I began my comments depended upon my reading of the teacher's willingness to participate in such lesson conversations. I focused on the use of strategies, time for students' ideas and discussions during the lesson, and inclusion of students' views in the direction the lesson takes as ways that I evaluated the success of lessons. However, my Kazakstani colleague took my questions and comments as critical, and instead of a dialogue about the lesson, our conversation was one-sided, with me doing almost all of the talking, and the teacher sitting quietly, hearing my honest questions and comments simply as criticism of her work.

Notice that even with an emphasis on asking for the teacher's goals and perspectives, the comments by the observer did not seek suggestions on how to support the Kazakstani educator. Furthermore, the comments by the observer did not seek to understand differences in presentation of self as a teacher to the lesson observer. Finally, such comments fell short of seeking accepted ways of communication that could have fostered relationships and built or clarified common goals. In summary, unpacking did not lead to a fuller appreciation by the American observer, because unacknowledged differences in communicative styles and topics affected reflections about the lesson.

One way to understand differences in the stances of the American and Kazakstani educators toward teacher reflection is to consider social and cultural norms that influence their uses of particular avenues of teacher reflection, such as the press conference and the recall of "the Soviet times." For teachers in Kazakstan, reflection and critique about their teaching and their lessons seems to occur within the context of decades of heavy emphasis on top-down, authoritative reviews of teaching and curriculum. The teacher's role in such a hierarchy is not to critique lessons and teaching, but to wait for higher authorities to take up those activities, to allow them to unpack the lesson before the teacher considers what to do next. In the case described above, the visiting American observer unwittingly assumed the role of the judging authority, even though he had hoped to act as a friend and colleague.

Some written reflections by the Kazakstani educators suggest that common understandings about teacher reflection could occur, albeit in small steps. Tamara explains, "Through communication we are enriching ourselves with new ideas. It is important to know how to listen, to accept ideas of others. All this is important to get rid of barriers...to learn how to speak openly." Such communicative steps should help us as RWCT participants understand the potential implications of the strategies and styles introduced by the project on the social and cultural relationships in Kazakstani classrooms, including ways of responding to others that emphasize discussion, debate, explanation of points of view, and give-and-take conversations—interactions clearly based on a theory of open, respectful communication within the classroom.

Crossing International Borders: Adopting and Adapting Teacher Reflection

Despite the differences in approaches to teacher reflection, American and Kazakstani educators seem to be developing hybrid, reflective practices that promote trust and understanding about teaching. Sometimes, for example, conversations about teaching have worked out successfully for participants. A recent conversation serves as an example of teacher reflection during which a number of sensitive areas were probed and explored. During the discussion, second-generation project participants at Gymnasium #6 displayed lesson planning and teaching that suggested potential for student-oriented lessons—a change from "the Soviet times." These participants were exploring some next steps with RWCT that move beyond what has been customary. One next step, which incorporates teacher reflection, is making visible certain types of teacher–student interactions that build lessons from students' comments. Analysis of the interactions makes visible a number of teacher–student conversational moves that build knowledge and understanding about reading and writing in the context of various academic content areas (such as reaching agreement, agreeing to disagree, extending and elaborating ideas, revising or reviewing previous understandings, asking why or asking for evidence, and predicting consequences and outcomes).

Such conversational moves in classroom settings are not always comfortable for teachers and students. Listening to views that we do not agree with or providing a rationale for our position on an issue is not always easy. However, exploring teacher-student interactions provides insights into students' involvement and into ways that teachers can support students' participation. Engaging in dialogue about teacher-student interaction represents an exciting potential avenue for teacher reflection.

Natalia explains that traditional modes of Kazakstani teacher reflection, coupled with RWCT emphases on critical thinking, have opened several new directions that encourage her understanding of her teaching. She is coming to understand many things: how the lesson will help the students to gain respect for themselves as learners; how the lesson can be more than a formality—going above and beyond what is required; how the teacher and students can develop emotional closeness through the types of teacher-student-student interactions that RWCT fosters; and how the alternative interactions open new possibilities for building knowledge about the content of the lessons.

Thoughtful, careful discussion and analysis of classroom teaching and learning, made visible through teacher-student interactions, refreshes our sense of the progress of RWCT and encourages us to challenge ourselves as educators to continue to grow in our understandings and applications of the spirit of student-teacher inquiry with reading and writing. Peter takes up this idea in the following section as he applies his experiences in Kazakstan to his U.S. university teaching:

Although I observed many lessons where teachers demonstrated RWCT lessons that richly captured the reflective component, as well as some that did not, the most memorable one occurred in a Kazak residential school. My American colleague, Bud Ogle, and I arrived at the school on a cold wintry afternoon. Located outside the city, the school operated its own farm to supply food for its residential students. When our escort opened the school doors, inside stood the students who greeted us with traditional Kazak music and song. On one side of the school lobby was a small orchestra of about 20 students playing dombra. Five adults in traditional dress and hats of bright colors stood at the center and sang Kazak folksongs. The orchestra and adult group alternately performed for us. Periodically other students recited Kazak poetry and threw colored candy as a symbol to welcome us to their school community. After a short break in the principal's room for tea and sweets, we visited several classrooms where teachers demonstrated RWCT methods.

The final lesson of the day proved to be the most exciting because of the rich exchange of political ideas among students. Twenty-five high school students sat in small groups of four and five. The social studies teacher began his lesson by asking students to recall what they had learned from the previous day's reading about the qualifications for high public office in Kazakstan. Then he distributed sheets of chart paper for the students to create a web of ideas about what they believed the qualifications for public office should be. Next he asked them to tape their webs to the classroom wall and participate in a Gallery Walk in which they would read and then write comments about the other groups' webs on the chart paper.

After about 10 minutes of participating in the Gallery Walk, they returned to their tables to summarize their thinking about the topic. It was at this point that they became very involved in the political topic of their study. They debated back and forth whether ethnicity, place of birth, or language should be considered criteria for high public office. Male and female students expressed equally strong and contrasting points of view about the topic. This lesson and particularly the final debate illustrated the value of reflection. The lesson was student-centered: Students used their prior knowledge, worked in groups to freely exchange ideas, committed themselves to a position, and publicly articulated their views about the issue with one another. The final component of the lesson generated a rich exchange of ideas illustrating the vital role reflection has in learning. Importantly, the teacher acted as a facilitator of student learning.

In my own teaching I have now learned to give reflection far more prominence and time than before. In my college classes with teachers in the United States, I now use reflection to evaluate and assess learning activities, just as I learned to do in Kazakstan. After simulating an activity with my students, I ask them whether the method could be used in their own classroom teaching. I encourage them to evaluate how they might modify the method to fit the needs of their own students. Sometimes these reflective discussions take as long as the actual simulation. However, I have learned that the time spent is invaluable because students hear a variety of interpretations from their peers, which deepens their own understanding of the method. This exchange of ideas requires them to participate in critical thinking about teaching.

Final Teacher Reflection: Opening Lessons That American Educators Are Learning

What does it mean for us, as American educators in particular, to think about our involvement with RWCT in Kazakstan? Among the lessons we are (re)learning is the importance of building relationships, building trust, and clarifying goals. Just now, for example, we are beginning to understand how various situations such as the press conference could help us establish relationships and build trust and common understandings of what we are to be doing. We begin to realize that one aspect of teacher reflection is to become aware of, and respond respectfully to, key assumptions and communicative styles of our Kazakstani colleagues. For the Americans, the past 2 years could be characterized as a crash course in learning the styles, assumptions, and cultural norms—in and out of school settings—expected of teachers and students in Kazakstan. Perhaps our Kazakstani colleagues have made similar discoveries about American assumptions and cultural norms. Such understandings are necessary, so that changes in teaching and teacher reflections can be sensitive and appropriate for the social and institutional situations within which we are working. Clearly, an ongoing task for all RWCT participants is to learn more about each other's educational views and interests and to seek ways to cross the social, cultural, and linguistic borders that shape teacher reflection within the contemporary context for education in Kazakstan.

Authors' Note

Sapargul Mirseitova, Zhanar Chakharova of the Soros Foundation (Kazakstan) Center for Democratic Education, and the Reading and Writing for Critical Thinking project supported the teacher research reported in this chapter. Thank you Sapargul and Zhanar for your leadership and support. Thank you to RWCT codirectors—Jeannie Steele, Kurt Meredith, Charles Temple, and Scott Walter—for their planning and international vision. Thank you also to Alan DeYoung and his colleagues for sharing their writing and research.

REFERENCES

DeYoung, A.J., & Suzhikova, B. (1997). Issues in post-Soviet secondary school reform: The case of Kazakstan. *International Journal of Educational Reform, 64,* 441–454.

DeYoung, A.J., & Nadirbekyzy, B. (1996). Redefining schooling and community in post-Soviet Kazakstan. *Politics of Education Association Yearbook, 1996,* 71–78.

Gilmore, P. (1987). Sulking, stepping, and tracking: The effects of attitude assessment on access to literacy. In D. Bloome (Ed.), *Literacy and schooling* (pp. 98–120). Norwood, NJ: Ablex.

Graves, D.H. (1984). *A researcher learns to write.* Portsmouth, NH: Heinemann.

Heap, J. (1981). What counts as reading? Limits to certainty in reading assessment. *Curriculum Inquiry, 103,* 265–292.

Kaiser, R.G. (1984). *Russia: The people and the power.* New York: Washington Square Press.

Lindfors, J.W. (1991). *Children's language and learning* (2nd ed.). Boston: Allyn & Bacon.

Olcott, M.B. (1997). Kazakstan. In G.E. Curtis (Ed.), *Kazakstan, Kyrgyzstan, Tajikistan, Turkmenistan, and Uzbekistan: Country studies* (pp. 1–97). Washington, DC: US Government Printing Office.

Orazalinov, S. (1994). *On the land of Abai.* Almaty, Kazakstan: Oner Press.

Scollon, R., & Scollon, S.B.K. (1981). *Narrative, literacy, and face in interethnic communication.* Norwood, NJ: Ablex.

Serikbaeva, K. (1995). *Kazakhstan.* London: Flint River Press.

Wilson-Keenan, J., Willett, J., & Solsken, J. (1993). Constructing an urban village: School/home collaboration in a multicultural classroom. *Language Arts, 70,* 204–214.

CHAPTER SIX

Documenting Critical Thinking Lessons Through Teaching Cases: Dilemmas and Achievements of Russian Teachers in Estonia

Janet C. Richards
with Neva Viise, Jodi Patrick Holschuh, and Hiie Asser

> Cases employed in teacher education are focused engaging narratives vary-
> ing in length from one to 30 pages. Usually written in the first person, they
> describe "a wide variety of [authentic] situations, decisions, dilemmas, and
> difficulties that routinely confront teachers and teacher educators."
>
> Sykes, 1992, p. ix

> Case writing may well bring special benefits to those who write them,
> prompting them to reflect upon their practices and to become more anal-
> ytic about their work. Teaching cases are not case studies. Teaching cases
> describe a context-specific incident or a series of related incidents. Like all
> good stories, cases portray characters that are real, contain dialogue and
> rich detail and are "contextualized in time and place."
>
> L. Shulman, 1992, pp. 9, 21

In the past few years, teaching cases have become increasingly important
to the field of education in many countries, such as Australia, Canada,
Great Britain, and the United States (Merseth, 1991; J. Shulman, 1992).
Authoring teaching cases is increasingly recognized as a potent vehicle for
stimulating teachers' abilities to identify, reflect on, and make informed
decisions about instructional concerns (J. Shulman, 1992; L. Shulman,
1992). Exploring and seeking solutions to teaching problems help teachers recognize that there is no one right answer in teaching (Richards &
Gipe, 2000). Equally important, authoring cases helps teachers discern
that they are problem solvers who are responsible for their students'
learning.

This chapter provides a brief rationale for educators' case writing and discussions. The chapter also discusses the attributes of well-written cases. The core of the chapter offers a narrative discourse study of authentic teaching cases authored by Russian primary, elementary, and secondary teachers who live in Estonia and participate in the International Reading Association's Reading and Writing for Critical Thinking (RWCT) project. (Following the disintegration of the Soviet Union in 1991, a large number of Russians remained in Estonia. Some became Estonian citizens. However, the Estonian public schools still remain quite separate, with 30% of the students in Estonia attending Russian schools and 70% attending Estonian schools [Haridusminissteerium Report, 1997].) The chapter concludes with a discussion of the implications of the research and its applicability to K–12 teachers everywhere.

The cases presented here were used for reflection on teaching and learning over a 3-year period. Following a short seminar devoted to teaching cases offered at the end of the second year of the RWCT program, the Russian teachers authored their own narratives. The first-person cases describe the teachers' quandaries, accomplishments, and reflective thinking pertinent to implementing student-centered, inquiry-oriented, critical thinking lessons across curricula in diverse teaching contexts. At the beginning of the third year of the project, the teachers worked in small discussion groups, brainstorming possible solutions to some of the encompassing dilemmas portrayed in the narratives. As they worked, they jotted down their ideas on large sheets of paper. Then each group presented their ideas to all participants.

Well-Written Teaching Cases

It is important to note that exemplary cases portray problems that warrant "serious in-depth examination" (Wassermann, 1994, p. 3). They begin with an appropriate title, include authentic dialogue, and contain sufficient contextual and background information (Richards & Gipe, 2000). Good cases are written in the first person, are "reader-friendly," and provide descriptions of a specific teaching quandary or a series of connected problematic teaching situations or accomplishments that are contextualized in time and place, but can be generalized to other teaching circumstances. Examples of such situations include teachers making incorrect assumptions about students, teachers neglecting to explain lessons fully, or students refusing to work to their fullest capacities. Exemplary cases conclude with teachers establishing some possible solutions to the problem described or some plausible reasons for a lesson's success.

When teachers complete the first draft of their cases, they ask themselves the following questions to assist them in editing their writing:

- Is the teaching problem easy to identify?
- Is there too little or too much contextual information included?
- Are some alternative solutions offered to the problem described?
- Is the title of the case interesting and appropriate for case content?
- Does the case contain authentic student and teacher dialogue? (Richards & Gipe, 2000)

Teachers Recognize the Value of Documenting Instructional Problems

Teachers who author cases clearly recognize the value of documenting instructional problems and specifying some possible solutions to teaching dilemmas. Teachers also recognize the benefits of discussing the concerns portrayed in their cases. For example, after small-group collaborations regarding some of the common problems portrayed in their teaching narratives, the Russian teachers listed their ideas about the benefits of case conversations:

It is good to know that others face the same situations.

It serves as a warning to me. I haven't faced some of these problems discussed yet, but they do exist.

I realize how useful group work is.

If I ever face a situation like the ones described here today, I will not be at a loss.

It is good to know that I have a resource...that I can turn to my colleagues for support.

The following case, authored by a Russian secondary teacher, details a Directed Reading-Thinking Activity (Stauffer, 1981) that went awry, and contains the specific attributes of all good teaching narratives.

Lilac or Blue: What's a Teacher to Do?

It happened in the fifth class in a literature lesson. The text was a fairy tale entitled, *Blue Puppy*. I intended to introduce a Directed Reading Thinking Activity (DRTA) to my students with this story. I had used the text in previous years with other students, and I thought this story about an unusual and very cute puppy was perfect for a DRTA lesson. I began the lesson by writing the title of the story on the blackboard. Immediately, I heard whispers and laughter. "What's the matter," I asked my students as I turned to face them.

Some of my students hid their faces and would not look at me as one boy blurted out, "I know what the word *blue* means. It means a boy who loves another boy."

A girl responded, "It's like the film, *Blue Men*."

I tried to explain that the topic of our text was entirely different and I endeavored to get my students to make predictions about events in the story. But another girl continued, "In the Estonian language, they say 'lilac' to mean that someone is gay."

Well, at that point, all of the students began to discuss their understandings of the words *lilac* and *blue* and the lesson got completely out of control. It would not have been the right thing for me to prohibit the students' interactions, so I let them continue to talk since the topic was so hot. But as far as I'm concerned, the lesson failed. In fact, we didn't even get to the lesson.

Later, I tried to analyze why things had gone awry. I came to the conclusion that students are better informed than ever before so in certain areas their thinking is quite mature. In addition, because of television and films, students are exposed to new ideas that are not always appropriate for school discussions. I also questioned myself about why I let the dialogue about *blue* and *lilac* go on so long. I guess it is because information offered in the Reading and Writing for Critical Thinking workshops and guidebooks have helped me understand how important it is for students to interact and discuss issues. But in hindsight, I think that maybe I should have brought the blue-lilac discussion to a close and started our DRTA lesson.

Cases as Rich Data Sources

As the case "Lilac or Blue: What's a Teacher to Do?" shows, authoring cases has the potential to promote teachers' professional thinking and problem solving. Equally important, the content of teachers' narratives can serve as rich data sources, documenting their planning, pedagogy, and reflections about a lesson. Cases also have the potential to illuminate teachers' decisions and understandings or confusions about educational goals and objectives, group management techniques, or teaching strategies. For example, in the case we learn why the teacher chose the text *Blue Puppy* (she was familiar with the story), and what strategy she planned to offer (DRTA). The case also poignantly delineates the disintegration of the lesson and the teacher's expanding frustrations and dismay as her students continued to voice their opinions and ideas about the meaning of the story title. More importantly, we discover why the teacher did not stop her students from talking ("It would not have been the right thing for me to prohibit the students' interactions so I let them continue to talk about it since the topic was so hot"). And finally, through the teacher's written reflections, we learn that while tenets of the RWCT project underscore the importance and benefits of promoting active, enthusiastic student discussions, RWCT tenets also recognize the importance of keeping these discussions focused. This case provided an excellent opportunity for workshop leaders to clarify when and how to focus classroom discussion to accomplish the goals of the lesson.

The Inquiry

Recognizing that authentic teaching cases can provide graphic, context-specific information about teachers' thinking, we decided to conduct a systematic, qualitative inquiry documenting the issues in the Russian teachers' narratives. We thought that examining and categorizing the cases according to thematic topics might pinpoint particularly cogent strengths of the RWCT project. We also had an idea that analyzing the cases might illuminate the teachers' increasing competence in planning and presenting instruction based on the philosophical and instructional frameworks of the RWCT project. In addition, we had a sense that scrutinizing the narratives might highlight gaps in the content presented to teachers in the project's workshop sessions, or target some potentially conflicting or ambiguous information printed in the RWCT guidebooks. Further, we had a strong hunch that the content of the teachers' narratives might illuminate subtle, albeit crucial aspects of teachers' planning, assumptions, and instruction that might require some fine tuning or further clarification. Like all educators, the RWCT participants have moved (and continue to move) through various stages of professional development as they encounter and embrace tenets of the RWCT program (see Fuller, 1969, for a description of stages of teachers' professional development). Moreover, as do all exemplary teachers, RWCT program participants want to accept responsibility for their practices and remediate rough spots in their pedagogy (Anderson, DeMeulle, & Johnson, 1997; Ryan & Cooper, 1998).

Conceptual Methodology

Three literatures informed our inquiry: (1) tenets of social constructivism that suggest that language reveals individuals' knowledge, perceptions, and beliefs (Goetz & LeCompte, 1984); (2) ideas from discourse analysis that describe written texts as true measures of experiences (Gee, Michaels, & O'Connor, 1992); and (3) views from social constructivism that suggest that as mature human beings encounter problems that emerge through their circumstances, they move to resolve those problems through thoughtful reflection and actions (Woods, 1992).

Research Questions and Methodology

In our qualitative inquiry, we sought to answer the following questions:

- What issues are visible in the teachers' cases?
- Do the issues portrayed in the teachers' cases illuminate gaps in the content presented in RWCT workshops or inconsistencies printed in RWCT guidebooks that program volunteer consultants and directors need to ameliorate?
- Do the contents of the cases provide a window into the teachers' expanded professional knowledge base and increasing competence as RWCT program participants?
- Do the content of the cases provide RWCT program volunteer consultants and directors with some narrative evidence to help plan future workshop sessions?

Data Sources and Mode of Inquiry

Working as a research team, we examined and categorized 19 teaching cases authored by the teachers during the final workshop of the second year of the program. First, we independently read and reread the narratives, looking for emerging categories and patterns that would "facilitate a coherent synthesis of the data" (Gay, 1996, p. 227). We made notes and highlighted what we considered to be vital dimensions of the texts as a way of revealing the dominant themes (for example "Satisfaction about the increased motivation of disruptive students when they participated in collaborative learning groups"; "Concerns about correlating RWCT lessons with state examination guidelines"). Then, working together through e-mail, telephone conversations, and face-to-face dialogue, we used analytic induction (Bogdan & Biklin, 1992) to code and categorize each narrative according to the prevailing theme. We settled any variances in perspectives through collegial discussions until we reached agreement.

Analysis revealed that irrespective of teaching context (primary, elementary, and secondary classrooms), the teachers wrote about eight major issues:

1. Complications involving cooperative grouping;

2. Satisfaction about the increased motivation of disruptive students when they participated in collaborative learning groups;

3. Concerns about correlating RWCT lessons with state examination guidelines;

4. Problems caused by teachers who neglect to model new strategies for students;

5. Predicaments associated with presenting teaching strategies that were incompatible with a specific lesson, text, or instructional task;

6. Dilemmas about students who did not take RWCT activities seriously;

7. Satisfaction about students who initially thought that RWCT strategies were difficult and confusing, but came to regard the strategies as helpful; and

8. Concerns about choosing an appropriate text for a specific lesson.

The following case excerpts illustrate some of these prevalent themes.

Theme 2: Satisfaction about the increased motivation of disruptive students when they participated in collaborative learning groups (authored by an elementary teacher)

Sasha

This year I was given a very difficult third-grade class. Most of the students appeared to have poor self-esteem, and they seemed to lack self-discipline and motivation for learning. Honestly, I did not believe that the wonderful RWCT learning strategies would help me and my students very much. I was especially concerned about a boy named Sasha. He appeared unstable, and in the middle of a lesson he would get under his desk and make a scene.

Dividing the class into learning groups worked like magic for all of my students. They stared at me and waited to see what would happen next. I distributed cards with words printed on them. The task of each group member was to make sound/letter analysis based upon the Round Table procedure (Kagan, 1992). This is a learning exercise where each student provides a written comment, and then passes on the card or paper to the student on the left until all students in the group have contributed written comments. In a culminating activity, the groups exchange cards and compare all of the statements written by their peers. This worked very well. Even unpredictable Sasha was involved! I was surprised to learn that he could write so well and do so many things! Now, my students do not want to work any other way except in groups.

In the case "Sasha," the teacher provides sufficient relevant context for readers to be able to understand her particular teaching situation (a difficult third-grade class). The teacher's expanded professional knowledge also is quite evident when she provides a description of the round-table procedure devised by Kagan (1992). Further, the teacher displays ability to recognize students' increased motivations for staying on task as they engage in cooperative learning groups (Slavin, Madden, Stephens, & Hannigan, 1990).

Theme 4: Problems caused by teachers who neglect to model new strategies for students (authored by a secondary biology teacher)

Why Didn't I Model?

I offered my biology lesson to my older students through the Enhanced Lecture format (Bonwell & Eison, 1991). I regarded myself as well prepared for the lesson. I knew the material and considered all questions. Everything seemed to be fine. But right before the lesson, I decided that since I had plenty of time, during the reflection stage of the lesson, we would write reflective five-line cinquains The lecturing part of the lesson went well, but the cinquain did not.

"Cinquains are short poems," I said after the lecture.

Then, I asked the students to write one. I also explained how to do it. My students sat very still. I asked them "Is everything clear?"

They replied, "Yes, everything is clear," but they still remained sitting very quietly.

"What are you waiting for?" I asked. "Why aren't you writing, then?"

The answer in chorus was, "How can we write a poem about biology?"

"What is bothering you?" I asked my students.

"Nothing," they said.

Then, in chorus they asked, "Can *you* write such a cinquain about biology?"

"Naturally," I replied, and immediately tried to write one.

Well, the cinquains were a success, but I realized how much easier it would have been if I had shared some of my reflective cinquains with my students before I asked them to write their own five-line poems.

We learn from the case "Why Didn't I Model?" that the teacher is quite sure about his preparedness for the lesson. The teacher also is exceedingly clear about when and how he made an instructional error during the planning stage of his lesson. Further, we also discover that the teacher recognizes the importance of teacher modeling.

Theme 5: Consider the lesson, text, and task when choosing a strategy (authored by a secondary English teacher)

I Should Have Used a Different Strategy

I was telling my older students about the writer Chekhov. It was a very hot day. I used an Enhanced Lecture format (Bonwell & Eison, 1991). The material was very comprehensive...many ideas, dates, events, and names. After about 15 minutes of work, the students refused to show any interest in the topic and I doubt they learned very much about the writer. Many boys were yawning and a few girls were looking out of the window.

Analyzing the lesson, I realized that it would have been more reasonable to use cooperative learning groups. Each group could have been responsible for reading and becoming an expert on different parts of the Chekhov text. After reading their particular portions of the text, the group could have created a cluster or semantic map on large sheets of paper based upon the information they read in certain paragraphs. Then, group members could have placed their papers on the classroom walls. All of the students in each group could have presented the information on their papers and taken responsibility for helping their classmates learn about Chekhov. The next time, I will certainly do it in a different way.

The author of the case "I Should Have Used a Different Strategy" supplies relevant, contextual information for readers, and links the specific teaching context to his instructional dilemma. As a reflective practitioner, he also explicitly states that after the lesson, he tried to analyze what went wrong. Further showing his teaching expertise, he describes how he might structure the class for future lessons and explains what strategy might have been more effective for that particular learning task. To conclude his teaching case, the teacher sagely applies what he learned in this lesson to future instruction.

Discussion and Implications for Teachers Everywhere

The study contributes several salient ideas to the body of knowledge regarding teachers' professional development and also provides insights into the RWCT teacher professional development model. First, the findings of our inquiry clearly indicate that case writing and discussion is a valuable venue for promoting teachers' professional growth. Authoring cases provided opportunities for the Russian teachers in Estonia to consciously identify a specific teaching problem or triumph. They were able to document classroom events through writing, and then supply possible solutions to the described dilemmas or plausible explanations for achievements. An added bonus is that sharing some of the dilemmas illustrated in the cases with one another in supportive communities contributed further occasions for the teachers to enhance their professional growth. Discussing educational concerns and sharing alternative actions and approaches in collegial circumstances empowers teachers and fosters their own capacities to think critically about their work. Talking collaboratively about dilemmas portrayed in cases, asking clarifying questions, and seeking alternative approaches to the problems portrayed all help teachers construct themselves as capable educators (Richards & Gipe, 2000). Discussing instructional problems with colleagues also promotes higher standards for teachers' inquiry and has the capacity to enrich teachers' pedagogy, thereby ultimately improving school communities (Lipsitz, 1984; Little, 1987).

Another contribution of the research is that the content of the teachers' narratives served as a window into their professional thinking. Analysis of the Russian teachers' cases highlights their abilities to solve dilemmas and offer alternative solutions to teaching problems. The cases also reveal the teachers' capabilities to discern teaching successes. In addition, the narratives disclose the teachers' strong and growing understanding of the RWCT philosophy and corresponding instructional strategies and techniques. The research also illuminates the eight distinct issues that concerned or intrigued the teachers outlined earlier in the chapter, so RWCT program volunteer consultants and directors now have some narrative evidence to help plan future workshop sessions.

Finally, the inquiry validates the RWCT project model. The content of these particular cases indicates that RWCT volunteer scholars offered well-developed, effective workshops and that the information in the RWCT guidebooks is consistent, practical, and based on sound theory. Further, the content of the cases show that the Russian teachers in Estonia are well on their way to becoming master teachers who are able to serve as instructional resources for their students and for other teachers who will join the program in years to come. In the 3 years in which they have participated in the RWCT program, these 19 teachers have made remarkable strides toward implementing classroom methods and approaches that promote students' critical thinking and group collaboration.

Implications of the research are applicable to teachers everywhere. Good teachers want to accept responsibility for devising and presenting lessons that promote students' critical thinking and abilities to work collaboratively. Teachers in all countries also appreciate the importance of documenting teaching concerns and successes and determining possible solutions to their pedagogical dilemmas. Because authoring teaching cases has the potential for promoting teachers' reflective thinking, professional attitudes, and inquiry, it is not far-fetched to suggest that in the near future, educators in countries throughout the world will write and share teaching narratives with one another through such global venues as e-mail and listservs, as well as through telephone calls and face-to-face meetings at scholarly conferences. Ultimately, through their collective wisdom and collaboration, teachers have the capacity to promote critical thinking and problem solving in all nations, regardless of governmental dictates or dogma.

Authors' Notes

Thank you to Tanya Suurkask, Russian/English interpreter for the RWCT project in Estonia, for translating the Russian teachers' cases into English.

A special thank you also to the Russian teachers who graciously wrote and shared their teaching cases with us.

REFERENCES

Anderson, R., DeMeulle, L., & Johnston, J. (1997, Winter/Spring). Plugging in: On-line collegial dialogue for self-study. *Teaching Education, 8*(2), 129–197.

Bogdan, R., & Biklin, S. (1992). *Qualitative research for education* (2nd ed.). Needham Heights, MA: Allyn & Bacon.

Bonwell, C., & Eison, J. (1991). *Active learning: Creating excitement in the classroom (AASHE-ERIC Higher Report No. 1)*. Washington, DC: The George Washington School of Education and Human Development.

Fuller, F. (1969). *Concerns of teachers: A manual for teacher educators: Increasing teacher satisfaction with professional preparation by considering teachers' concerns when planning preservice and inservice education.* Austin, TX: Texas University, Research and Development Center for Teacher Education (ERIC Document Reproduction Service No. ED 040 143).

Gay, L. (1996). *Educational research: Competencies for analysis and application* (5th ed.). Englewood Cliffs, NJ: Prentice Hall.

Gee, J., Michaels, S., & O'Connor, C. (1992). Discourse analysis. In M. LeCompte, W. Millroy, & J. Preissle (Eds.), *The handbook of qualitative research in education* (pp. 227–291). New York: Academic Press.

Goetz, J., & LeCompte, M. (1984). *Ethnography and qualitative design in educational research*. Orlando, FL: Academic Press.

Haridusminissteerium (Education) Ministry Report. (1997). Tallinn, Estonia.

Kagan, S. (1992). *Cooperative learning*. San Juan Capistrano, CA: Kagan Cooperative Learning.

Lipsitz, J. (1984). *Successful schools for young adolescents*. New Brunswick, NJ: Transaction Books.

Little, J. (1987). Teachers as colleagues. In V. Richardson-Koehler (Ed.), *Educator's handbook: A research perspective* (pp. 491–518). New York: Longman.

Merseth, K. (1991, September/October). The early history of case-based instruction: Insights for teacher education. *Journal of Teacher Education, 42*(4), 243–249.

Richards, J., & Gipe, J. (2000). *Elementary literacy lessons: Cases and commentaries from the field*. Mahwah, NJ: Erlbaum.

Ryan, K., & Cooper, J. (1998). *Those who can, teach* (8th ed.). Boston: Houghton Mifflin.

Shulman, J. (Ed.). (1992). *Case methods in teacher education*. New York: Teachers College Press.

Shulman, L. (1992). Toward a pedagogy of cases. In J. Shulman (Ed.), *Case methods in teacher education* (pp. 1–30). New York: Teachers College Press.

Slavin, R., Madden, N., Stephens, R., & Hannigan, M. (1990). Cooperative learning: Models for 3 R's. *Educational Leadership, 47*(4), 22–28.

Stauffer, R. (1981). *Teaching reading as a thinking process*. New York: Harper & Row.

Sykes, G. (1992). Foreword. In J. Shulman (Ed.), *Case methods in teacher education* (pp. vii–ix). New York: Teachers College Press.

Wassermann, S. (1994). Using cases to study teaching. *Phi Delta Kappan, 75*(8), 602–611.

Woods, P. (1992). Symbolic interactionism: Theory and method. In M. LeCompte, W. Millroy, & J. Preissle (Eds.), *The handbook of qualitative research in education* (pp. 337–404). New York: Academic Press.

CHAPTER SEVEN

"The Atmosphere Is Completely Different": Students' Perceptions of RWCT in Action in Macedonian Classrooms

Alison Preece
with Elena Ackovska-Leskovska, Suzana Miovska, Ruth F. Longman,
Daniel R. Hittleman, and Jill Lewis

Michael Fullan (1991) once noted that we know very little about how students perceive school reform because *we so rarely ask them.* The observation is more than simply ironic; it acknowledges a sorry loss of invaluable information. The success or effectiveness of any program of school reform directed at the classroom level cannot be fairly or fully assessed if the students who experience those reforms are not consulted about them. Convinced of this, we felt we needed to find out how the students touched by the RWCT project in Macedonia perceived and experienced it. We wanted to learn about *their* responses to the efforts of their teachers to implement the strategies and approaches promoted by the project: Had they noticed any difference? If so, what sort of difference? How did they feel about the changes being made? Heeding Fullan's point, we asked them.

The views presented here are derived from a variety of sources. During the first year of implementation (1997–1998), 90 elementary and secondary students anonymously completed an open-ended questionnaire devised and distributed by the in-country project directors, Susana Miovska and Elena Ackovska-Leskovska. The questions invited them to describe the positive and negative aspects of the new approaches and to comment on any changes they may have noted in their in-school roles and relationships and in the role of their teachers. They were asked to compare the new approaches with their previous experience of school in terms of their interest in the lessons, the acquisition and retention of the material to be learned, their cooperation with classmates, and their communication with their teachers. In the second year of implementation (1998–1999), this same questionnaire was completed anonymously by 54 elementary students and 33 high school students taught by teachers newly involved in the project. In the third year of the project (1999–2000), 33 postsecondary education students who had experienced the strategies during an intensive 6-day professional development institute were asked to describe in writing their reactions to the strategies from their perspective as learners. The statements were unsigned to ensure a frank response. Throughout the 3 years of our involvement in the project, we also recorded the comments made by students and noted their reactions during our many visits to observe lessons taught by project participants. In addition, all the teachers involved were surveyed and asked about the responses of their students and whether they had perceived any changes in their students that they could attribute to the RWCT project.

The Context

Macedonia is a tiny, rugged, culturally rich, land-locked Balkan nation bordered by Albania, Yugoslavia, Bulgaria, and Greece. At the introductory planning meeting, our Macedonian project leaders proudly and laughingly described their country as having "the most beautiful women, the best dancers, the tastiest tomatoes, and the loveliest lakes!" Many readers will recall the devastating earthquake of the early 1960s that leveled the capital city, Skopje. For others, Macedonia is more recently recognized for its disproportionately generous provision of shelter to the refugees from Kosovo in 1999. Since becoming proudly and precariously independent from Yugoslavia in 1991, Macedonia has been faced with harsh economic conditions that have tempered and deflated early post-independence dreams of better times. Life is hard, the social and political changes have been slow to bear tangible fruit, and the future is uncertain. Nevertheless, as their history makes plain, the Macedonians are a resourceful, resilient people who are determined to make their country work on their own terms. For the four of us (Alison, Ruth, Dan, and Jill) who came to Macedonia as "North American volunteers," the reality of the challenges faced by our Macedonian colleagues has been sobering. At the same time, their response to those challenges, their professionalism, day-to-day dedication, and unflagging willingness to work for changes in their schools have deeply impressed and moved us—and taught us lessons they, and perhaps we, may not have been aware we were learning.

A note about the educational context should help provide an interpretive backdrop for the students' reactions. Since independence, many teachers and administrators have been actively attempting to expand and experiment with their repertoire of instructional practices. Interest in externally funded professional development projects, such as Step-by-Step for early childhood and the Debate Project, has been keen. All the teachers invited to join the RWCT project had been selected on the basis of their professional commitment and their interest in refining their pedagogical practices. We were therefore working with a highly skilled and dedicated group who, prior to the project, had invested considerable effort in providing quality learning experiences for their students.

However, the curriculum was, and remains, rigidly prescribed, materials are scarce, and the predominant instructional style (both observed and reported) is teacher-directed and textbook-centered with students responsible for memorizing the information presented. Orientation visits arranged to help the North American team members familiarize themselves with Macedonian schools had provided striking examples of "traditional" practices. In almost all cases observed, the teacher dominated the interactions, and the lessons consisted of a barrage of questions designed to elicit a replay of the passage or content assigned in the text. Usually the more able students were called on to stand and deliver their answers, while the rest of the class listened. Answers, almost uniformly fact-based, were evaluated publicly by the teacher, corrected where necessary, and the next question then posed. We were impressed with the confidence and articulateness with which the selected students responded, and with the amount of factual information they appeared to have at their command. Nevertheless, prior to the RWCT workshops, we saw little variation in this pattern, no evidence of group work, and almost no examples of students being asked to independently research, interpret, reshape, or provide their own opinions about the target material. In every case, the most active person in the classroom was the teacher.

Positive Responses

Our impression that the students were positively embracing the new approaches was absolutely confirmed by the data gathered. Overwhelmingly the students reported finding the strategies interesting and useful (97% of the first-year group; 100% of both the second-year group and the post-secondary students), and their lessons more dynamic, involving, and enjoyable because of them. Their comments repeatedly note their high level of engagement in the activities, their surprise at how quickly time passed as a consequence ("I did not even think about lunch!"; "Not for one minute…did I feel tired or bored"), and their awareness that *all* rather than just *some* were actively involved in the tasks assigned. More than 95% of the second-year group specifically reported that they were more involved in their "new" classes, with only 3% claiming no change. A post-secondary student put it this way: "In all of my experience until now as a student, I've never been so involved in the learning process, which means to be always active, to think, to compare, to listen and to make conclusions." Another stated,

> These new strategies are more interesting than the traditional.…. I am always active without the possibility of thinking about something outside of the topic. That is a great advantage because the student is not only physically present at the lesson, he's also mentally engaged and developing.

The evidence that the students found the new approaches more enjoyable was persuasive. The adjective *fun* was common in the data, and our observations provided us with many examples of lessons that crackled with energy and were fueled by the enthusiastic responses of the students. On several occasions we had been amused by students' demands of their teachers, following an absence due to attendance at one of the seminars, for the new strategies the teachers had learned at the workshop. These requests were always made with a sense of happy expectation ("You said you'd learned something new…so show us!"). However, while certainly relevant and revealing, enjoyment is only one aspect of program effectiveness. We were eager to know whether the students perceived any impact on their learning as a result of the strategies implemented.

"They *Like* These Strategies, But Are They Learning Anything?"

Almost all those surveyed attributed clear learning advantages to the new methods. The entire second-year group (100%) reported use of the strategies made learning easier and 97% of the first-year group confirmed them as beneficial. One of the postsecondary students stated, "This way of learning helps us to learn the material easier and faster but also it motivates us to work more and better"; another wrote, "My experience with the strategies is wonderful. They helped me to learn and fulfill the tasks much more easily." All groups claimed that the strategies made it easier to retain the knowledge learned; all 87 of the students surveyed in the second year agreed that lessons with applied critical thinking strategies were remembered longer than traditional lessons. There were many reasons given as to why this was so. High on the list were the advantages that resulted from being able to collaborate and confer with classmates. The students gave cooperative group work a very strong endorsement; it ranked first on the list of positive changes noted by both the first- and second-year student groups. In fact, the opportunity to work with one's peers, classmates, and colleagues was resoundingly endorsed and appreciated by all the educators who participated in the project. Sadly, both students and their teachers noted that such opportunities had been rare events in their educational and professional experience prior to RWCT.

The project teachers were encouraged to include many partner and small-group activities in their lessons and to regularly invite students to share and compare their responses with those sitting beside them. The students clearly recognized the contribution that such exchanges made to their learning. Having to articulate a position or viewpoint so as to communicate it, and then having to elaborate or defend it in response to a classmate's questions meant that the material was more thoroughly (and likely more meaningfully) reviewed. As one student put it, the result was "more durable knowledge." In contrast to the public pattern characteristic of the traditional model, in which the teacher asks the questions and only one student at a time answers, partner and small-group conferences permit *all* the students to simultaneously share their remarks in a more private and less intimidating context. This difference was an important one. Students repeatedly noted that it granted them more freedom to express their own opinions, and just as importantly, to become aware of the opinions of others. Striking in the data is just how much this was valued. One student commented, "We found out how much it means to be listened to by the others, to express your feelings, beliefs, and to hear those of others." Many acknowledged that they learned from each other. Others stated that they had gained confidence from having their ideas accepted and taken seriously by their classmates, and by having "the opportunity to be heard out by others."

Creativity, Imagination, and Inventiveness

A recurring theme was the increased creativity and inventiveness unleashed by the strategies. Students included references to imagination, originality, innovation, and variety in their descriptions of the positive effects of the application of the critical thinking strategies. One reported, "I was thinking in a new way—more free and more creative!"; another stated, "For me as a student these strategies are very productive and inventive." Interestingly, these descriptors were not limited to the students. When asked if they had noticed any change in the role of their teachers, some responded that their teachers were more creative in designing and delivering the lessons, and more encouraging of their students' creativity. For their part, the teachers were quick to recognize the creativity and quality of the work produced by their students, and some were endearingly honest in admitting their initial surprise at just how good this work was. It was a rare school visit that did not result in a teacher proudly showing off examples of student work. Observational notes capture one visit during which a high school history teacher gleefully displayed piles of graphic organizers and visual charts created by her students, using them to illustrate the contrast with the type of assignment she had given previously. The work was impressive and her reaction, noted in the account of the visit was, "so enthusiastic and excited she was almost exploding with it."

The opportunities inherent in techniques such as brainstorming, clustering, and the building of K-W-L charts for students to uncover and contribute their previous knowledge of the focus topic were pointed to as facilitating the learning that occurred. Such techniques also were credited with helping students deepen and extend their understandings and make connections among the new and the already known. As one student put it, "I could learn more—my knowledge became richer—clearer." In stark contrast to the still commonly held perception that "active" student-centered pedagogy is an invitation to waste precious school time on socializing rather than learning, these students had no doubt that by working together and by sharing their efforts and understandings, they had enhanced their learning. Further, several made explicit their conviction that the approaches being adopted by their teachers demanded more rather than less of them, and placed greater responsibility on them for making sense of the concepts and materials featured in their curriculum. This view was echoed by a group of seventh-grade students who spoke to us after we had observed a directed reading lesson in their classroom. Their teacher had elicited their predictions about the events and outcome of the story and had them craft cinquains to synthesize their responses to the text. The students were effusively positive about what they had just experienced, claiming it was their "best class all year" and calling for more classes just like it. To the accompaniment of confirming nods from the others, one boy stated that "it obligates us to think a lot more than the traditional way, and we are all *in* the text." Picking up the theme, another stated that "in groups, we *all* think about the questions." A third boy added that "working in this way we talk less," and when questioned as to his meaning he explained that they engaged in much less off-topic talk because they were so interested in what they were doing.

Changed Relationships

We were curious as to whether the students perceived any relational shifts resulting from their teachers' efforts to enact the RWCT philosophy and goals. Our observations had suggested that many of the teachers appeared energized by the freshness of the new approaches and seemed to be clearly enjoying presenting these to their students. Some admitted to having been a little apprehensive at first, unsure of how their students would respond; others had been concerned about the reactions of their colleagues if their classes became noisier or looked disorganized when the students worked in pairs and groups. One of the genuine pleasures of observing the teachers' early efforts at incorporating the strategies into their lessons was seeing them happily surprised and reassured by the positive reactions of their students. Often a marvelously symbiotic response would be evident, with the teachers relaxing and opening things even more as their students met and exceeded "performance expectations" and signaled their pride and pleasure in doing so. We wondered whether the students would confirm our impressions, or whether their view would be that only technique, rather than tone and tenor, had changed.

Seventy-two percent of the 90 students polled in the first year reported experiencing better communication with their teacher, with 11% stating directly that they felt their teacher had become "a much better friend." In the second year, 95% of the 87 surveyed students listed an improved teacher-student relationship as one of the positive results of the RWCT project. Many stated that they felt greater freedom to express their own opinions. Others reported less fear of their teachers, and 10% stated they felt their teacher had become more of a friend to the students. One of the postsecondary students wrote, "Each of us was very active and put in a position to express his opinion about some problem. I felt a different relationship, teacher to student, which differs from the relationship I knew until now."

One classroom observation stands out and exemplifies the shift described by the students. During a Grade 4 mathematics lesson, the teacher, Jordan Dudeski, had skillfully engineered a debate about the characteristics and defining qualities of polygons. The atmosphere was electric, and sides were drawn. Intent on provoking the children to think through their answers, the teacher deftly played devil's advocate, disputing and questioning the points students raised in a way that forced students to explain and defend their positions. What impressed all of us who watched this unfold was the confidence and energy with which several of the children challenged and countered their teacher's statements. Much to his thinly veiled delight, his rebuttals met the same response. It was quite apparent that the children felt comfortable—even gleeful—contradicting their teacher, and it was equally evident that their teacher applauded their willingness to do so. The contrast with traditional classroom practice could not have been greater.

Relationships with teachers were not the only relationships claimed to be changed. One of the features of "active learning" most valued by the students was the frequent opportunity to confer and collaborate with each other. Their awareness of the contribution such collaboration made to their knowledge and understanding has already been noted. Just as significant is their recognition of how this changed the atmosphere of their classes and their relationships with each other. Lessons were more engaging and involving in large measure because they were now permitted to work on assignments together, to share their ideas with each other, and to use each other as resources and sounding boards. Interest was heightened and anxiety lessened. As one student emphatically put it, "the atmosphere is completely different."

Both the classroom observations and the survey data provide ample evidence of the students' appreciation of their classmates' ideas, skills and talents, and their pride in the results of group tasks and projects. Students were generous in their praise of their peers' creative efforts, and eager to hear what their classmates had produced. The only complaint was that there was rarely sufficient time to hear everyone's ideas or to read aloud what every student had written. Many commented that the strategies had helped them to get to know each other better and to be more comfortable with each other. Discussion circles earned a particularly warm response; one student listed this as a favorite new activity because "when we sat down in a circle facing each other we all felt equal." Perhaps the most affirming aspect of all this is the clear message that the students felt their peers had worthwhile things to say, and that they recognized the power and pleasure of learning with and from them.

The implications of such changed relationships are potentially far-reaching. The foundation of a democratic society is the belief in the individual right to a voice and a vote, and a sense of collective responsibility for the decision making that shapes that society. Power and authority, at least in theory, reside with the people. To achieve and sustain any such democratic system, *each person* needs to feel entitled to take a position on issues that touch his or her life, and responsibility for supporting that position with reasons that can be defended logically. Each person needs to believe he or she has a right to be heard, and that he or she has an obligation to listen to the views of others. Such behaviors need to be learned and experienced directly, and that experience needs to begin early—in our schools. The unquestioned authority of the views of the teacher and the textbook has to be replaced with opportunities for questions, for dialogue, for personal interpretation, and for debate.

Supporting Critical Thinking

The major goal of the RWCT project is to foster and support the disposition and the skills necessary to think critically. The data provide some evidence of enhanced student awareness of critical thinking, but this evidence tends to be more indirect than explicitly stated. A recurrent theme is appreciation for the greater encouragement of and more opportunities for free expression of individual views, ideas, and opinions. One of the postsecondary students summarized her experience of the strategies by announcing, "I feel free—I choose—I have a great possibility to express myself, to be creative." Sounding a more poignant note, another wrote, "If these techniques had been used by all my teachers, maybe today I would be more free." A few of the students made specific reference to critical thinking. One noted, "The strategies are good because they really motivate the student to think critically, to tell his opinion, and of course to defend what he has told." Echoing these sentiments, another stated, "we had the opportunity to learn strategies that encourage critical thinking in ourselves."

The questionnaire asked the students if they had noticed any change in their interest in reading beyond the material assigned in the textbook as a result of the strategies. Had they used supplemental literature? Sixty percent of the first-year group claimed an increased interest in "additional" reading, while 93% of the second-year group reported that the RWCT strategies had motivated them to expand their knowledge of the topics treated. A heightened desire to conduct independent research and increased motivation to seek out materials other than the ones put in front of you are certainly behaviors that engender critical thinking. A number of the students noted that the strategies had made them more aware of their own thinking. The expectation that one would share an interpretation or opinion meant that one had to formulate and articulate that interpretation or opinion. One of the postsecondary students noted that "we are able to know ourselves better," while another wrote, "I learned new things about myself that I didn't know I knew."

Confirmation From Their Teachers

All the teacher participants in the project were surveyed and asked to describe the responses of their students and to comment on any changes they had noticed in their students that they felt were a result of their efforts to implement the project goals and strategies. Their responses are strikingly congruent with those of the students. The teachers saw their students as much more active, involved, and interested in learning and more motivated to learn independently. Some noted that even their weaker students were more active when the lessons incorporated the critical thinking strategies. They strongly confirmed the view expressed by the students that learning was easier and agreed that the material appeared better retained with the new methods. The teachers who joined the project in its second year of implementation provide powerful evidence that real changes have occurred. Ninety-three percent noted greater cooperation among students, with more tolerance and patience evident. Some noted students had developed a greater respect for others' opinions and had become more willing to listen to what their classmates had to say. Ninety-one percent of the teachers claimed an improved teacher-student relationship, with some describing it as friendlier and more of a partnership. Students were seen as feeling freer to express themselves and less anxious about assessments and grades. Overwhelmingly, the teachers endorsed the active-learning strategies as having made their instruction more effective and their experience as teachers richer and more rewarding. It is an understatement to claim they were pleased with the differences noted.

Some Caution, Some Ambivalence, Some Negatives

Although generally very positive, some students raised questions and concerns that need to be noted and considered. Six percent of those surveyed in the second year felt that their class periods were not long enough to permit them to do justice to the strategies; they felt rushed and pressured by time. Others (2%) felt that the new methods resulted in heightened noise levels in their classes that they found distracting and uncomfortable. Several stated that they felt collaborative work made the class "less disciplined," but again this appeared more a concern about noise than the quality of the work produced. A few expressed concern that some students might not pull their weight during group work, placing an unfair burden on the others. One student noted that over-use of the same few strategies would result in boredom; this appears, however, not to have been a condition experienced, but rather one anticipated.

Time is always problematic in teaching no matter the context. At first, many teachers tended to "stuff" lessons with strategies, often moving from one to the next before students had sufficient time to interact or complete the task assigned. This changed with experience, however. Concern about noise was shared by many of the teachers at the outset of the project. The North American volunteers had to explicitly counter a misconception that active learning equated with and sanctioned high noise levels and free movement. However, as expectations were modeled and defined, and the difference between a productive working buzz and unacceptable bedlam was made clear, concern about noise abated.

Novelty, Halo Effects, and Too Good to Be True?

Survey results as overwhelmingly positive as these inevitably invite questions as to their trustworthiness: Can such results be taken at face value? How much are the responses positively skewed by the impact of novelty? Do the results simply reflect a situation in which *anything* different would be positively rated simply because it offered a change? Do the results benefit from the halo effect, from the "specialness" that inclusion in such a project affords?

There is probably no question that the novelty of the strategies and their difference from the standard practice contributed to the positive ratings they received. However, it is also clear that the differences were embraced because they permitted ways of being and thinking in the classroom that were wanted and valued by the students who experienced them. Further, the surveys were completed at the end of the school year, by which time most of the students should have become familiar with many of the strategies and would have had multiple exposures to them. Thus any initial novelty effects would likely have diminished. However, the issue hinges on whether students are simply responding to change for change's sake. Based on the data presented here and corroborating evidence provided by many classroom observations, our perception is that the strong, positive response is a genuine one, based on first-hand experience of the difference to learning that active engagement can make.

Lessons Learned, Messages Heard

It is almost impossible to engage in any cross-cultural experience without feeling that you are in some ways playing with mirrors; any examination of what others are doing in their classrooms raises questions about what we are doing in ours. Although the focus here is ostensibly the impact of a professional development project in Macedonia, the students' reactions and evaluations have implications for all of us who care about teaching.

The concept of "active learning" is one that most North American teachers take as a given (Bredekamp & Copple, 1997; Goodlad, 1984). Few would challenge its merits, and most teachers would likely claim that their classrooms were active and engaging environments, or certainly that they were trying to make them that way. However, it is easy to forget or to overlook just how much of a difference practices that invite and value student participation actually make. In Macedonia, the contrast has been a stark one. The differences are visible and felt. In most North American classes, the need for such dramatic changes would likely be far less pressing. Nevertheless, the Macedonian students remind us just how much student-focused pedagogy matters, and how much of a difference it can make to the quality of the learning experienced. An honest scrutiny of our own teaching contexts may well reveal that they are not as supportive of active learning and full student participation as they might be. As the data presented here make clear, any effort we can make to genuinely involve our students in their learning is effort wisely invested.

The pressure to cover the curriculum is a pressure felt by all of us. Far too frequently it becomes the justification for content-dominant instruction that leaves little room for students to interpret or share and compare their views of the material presented. Ironically, students then learn less, and the process of learning is diminished and devalued. Much of the time, content coverage is an illusion, the naïve and erroneously optimistic equation of presentation with learning. If content is to be integrated usefully into our understanding, then it must be discussed, dissected, worked over, connected to things that matter to us—digested, not just "received." This takes time, but as the Macedonian students quoted here confirm, it is time that translates into learning that lasts.

Research has convincingly documented the wide array of benefits that can result from cooperative learning (Johnson & Johnson, 1985; Slavin, 1990). Large-scale workplace surveys of employers repeatedly note the value placed on employees who can communicate effectively and work collaboratively. These are skills that are learned, however—and common sense tells us they are more easily learned if explicitly taught and fostered at an early age. Although most North American teachers are well acquainted with the rationale for cooperative learning, it is fair to question whether its potential is exploited as frequently or as richly as it could be. As these Macedonian students so strongly remind us, students *want* and *need* to work with each other; they value opportunities to hear the opinions and perspectives of their classmates; and they learn better when things are set up so they can collaborate and contribute to the instructional conversation. Just as clearly, they respect and appreciate teachers who make it possible for them to do so.

One of the most resonant lessons carried home from Macedonia by the four of us from North America is that the health and viability of an open society depends more than most of us realize on what our young people experience in our schools. If we want a participatory democracy where all voices have a right to be heard, and where authority can be challenged by right, reason, and logical argument, then our students need to have experienced and lived those values in our schools. In Macedonia, history has made the connection obvious. Our lesson from Macedonia is that we dare not forget how direct that link is.

Authors' Note

All the student comments have been translated from Macedonian, and any awkwardness of phrasing or wording is a consequence of the difficulties of converting the meaning into another language.

REFERENCES

Bredekamp, S., & Copple, C. (Eds.). (1997). *Developmentally appropriate practice in early childhood programs serving children from birth through age 8* (Rev. ed.). Washington, DC: National Association for the Education of Young Children.

Fullan, M. (1991). *The real meaning of educational change* (2nd ed.). New York: Teachers College Press.

Goodlad, J.I. (1984). *A place called school: Prospects for the future.* New York: McGraw-Hill.

Johnson, D.W., & Johnson, R.T. (1985). Motivational processes in cooperative, competitive, and individualistic learning situations. In C. Ames & R. Ames (Eds.), *Research on motivation in education* (Vol. 2). Orlando, FL: Academic Press.

Slavin, R.E. (1990). *Cooperative learning: Theory, research and practice.* Englewood Cliffs, NJ: Prentice-Hall.

CHAPTER EIGHT

"I Feel Like a Bird": How the RWCT Project Supports Motivations

Jodi Patrick Holschuh, Cynthia Hynd, and Penny Oldfather

It was a very big decision I made. I understood I had to do something new. When I came from the workshop, I had this decision with me. I remembered when I entered the classroom I asked for a piece of chalk, which I had never done before. The children were looking at me in surprise, because I hadn't warned them beforehand, and I could feel that the children were prepared for something new also. Before that time, I was in quite a static role. I was explaining the lesson and enjoying myself, my rule, my speech. Actually, I wasn't very interested in the other counterpart in the classroom. The important thing was that my role was successful, that I was efficient in implementation of my role. I was sort of using my students for expressing my own ability and skills as a teacher. And now I was quite convinced that this had been my teaching process.

After the experience, I started teaching and provoking students' thought. My role became more dynamic. I involved my students. Before those times I never used chalk and blackboard, and they became a central part in my teaching. Through the blackboard I had very close contact and communication with my students. That was the first time I applied these methods. I was using the method of evocation. The topic was one of the short stories of a 20th-century Georgian writer.

The questions were: "What do you know about women's role in society? What is your perception of a woman as a mother?" I told them that my next lesson would be about the life of a woman. And very interesting material came from the students. And we tried to put it up on the blackboard. Of course, they were also writing in their notebooks. All of them were trying to participate, to contribute somehow to the lesson. I couldn't make any division between excellent or poor students. Before the lecture that day, I had always somehow divided the class in my mind between excellent and poor students, and now that division was eliminated. And actually...I was speechless. I was enjoying the lesson, and I was amazed at the knowledge of my students. In the past, I would never have believed that they would have known so much. So, the students became my partners. There were no boundaries between students and teacher. Actually, I used the whole class period for evocation—the whole lesson! We filled up three blackboards and five pages in students' notebooks. We have never done that much before. And it was such a busy environment. You could hear the notebooks, turning pages, making noise. It was very busy. Everybody was trying their best. And after the lesson was over, I felt great exhaustion. I must say that the lessons you taught [in RWCT] encouraged me to discover a new type of teaching.

This story, written by a teacher named Mzia, reflects a transformational experience for her and her eighth-grade students that took place as a result of what she had learned through the Reading and Writing for Critical Thinking (RWCT) project in the Republic of Georgia. She describes how the simple but dramatic shift in her role as teacher had enormous impact not only on her students' critical thinking, but on how she understood her students, their abilities, her relationship to them, and their intrinsic motivation for learning. Her story is one of many that we have heard during our involvement in RWCT in the Republic of Georgia and Estonia.

In Georgia and Estonia, as in many of the new democracies once part of the Soviet Union, educators and policy makers involved in the RWCT project understand the necessity for teaching citizens to think critically. A focus on critical thinking, taught through active learning strategies, is a vital component to schooling. These abilities will provide tomorrow's citizens with the ability to solve complex problems, a necessity for the continuance of democratic practices.

Because critical thinking was not encouraged in the Soviet Union, many students in Central and Eastern Europe and Central Asia have difficulty thinking critically and approaching learning in an active manner. But the problem is not confined to former Soviet Republics. Students in U.S. schools who have been taught mainly to "memorize the facts" also have difficulty. RWCT attempts to change that situation by promoting teaching practices that help students think critically, learn problem solving, work collaboratively, and become lifelong learners. This model has the potential to change the way in which students experience schooling.

The mere fact that teachers and students are taught strategies is not enough to effect this change. Motivations are both tools and outcomes that play a key role in the success of the project on multiple levels. A healthy and vibrant democratic society has citizens who experience positive motivations that spring from a sense of hope, a sense of empowerment, a sense of connectedness to community, and the belief that individuals and groups can make a difference. Motivation is crucial to all aspects of RWCT, and it influences the quantity and quality of learning and the interactions surrounding learning for both instructors and students. It is our belief that the type of instruction and learning RWCT promotes is inherently motivating. The purpose of this chapter, then, is to explicate theoretical and practical ways in which RWCT supports motivations of the educators and their students and, potentially, the larger societies in which they are situated. To do this, we will show links between the framework used in the RWCT project (Evocation, Realization of Meaning, and Reflection [ERR]; Steele & Meredith, 1995; see also Steele, Chapter One in this volume, for further discussion of ERR) to several current motivational theories, and we will provide examples of this connection through observations and through the comments of the participants with whom we worked in Estonia and the Republic of Georgia.

Current theory suggests that motivation is not a unidimensional construct; instead, it is integrative and involves multiple dimensions (Alexander, 1998; Paris & Turner, 1994). For example, McCombs (1996) said that children are more motivated to learn when they have appropriate strategies for learning (the skill), the desire to learn (the will), and interaction with their peers (the social support). Motivation also comes from feelings of empowerment. Oldfather's (1992) research suggests that students who are involved in reflecting on their own thinking and who are allowed ownership of their learning are likely to be more intrinsically motivated, as well as deeper thinkers and problem solvers. These theories describe conditions for motivation that are fostered by the RWCT and embodied in the ERR framework.

In this chapter, we present several current motivational theories, discuss their connection to the RWCT project, and provide examples of this connection through observations and through the comments of the participants with whom we worked in Estonia and the Republic of Georgia. Jodi is in her third year of working with Russian teachers in Estonia (the names of the Estonian teachers presented in this chapter are pseudonyms), and Penny and Cyndie are in their third year of working with teachers in the Republic of Georgia. The comments we share in this chapter come from our efforts to document the kinds of changes that are taking place in the RWCT participants' lives and are taken from interview and questionnaire data that we have gathered systematically over the course of our work in these countries. These are data supplemental to the overall assessment data collected to document the effectiveness of the entire RWCT project.

Model of Domain Learning (MDL) Viewpoint

Alexander and her colleagues (Alexander, 1998; Alexander, Jetton, & Kulikowich, 1995; Alexander, Kulikowich, & Schulze, 1994) suggest a Model of Domain Learning, or MDL. This model has relevance to motivation theories because like other integrated theories, a facet of motivation (in this case *interest*) is combined with other aspects of learning (such as *knowledge* and *strategy use*) to explain differences in learning. Alexander describes three stages of development in domain literacy: acclimation, competence, and proficiency. She uses this model to describe changes in knowledge, strategic processing, and interest that occur simultaneously as someone progresses from being a novice or acclimated learner to one who is competent or even an expert in a knowledge domain.

Acclimated learners have little knowledge, use general, inefficient strategies, and may have minimal interest in the domain. They know little about the domain in question, and what they do know tends to be fragmented, disorganized, and poorly related to central principles. Because they do not have an understanding of the relations among ideas, acclimated learners do not realize when ideas agree or compete, they do not connect details with an overarching frame, and they have difficulty in engaging in critical thinking.

Acclimated learners rely heavily on general strategies, but may not use them effectively because their lack of knowledge hinders their strategy use. For example, a student reading a biology text may think that all ideas are equally important and so will not highlight or annotate the text appropriately. In addition, acclimated learners may have lower levels of personal investment in learning. Thus, if they are to exert strategic effort, it may be more in response to external forces (such as grades or recognition) than to a deep-seated interest. Of course, some situations (such as an interesting topic) may spark interest; this interest, unfortunately, may not be maintained unless the student can relate that interest to personal goals.

To reach competence, acclimated learners can accumulate more knowledge, apply intense strategic effort, or exhibit a strong will to learn or achieve. Competent learners, in contrast to acclimated ones, have a knowledge base on which they can begin to learn key concepts about the domain they are studying. They also begin to develop a repertoire of specific strategies that they can use efficiently, and they have an increasing all-encompassing interest in the domain, which sustains them when their situational interests are low. Students who are competent learners begin to develop and recognize opportunities to use routines. Thus, cognitive effort can be used to add more to the knowledge base, develop further routines, and connect ideas. A competent learner will begin to be able to think critically about ideas, see the relations among them, and apply and evaluate knowledge. He or she may be motivated by more intrinsic interests, yet still look toward extrinsic motivations on some occasions.

Proficient learners not only have high levels of interconnected knowledge, but also are highly efficient strategy users who have abiding interests and personal investments in the domain. Oftentimes, expertise comes after formal schooling as one becomes immersed in a profession. Learners at this level engage in a great deal of critical thinking; they constantly evaluate and extend their understandings and even add to the knowledge of others.

Alexander (1998) makes the point that students at acclimated levels need scaffolding and support to become independent learners. They also need instruction that will "hook" their interests, and will explain concepts in ways that allow students to make connections to other concepts and to their own interests. With its focus on the interplay between interest, strategy use, and knowledge, the Model of Domain Learning extends our understanding of the interactions affecting motivation. Other theories we review here do not emphasize domain knowledge except as a characteristic of the learner.

How RWCT and the ERR Framework Support Key Dimensions of the MDL

Although Alexander does not deal specifically with critical thinking or active learning, it is easy to imagine that students engaged in active learning strategies would be more interested in learning and also would develop a critical sense of the discipline in which they are engaged. The growth of critical thinking, the use of active methods of thinking, and increases in motivation would be reciprocal.

Alexander's theory is useful in explaining both teacher and student motivations. When we discuss teachers, we will discuss their knowledge, strategy use, and interest in being teachers of critical thinking, rather than confounding it with their subject matter knowledge or teaching expertise in general.

The MDL as Applied to Teachers' Learning

The teachers in the RWCT program in both Estonia and the Republic of Georgia have seemed interested in being good teachers and in teaching critical thinking. One comment that has recurred in the Republic of Georgia is that teachers teach as an act of patriotism. They believe in what they are doing, feel that it is vital for their country's future, and truly desire for their students to grow up to be problem solvers. For example, Irena, a Georgian participant, said, "In chemistry, my students are becoming good chemists. That is good for the economy and for the country." Nino R. joined in, " The same about history." And Tsitsino added, "We feel that we can build the knowledge base that can help the country." Nino J., another Georgian participant in the project, commented about herself and her fellow teachers that, "Our goal is the same. We have [a common interest]. If any of us doesn't do well, it's a problem for everyone."

So, the teachers were interested. Also, they had some theoretical knowledge about the values of critical thinking and active learning. What were they missing that RWCT provided? Our work in RWCT provided a set of strategies for accomplishing active learning and critical thinking and a framework to use as a guide for applying those strategies. Mzia's story that begins this chapter illustrates how the workshops helped teachers put into operation ways of teaching that they had heard about but had not experienced, and she used Evocation, the first part of the ERR framework, as a starting point in her lesson. Others have expressed the idea that the systematic framework is what helped them use what they already knew but had used only haphazardly. Tea, from the Republic of Georgia, said, "So what was unconscious for me became conscious. Take Bloom's taxonomy. I used to challenge higher order thinking, but it was very unconscious. I tried questioning before, but now I can use it in an organized way." Nino J. said, "We were already practicing [what you have taught us], but not systematically. You have named it. You see, the most surprising new thing for us was that you separated things in detail in the thinking process. That is quite difficult for us.... Our emphasis was on the whole, not so much on the parts." Pati, a teacher in the Republic of Georgia, commented, "I graduated from college, and I learned *what* to teach but I didn't know *how*. I had lots of thoughts in that direction [of the RWCT pedagogy], and some things were not quite new, but you gave me a structured and systematized whole that helped me, which should be very important and acceptable to all of the creative teachers who are novices." Finally, Nadia, an Estonian teacher, commented, "Teaching in the RWCT framework motivated me to use strategies more often. My lessons go beyond the framework of a traditional lesson and I am more comfortable using strategies."

Previously, what they knew about the strategies for teaching critical thinking, by their own admission, was somewhat fragmented or unstructured; that is, their existing concepts were somewhat disorganized and poorly related to central principles. Thus, we believe that the teachers we worked with were ready to move from acclimation to competence as critical thinking teachers, but lacked a systematic approach or schema that tied ideas together, and lacked a set of strategies to accomplish these goals. The strategies and the ERR framework we taught seemed to help things fall into place. The outcome of this learning was that the teachers themselves increased their levels of interest in their own teaching of critical thinking and began to see themselves as more knowledgeable, as the theory would predict. Mzia's story illustrates this point dramatically, as do these other comments. For example, Nino J. said, "I feel myself to be more energetic.... If I studied everything from the books, many things would be vague. But now, with [this experiential] practical work, it's more productive." Svetlana, from Estonia said, "All of a sudden I realize I can present my lessons in a way that I can be sure will be a success. It is a real breath of fresh air. This is what is motivating for me." Larissa, another Estonian teacher, commented, "I feel that there is an experiment going on inside me as a result of learning new strategies for teaching."

Program participants began to develop their own strategies to fit into the framework. It has been exciting for them and for us to see how they could apply the framework in ways that support their existing curriculum. Participants have been eager to teach their colleagues about the principles and applications to Georgian and Estonian schooling.

The MDL as Applied to Students' Learning

The students in RWCT represent varying age and ability levels and are studying a number of different subject areas. Through the teachers' reports and our own classroom observations, we have come to understand that most students are quite competent at answering lower level questions and seem motivated to learn. A typical experience visiting a traditional class is that the students eagerly raise their hands to answer questions the teacher poses, recite answers when called on, and seem quite pleased when they do well; they seem quite chagrined when they do not. We rarely noticed off-task behavior in any of our classroom visitations.

Just as teachers' knowledge prior to RWCT training was unstructured, students' knowledge seemed fragmented and poorly related to central concepts. Thus, students did not have a systematic way to approach higher order questions. Because of their RWCT training, the teachers provided students with instruction in applying critical thinking to their lessons and in becoming reflective learners who think about knowledge and the strategies they use to develop deeper understandings. One Georgian literature teacher, for instance, taught her eleventh-grade students to apply Bloom's taxonomy to the texts they read on their own. The teachers reported that when they began using active learning strategies and teaching critical thinking not only did the students' thinking and knowledge improve, but so did their interest, which already seemed quite high.

Alexander's Model of Domain Learning predicts that an increase in one area—knowledge, strategy use, or motivation—will support increases in the others as a result. This is what we have observed happening with both the teachers in RWCT and their students. We offered teachers knowledge about critical thinking and provided them with strategies to use. They reported increased interest and competence in teaching critical thinking. They helped their students see the interrelations among ideas by focusing on higher level thinking, and they provided students with active learning strategies to help them engage in that thinking. The teachers reported that the result was increased interest and competence in their students. Mzia noted how feverishly her students worked and how competent they felt when they focused on critical thinking strategies. Other teachers reported similar information about their students.

The following teachers' comments illustrate how students' enjoyment, active participation, and knowledge intertwined. These comments exemplify Alexander's point that knowledge, strategy use, and motivation are developed mutually. Irena reported that her students' thinking "has become definitely freer…and they are asking questions to themselves like 'why, what for?' For my subject, chemistry, these questions are really quite essential." Sasha, an Estonian participant, said, "RWCT motivates students to participate in the lesson. It involves the student in the work in the course of the lesson. So the object of learning becomes the subject of learning." Katya, another Estonian participant, added, "Students enjoy and want to have these lessons. They are more relaxed and they enjoy learning. They read more and want to learn more to demonstrate their knowledge during the lesson.

Finally, the lessons, as reported by the RWCT teachers, have had a positive impact on students' levels of knowledge or achievement. For example, Nino B. explained, "The children get a very deep and thorough knowledge about the content." Marina, a Georgian participant, discussed her students' performance at a school competition: "Forty different works were sent to a competition from our school, and all 40 of them were rewarded. And it was a big thing." Patti reported a higher rate of success in her students than normal: "In my classroom, I had 15 highly successful students. They had all excellent marks in one class, which is quite a high number.... And this happened in a class where my lessons were critical thinking lessons." In fact, the teachers were so pleased with their students' achievement that they expressed sincere dissatisfaction in the schooling their own children were receiving. Manana, a Georgian participant, complained, "We are teaching other children, and our own children are lagging very far behind. I want other teachers to think about our children in this way. I'm very nervous and angry about this." At that point, others joined in expressing their own dissatisfaction.

Thus, many of the participants' comments illustrate the recursive nature of growth in knowledge, motivation, and strategy use. The teachers discuss students' interest, attention to critical thinking, and competence together. Therefore, we believe that Alexander's theory is supported by the findings of the RWCT project in both Estonia and the Republic of Georgia.

Situated Motivation Viewpoint

Paris and Turner's (1994) theory states that motivation is "situated," or dependent on specific situations. In this theory, there are four characteristics of personal motivation. First, motivation is a result of the cognitive assessments of individuals in situations. For example, learners think about and evaluate the way they perform while engaging in specific tasks in classrooms ("I'm good in history, but not so good at math"; "I like to do experiments, but I can never understand the formulas"). Second, motivation depends on context because the learner creates unique interpretations of events, goals, and outcomes in different situations. Third, motivation is an unstable state because a learner's goals are not the same in all settings and may vary as a consequence of his or her assessment of affective dimensions such as expectations, values, goals, rewards, and efficacy in a particular setting. Fourth, these cognitive interpretations are constructed by the learner and represent his or her perceptions rather than an objective assessment.

Situated motivation emphasizes that motivation is highly personalized. Paris and Turner's (1994) work draws from previous research on motivation to describe four characteristics that influence situated motivation—choice, challenge, control, and collaboration. First, *choice*, based on intrinsic value or interest, plays a role in student motivation. Students who have a personal interest in text information use appropriate learning strategies to process text more deeply and report a higher quality of experience (Schiefele, 1991). Second, *challenge* is an important characteristic because students are not motivated when they experience success at tasks that do not require effort (Clifford, 1990). Csikzentmihalyi (1990) emphasized the importance of optimal challenge in which one is involved in an activity that is neither too easy (provoking boredom) nor too difficult (provoking anxiety). A third important characteristic is *control*. Tasks that allow students to feel control over their learning are more motivating than those that are under the control of the teacher. The factors of choice and control can affect an individual's ability to experience optimal challenge. (These factors are also central to Deci and Ryan's (1987) self-determination theory.) Fourth, *collaboration*, or social interaction with peers, affects motivation for many reasons. For example, talking to peers can enhance learners' interests, stimulate and challenge their thinking, and support their sense of belonging (West & Oldfather, 1993). In addition, collaboration goes beyond interaction with peers; collaboration may lead to feeling connected to something beyond oneself (Deci & Ryan, 1990).

These attributes of motivation—choice, challenge, control, and collaboration—interact in any given situation to produce unique motivations for learning. The same activities do not always elicit the same motivation, nor are individuals consistently motivated across situations. Thus, situated motivation adds to our understanding that motivation is unstable within a context. The theory helps explain why students in our classrooms may be motivated to learn some topics and not others, or why students are motivated by some activities and not others. It also helps explain why some students maintain motivation when the content becomes difficult and others do not. For example, a student who is interested in a topic because he or she chooses to study it and who feels successful at learning similar topics will be more likely to learn information about the topic.

How RWCT and the ERR Framework Support Key Dimensions of Situated Motivation Theory

The elements of the RWCT project and ERR framework promote motivation according to the four characteristics offered by Paris and Turner. For example, because teachers feel equipped with a repertoire of strategies for teaching and learning, their own sense of control is supported in concrete ways. Also, as depicted in Mzia's story, thinking critically is challenging for teachers. Nino J. also spoke of the challenge of thinking analytically about her teaching when she said "you separated things in detail in the thinking process. That is quite difficult for us." Moreover, collaboration is an integral component of many of the strategies presented in the RWCT workshops. This emphasis on collaboration allows teachers to examine multiple viewpoints and to receive feedback from peers. As Nino B. said, "While working in groups, I felt that my fellows were sharing my ideas." Additionally, when teachers select strategies for learning, they are exerting their choice. Thus, the RWCT methods are useful in explaining the situational nature of teachers' motivations.

Situated Motivation Theory as Applied to Teachers' Learning

Paris and Turner (1994) suggest that motivation increases when learners assess their expectations, values, goals, and self-efficacy positively. The RWCT teachers made clear their rising expectations and sense of self-confidence and expressed these feelings in several ways. Some found the strategies increased their confidence. Tatiana said that she now knows many methods for teaching. Nino B. said, "[Even] if someone gives me an unfamiliar text, I feel that I am able to plan a lesson. I feel like a bird." Participants liked knowing these strategies because it made them feel special. Ludmilla, a teacher in Estonia, remarked, "I enjoy thinking about the fact that only I know these strategies in my school." In addition, several teachers expressed their motivation to teach colleagues the strategies.

Motivation results when there is an optimal balance of choice, control, challenge, and collaboration for the learner. RWCT provides a structure in which teachers can be flexible in their lessons to maximize this balance for their students. Just as Mzia found that the distinction between poor and excellent students disappeared during her lesson, Tatiana commented that now she realizes that she can present her lessons in ways that she is sure will be a success for all students.

Situated Motivation Theory as Applied to Students' Learning

Not only does the theory of situated motivation explain teachers' motivations, it explains students' motivations as well. Teachers expressed the belief that working with the ERR framework enhanced student motivation for learning in several ways. First, students were motivated to work in groups. As Irena said, "They are more used to listening to each other, to taking each other's ideas into consideration." Aleksander, a teacher in Estonia, said, "RWCT has had a positive impact on participation in my lessons. Why? Because students are not afraid to become a laughing stock; it is not one student against the rest of the class." The students found the material more interesting and liked the fact that they all participated in the learning.

Second, teachers found that the strategies increased a sense of collaboration between themselves and their students in the classroom. Like Mzia, teachers in Estonia found that students increasingly trusted their teacher as they shared in the learning. As one teacher explained, "I'm not the 'truth' anymore. Students like having their ideas be equal to the teacher and being equal they feel more responsibility for being well prepared for the lesson."

Third, the teachers felt that, perhaps because of the sense of collaboration, students became more responsible, thus feeling in control. As Nino B. said, "I am now in the role of supervisor, and the students guide the lessons." And Nino R. commented, "Responsibility is shared. My students are partners. You can feel this partnership in their attitudes, their gestures." One Georgian teacher told us how, when she was feeling ill, her students told her that she should rest because they could do the lesson by themselves.

Fourth, teachers found that the students felt that the work was more challenging. Nino R. commented, "Our students are becoming much more hard-working, because they are competing on a plane with their teachers. In the past, we were delivering ready information. I was thinking on their behalf. It wasn't challenging for them."

Finally, the teachers found that students were more eager to learn for their own sakes. Nina, an Estonian teacher said, "My students are more eager to learn for themselves and not for the teacher or for a grade." Thus, the elements of challenge, control, and collaboration led to intrinsic motivations for learning. Teachers' thinking about their own teaching and their students' engagement in learning reflect ways in which the RWCT framework and strategies support the dimensions of situated motivation to enhance student learning.

A Sociocultural Viewpoint

The motivation theories previously discussed are based on predominantly cognitive/affective processes of individuals. As illustrated earlier, we find them very helpful in understanding aspects of how the RWCT program and the ERR framework support critical thinking and motivated, active learning. However, we argue that for the fullest understandings, sociocultural and sociopolitical lenses are required. Such lenses contribute an important complement to the large body of motivation research in general and literacy motivations in particular (Oldfather & Dahl, 1994). For example, in seeking to understand how learners might become engaged readers and writers, these approaches look beyond the individual learner or specific teaching strategies and take into account the ways in which the culture of a particular school, classroom, neighborhood, family, and society may contribute toward such outcomes. A person taking a sociocultural approach to learning might ask,

- Is it "cool" to be an active learner in this classroom?
- What are the expectations about what it means to be a "good" student? Is being a good student a matter of listening quietly, or is it about sharing ideas with others? Is it about knowing the "right answers"? Is it about being able to generate interesting questions and creative answers about the real world?
- What counts as knowledge and whose knowledge counts in this learning environment and in the larger culture?
- How is the teaching and learning environment influenced by the religious, racial, and political histories of this school, community, and nation? How are gender roles constructed? To what degree do people within this culture feel free to examine and express their own ideas? Do they feel optimistic or despairing about their abilities and responsibilities to effect change?

These questions only scratch the surface of those that can be explored. They get at fundamental aspects of beliefs, values, and taken-as-shared understandings within cultures that can have an impact on motivations (Oldfather, West, White, & Wilmarth, 1999). Of course there are varying responses by individuals within particular cultures, but it is clear that it is helpful to look beyond individuals' cognitive and affective experiences to sociocultural factors in considering motivations.

Sociocultural Dimensions of Motivation and Empowerment

The questions framed earlier relate to some other important motivational theories, particularly key aspects of the self-determination theory of Deci and Ryan (1990). In their synthesis of research, Deci and Ryan posit that the most fundamental aspects of intrinsic motivation are a person's perception of self-determination or autonomy, one's perception of self-competence, and one's social relationships to others or to a cause beyond oneself. Their theory is relevant to (although not originating from) cultural considerations. Consider, for example, the impact on students' motivation when they experience the emancipatory aspects of knowledge construction. Their very relationship to learning is affected. Consider the potential for deep motivation when a cultural environment supports a sense that one can make a difference in the world and that one has responsibility to try. Consider the potential effects on people's sense of self-competence and self-determination when they are challenged to think critically and creatively and are supported in those efforts. There are indications that a number of participants have experienced these emancipatory motivational dimensions through the RWCT project. Note Nina B.'s statement that she felt like a bird. Nino J. felt so empowered that she decided to give up her work in other fields (law and journalism) and concentrate on teaching. Such experiences have potential to affect the culture of schooling, as well as the cultural, social, economic, and political dimensions of these new democracies. These outcomes are at the core of the purposes that we and the participants are pursuing both for educators and for their students.

Oldfather (1992) has conceptualized these experiences as *epistemological empowerment*. Epistemological empowerment is a sense of intellectual agency in which learners understand that they can make sense of the world and make judgments based on their own constructed knowledge. They also understand that knowledge is not "out there" to be transmitted from teacher (or other authority) to learners. One who is epistemologically empowered assumes responsibility for developing criteria for making choices and understands that there can be more than one legitimate viewpoint. These qualities of epistemological empowerment are also qualities found among critical thinkers and are among the goals of the RWCT project. The implications are clearly emancipatory and have important relevance for the countries that are striving toward democratic ideals.

We believe that the sociocultural context has a great deal to do with how epistemological empowerment develops. In a learning culture in which teachers and classmates are able to "share ownership of knowing" (Oldfather & Dahl, 1994, pp. 144–145), learners can experience their own sense-making in emancipatory ways. A teacher who shares ownership of knowing facilitates understandings through classroom interactions. Such a teacher needs to seek and understand learners' logic, rather than to focus on whether learners provide the so-called "right answers" (Duckworth, 1987). Such a teacher helps students to engage in metacognitive activities through which learners reflect on what they are learning, how that learning relates (or does not relate) to their previous understandings, what their own reasoning is, and whether or not they are engaged in meaningful learning. Within this framework, the teacher's role includes a great deal of listening; skilled question-posing; structuring interactions among the learners that enable them to learn from each other; and challenging them to pose their own questions, to find connections, to examine evidence, to apply what they learn to the real world, and to generate creative products.

How RWCT and the ERR Framework Supports Key Dimensions of Sociocultural Theories of Motivation

In order for educational environments to support learners' intrinsic motivations through enhancing self-determination and competence, these environments need to be deeply responsive to learners' ideas. The ERR framework implemented by the RWCT project supports teachers in achieving such an environment. We not only taught teachers to use the ERR framework with their students, but we also used the framework to guide our workshops. Thus, teachers as well as students experienced enhanced feelings of self-determination and competence. In Evocation activities, teachers facilitate thought and expression of students' existing ideas, their prior knowledge, and their current viewpoints. During these exchanges, students' ideas are offered and accepted in a respectful environment. The students understand that learning is about sense-making, and that they are respected and active participants. They are able to see that there are multiple perspectives. They activate their own prior knowledge and identify gaps and questions. Curiosity is aroused. They become primed for meaningful learning. Our use of Evocation with the workshop participants had these aims of supporting learners' sense of empowerment and intrinsic motivation, and the participants carried the same aims into their own classrooms. Mzia's story is a powerful illustration of the results of such priming.

The Realization of Meaning phases of the framework build on what has been established in the Evocation phases. Realization of Meaning activities are structured in ways that place students in positions of responsibility for their own learning, in which they will create products through a variety of formats that are shared with others and that represent their own new understandings and plans of action. The teacher does present information at times—but this is done within the ERR framework so that it is not "delivered" in a way that places the students in the role of passive recipients of knowledge. The Reflection phase of the framework similarly places the students in empowered metacognitive roles in which they apply critical thinking abilities to integrate, assess, internalize, make connections, and create plans for action. As you have read, many teachers noted the shift in responsibility from teacher to student as they used RWCT strategies in the classroom. They also expressed a growing sense of responsibility in their own lives as they began to reconceptualize their roles as teachers. They have taken on the responsibility to let others experience what they know as teachers, and they are engaged in plans of action to carry out that goal. Nino J. explained that "the system of education [in the Republic of Georgia] seems frozen. The teachers need something to do to get out of that frozen area. Some think there is no way out. Some of them think that there might be a way, but don't know the way. And some don't want to go out because they don't see the possibility. If I can help them, that's good." Participants' epistemological empowerment is supported by all phases of the ERR framework. Many of the RWCT participants report that they and their students gain a new sense of competence and self-worth (Covington & Beery, 1976) through these approaches, as you have already seen from their comments.

Establishing a Culture of Listening

We have learned through our experiences with RWCT that one major hurdle had to do with the typical discourse patterns found within groups in Eastern European countries; that is, there are different "rules" or expectations about the ways in which participants speak and listen to each other. We often saw participants stand and "hold forth" for extended periods of time without thinking particularly about the need for turn-taking. On the other hand, this practice often did not appear to be particularly bothersome to other participants, as they did not feel constrained from talking (often in normal speaking voices) during the turn of the person holding forth. We knew that in order to accomplish many of the goals of the RWCT project, we needed to be very explicit about the rationale and strategies for turn-taking, as this kind of teaching and learning requires a classroom culture that is deeply responsive and respectful, one that honors students' voices (Oldfather, 1993). This sense of respect is an essential element in feelings of epistemological empowerment, and is thus central to motivation as conceptualized in sociocultural theories.

Very gradually we were able to help participants change their discourse patterns. They began to speak for shorter periods of time and started really listening to each other. We became particularly aware of the progress we had made in this regard when some newcomers joined the group. They had not internalized the new ways of listening and turn-taking within the workshop culture. Other group members became very distressed, voiced their concern about the lack of listening, and tried to influence the newcomers to participate differently. For many teachers, one of the most important achievements that has come out of participating in the RWCT project is that they have become part of a "culture of listening."

Other Problems and Challenges

We need to emphasize that our efforts are not entirely successful. We are asking that our international colleagues in the RWCT program make major epistemological shifts, and this is a large undertaking. Additionally, the ERR framework requires significant reconceptualization of teachers' roles. Some are not easily able to share ownership of knowing—to listen and be responsive to their students' ideas—yet this reconceptualization is at the heart of the kinds of the motivational changes we have noted in other participants. We particularly noted this difficulty in reconceptualizing roles within the RWCT workshops recently begun with university professors—and we suspect that this problem also exists in the universities in the United States and elsewhere (Maher & Tetreault, 1996).

Furthermore, even though teachers in Estonia and the Republic of Georgia have been extremely positive about the effect of critical thinking and active learning strategies on their students and on themselves, some will detect danger in the feelings of empowerment that have surfaced, a danger that may dampen their motivation in the future. The danger is that because teachers are looked on by their peers as having specialized knowledge, they can be objects of jealousy. This jealousy may be fueled by students who, at times, openly criticize the traditional lessons they are receiving from their non-RWCT teachers and ask for better teaching. In addition, critical thinkers think critically about all kinds of things, and in essence can bring up for discussion topics that are not pleasant or easily handled. It may be that other teachers are not yet ready to deal with these issues, and that the RWCT participants, in their enthusiasm, may appear pushy. If other teachers evaluate them negatively, motivation theories suggest that these evaluations can dampen motivation among all involved.

Conclusion

The RWCT project in Estonia and the Republic of Georgia has fostered an increased motivation for both teaching and learning. This motivation, in turn, has fostered important changes in the quality of teaching and learning. Furthermore, the relationship between motivation and the quality of teaching and of learning seems to be reciprocal: The changes in the quality of teaching and learning are helping to sustain motivation, and motivation, in turn, is improving the quality of teaching and learning.

What are the changes that we have seen taking place? First, the relationship between teachers and students has improved. Teachers overwhelmingly report a closer, more equal relationship with their students. As Mzia's story illustrates, teachers have a new respect for their students, and their students appear to have a keener respect for them and what it means to take on the role of teacher. Teachers expressed amazement that their students knew as much as they did, and the students felt as though they could help the teacher in planning and implementing lessons.

Second, the relationship between the teachers and their colleagues changed. Teachers expressed feelings of increased collegiality with their RWCT peers and a sense of competence in relation to their fellow non-RWCT teacher-colleagues. Teachers saw that they were sought out by others for their teaching advice and were asked to share their new knowledge. Their problem-solving discussions with their RWCT peers brought them closer together with a sense of shared responsibility.

Third, the teachers' relationships to self changed. McCombs (1996) discusses how feelings of self-competence arise from one's perceptions of the negative and positive evaluations of others over time. These teachers were rewarded for their hard work with the positive evaluations of their RWCT colleagues, their fellow non-RWCT teachers, and their students. Thus, they increased their self-confidence and felt a sense of control over their own lives.

What in the RWCT project has supported the important changes that have taken place? Perhaps one of the most powerful supports teachers received was strategic support. Teachers were able, through the workshops, to see how critical thinking theory is instantiated in practice. Being able to experience how it works, they felt more confident in trying it with others. Two of the key features of this strategic support were modeling and practice. For example, when Penny and Cyndie worked on strategies for sharing information in order to instantiate a culture of listening, they modeled a situation in which sharing had a time limit. The teachers then practiced timing their sharing within groups and with the whole class.

Another powerful support was the ERR framework itself and the focus on active learning that is a part of the framework. The ERR framework allowed the teachers to connect the hodgepodge of theories and practices they had previously only implicitly held into an articulated, principled network that could be used for lesson planning. It was no accident that we used the same principles when we ran the workshop—Evocation, Realization of Meaning, and Reflection—that we wanted the teachers to use when they were teaching. We believe that the framework allowed us to carry out our lessons in ways that deepened the teachers' understanding of ERR by increasing their interest, which led to deeper understandings of the concepts and strategies. Alexander (1998) describes the reciprocal nature of these three elements of competence leading to expertise. Also, Paris and Turner (1994) describe how the elements of challenge, choice, control, and collaboration are part of the most motivating situations. Evocation, Realization of Meaning, and Reflection realized through active learning strategies inherently build on these elements. Critical thinking and the development of deep understandings that are the outcomes of the ERR framework require that one is *challenged* to be in *control* of one's own learning, and to exercise informed *choices* based on *collaborative* understandings. In addition, the sociocultural impact of the framework is notable. The emphasis of such a framework is on self-determination, self-competence, and epistemological empowerment, brought about through sharing the ownership of knowing through classroom interactions (active Evocation and Realization of Meaning) and one's metacognitive reflections about knowledge (Reflection).

Thus, although the RWCT Project is aimed at developing critical thinking in students, it has had a motivational outcome as well. The outcome is explained by several integrated motivational theories. But the motivating nature of the project is most obviously exemplified by the words of the teachers themselves, which we have shared with you. To "feel like a bird" is what we all wish for as we think about our teaching and learning.

REFERENCES

Alexander, P.A. (1998). Stages and phases of domain learning: The dynamics of subject-matter knowledge, strategy knowledge, and motivation. In C.E. Weinstein & B.L. McCombs (Eds.), *Skill, will, and self-regulation.* Mahwah, NJ: Erlbaum

Alexander, P.A., Jetton, T.L., & Kulikowich, J.M. (1995). Interrelationship of knowledge, interest, and recall: Assessing a model of domain learning. *Journal of Educational Psychology, 87,* 559–575.

Alexander, P.A., Kulikowich, J.M., & Schulze, S.K. (1994). How subject-matter knowledge affects recall and interest. *American Educational Research Journal, 31,* 313–337.

Clifford, M.M. (1990). Students need challenge, not easy success. *Educational Leadership, 48,* 22–26.

Covington, M.V., & Beery, R.J. (1976). *Self-worth and school learning.* New York: Holt, Rinehart & Winston.

Csikszentmihalyi, M. (1990). *Flow: The psychology of optimal experience.* New York: HarperCollins.

Deci, E.L., & Ryan, R.M. (1987). *Intrinsic motivation and self-determination in human behavior.* New York: Plenum.

Deci, E., & Ryan, R. (1990). A motivational approach to self: Integration in personality. In R. Dienstbier (Ed.), *Perspectives on motivation* (pp. 237–288). Lincoln, NE: University of Nebraska Press.

Duckworth, E. (1987). *The having of wonderful ideas and other essays on teaching and learning.* New York: Teachers College Press.

Maher, F.A., & Tetreault, M.K. (1996). Women's ways of knowing in women's studies, feminist pedagogies, and feminist theory. In N. Goldberger, J. Tarule, B. Clinchy, & M. Belenky (Eds.), *Knowledge, difference and power.* New York: Basic Books.

McCombs, B.L. (1996). Alternative perspectives for motivation. In L. Baker, P. Afflerbach, & D. Reinking (Eds.), *Developing engaged readers in school and home communities* (pp. 67–87). Hillsdale, NJ: Erlbaum.

Oldfather, P. (1992, December). *Sharing the ownership of knowing: A constructivist concept of motivation for literacy learning.* Paper presented at the annual meeting of the National Reading Conference, San Antonio, TX.

Oldfather, P. (1993). What students say about motivating experiences in a whole language classroom. *The Reading Teacher, 46*(8), 672–681.

Oldfather, P., & Dahl, K. (1994). Toward a social constructivist reconceptualization of intrinsic motivation for literacy learning. *JRB: A Journal of Literacy, 28*(2), 139–158.

Oldfather, P., West, J., White, J., & Wilmarth, J. (1999). *Learning through children's eyes: Social constructivism and the desire to learn* (Psychology in the Classroom Series). Washington, DC: American Psychological Association.

Paris, S.G., & Turner, J.C. (1994). Situated motivation. In P.R. Pintrich, D.R. Brown, & C.E. Weinstein (Eds.), *Student motivation, cognition, and learning: Essays in honor of Wilbert J. McKeachie* (pp. 213–238). Hillsdale, NJ: Erlbaum.

Schiefele, U. (1991). Interest, learning, and motivation. *Educational Psychologist, 26,* 299–323.

Steele, J.L., & Meredith, K.S. (1995). *Democratic pedagogy national staff development manual.* Bratislava, Slovakia: Orava Foundation for Democratic Education.

West, J., & Oldfather, P. (1993). On group work: An imaginary dialogue among real children. *Language Arts, 70*(5), 33–44.

SECTION III

How Practices and Paradigms Change

CHAPTER NINE

The Teaching of Writing in the Czech Republic

Zuzana Šaffková

I recently opened my daughter's exercise book to look at her writing. As a teacher of writing myself, I was interested to see what my elementary school-aged daughter was working on. I found a vivid description of her grandmother's loft, which led into an interesting essay reflecting on the beauty of old things. Although my daughter's style lacked perfection and although the structure of the piece was not faultless, the whole essay suggested a writer deeply involved in her task and eager to convey a discovery.

However, two red lines in the margins of the essay warned the reader that the teacher had found something wrong. Several underlined pronouns showed unforgivable repetition, and the only comment was "Inappropriate stylistics." The overall grade was unsatisfactory. When I later discussed this essay and her teacher's response to it with my daughter, I found out that the children in her class generally accept the teacher's "evaluation" without question. They understood the role of the teacher was to judge their effort, and the role of the student writer was only to please the teacher. Because these student writers have not experienced a different approach, they think that in order to succeed they have to meet exactly the teacher's preferences—to the detriment of their own expression. They are also used to the unchangeable system of grading based on this scheme: one grammar error, Excellent; two errors, Good; more errors, Unsatisfactory. Both as a mother and as a teacher experimenting with new ways of teaching writing, I felt sad for my daughter. Her effort to communicate something meaningful was met with a reductive, narrow emphasis on grammar, and her ideas were never acknowledged by her teacher. This realization made me scrutinize the situation in detail in order to know more about my own students' writing background, to reexamine the ways in which writing is taught and learned, and to understand the preconceived ideas that students have to overcome.

For a number of years in my work in the English department of a teacher training college in the Czech Republic, I have been tailoring the reading/writing course to offer students as much encouragement as I can to improve their writing skills. I offer my students a variety of invention strategies such as brainstorming, clustering, and freewriting. I ask students to write multiple drafts of their essays. I encourage students to read and respond to one another's writing. Yet despite these innovations in my teaching of writing, I still find most of my students unable to form their own original ideas. Recently when I evaluated a set of essays from my university students, I realized that although they had obviously improved the structure of their essays, the coherence of their thoughts, and the precision of their grammar, the content of their papers was still inadequate. Their ideas lacked originality and attractiveness, and the students seemed not to be very involved in their own writing. They often resorted to parroting overused issues and trite topics. Sometimes I even read similar sentences conveying similar ideas expressed in almost the same words by different students. The clash between the thorough preparation of the final products and the seeming emptiness of the prose aroused an array of questions for me. The most crucial question had to do with the connection between my daughter's school experience and the university-level performance of the future teachers in my class. How will large numbers of Czechs become competent, independent writers if there is little or no tradition of teaching writing in such a way as to value ideas and to encourage creative and critical thought? How did our system of language instruction come to emphasize only grammatical correctness? How can we move forward into more successful ways of teaching writing?

These questions take on a special urgency as I see the approach to writing advocated by the Reading and Writing for Critical Thinking (RWCT) program. In many ways, this approach matches what I have adopted and modified from U.S. models of teaching reading and writing from previous teacher workshops. The multiple drafts, the invention exercises such as clustering and freewriting, the emphasis on communicating something meaningful to real audiences, the recognition that good writing is much more than simple grammatical correctness—all these RWCT ideas coincide with the approach I have been trying to implement in my teaching for a number of years. The RWCT program places this approach to writing in a larger framework of critical thinking skills, of course. Yet my previous experience suggests that the prevailing educational context in my country prevents individual initiatives by a single teacher from being wholly successful. As students come to my writing classes from many years' experience in traditional Czech classrooms, they seem unable to accept fully the freedom and the responsibility of these new opportunities. Why is this so?

The Tradition of Rhetoric Instruction in the Czech Republic

The area now called "The Czech Republic" has been governed in a variety of ways and called by many different names over the last 1,000 years. Between the years 993 and 1212, the Czech lands (Bohemia and Moravia) were gradually united into a kingdom under the rule of the Přemysl dynasty. In 1346, Charles IV became king, and under his enlightened rule, the country reached its first golden age. This area was controlled on and off by the Hapsburg Austro-Hungarian Empire from the 16th century until the end of World War I when a democratic Czechoslovakia was formed. Czechoslovakia remained a democratic nation until the turmoil of the Nazi era. At the end of World War II, it fell under the control of the Soviet Bloc and acquired a socialist government. In 1989, the "Velvet Revolution" restored democracy to Czechoslovakia, and on January 1, 1993, the Czech and Slovak Republics peacefully separated into independent countries. I use the term "the Czech countries" or "the Czech lands" to refer to the area that today is called the Czech Republic.

The teaching of rhetoric as a school subject in the Czech countries has a long history that dates back at least to the year 1775 when Theresian school reformation was adopted. Under the reign of Empress Maria Theresa of the Austro-Hungarian Empire, schools throughout the Czech lands adopted uniform curricula and methods for the general education of all (or nearly all) children in state-sponsored schools. Because the teaching of rhetoric focused at that time exclusively on the practical needs of society, such as the ability to write business letters or to produce an account for work or a receipt for payment, writing became a separate, independent subject within the national curriculum. Eventually, this exclusive focus on pragmatic uses of writing was understood as an obstacle in the development of children's general writing skills.

In the 19th century, educators tried to improve the teaching of writing by urging teachers to focus on simple grammatical, semantic, and stylistic exercises, and by introducing other forms of writing such as description and narration. A new national curriculum in 1869 even emphasized developing thinking skills and strengthening memory, which were to be achieved by imitation, reproduction, and modification of a text. Observation and analysis of texts from history, geography, and literature were to serve as instruments to develop children's knowledge about real-life circumstances, and students' use of elaborate outlines was intended to contribute to the improvement of articulate communication. However, the requirements of this new curriculum were too ambitious, and instruction in rhetoric often fell to the side as teachers resorted to mere training of syntax and revision of grammar rules. Practicing writing itself as an act of creation and communication almost disappeared. In addition, the main idea of the innovative curriculum—that rhetoric should teach an understanding of a variety of things—gave way to a one-sided orientation of analyzing and writing in a rigid structure about issues from geography and history or about themes dealing with nationalistic and regional problems. Finally, the majority of teachers turned to mere copying of sample texts from textbooks as the easiest way to meet the requirements of the curriculum. All these approaches to teaching writing were later criticized both by experts in the theory of writing and by the teachers themselves. Various efforts to improve the teaching of rhetoric at schools culminated at the beginning of the 20th century in the rejection of preparative and sample exercises and the adoption of a more learner-oriented approach.

"Free rhetoric," as the new approach at the beginning of the 20th century was called by its proponents, encouraged students' interest in writing and a creative atmosphere in the writing class. "Free writing" became a synonym for pupils' free choice of themes, yet students were allowed to choose only from a list controlled by the teacher, and there remained a strong emphasis on the product. Thus, "free rhetoric" was not as free as it seemed. Unfortunately, teachers were unable to achieve a truly learner-oriented and creative atmosphere in writing classes. They lacked adequate teaching methodology to support this new approach to writing, and most teachers quickly returned to the use of sample texts in pupils' textbooks as the only source for this new approach. Paradoxically, their use of old methods to achieve new goals contributed to the restitution of the traditional way of teaching. The "free rhetoric" movement, although a promising innovation even by contemporary standards, failed to thrive in the fertile ground of the new Czechoslovak democracy of the early 20th century. The lesson of this failure might apply to current RWCT pedagogical innovations as well. If new approaches to teaching writing are not supported adequately by suitable textbooks, by systemic changes in institutions, by cooperative headmasters and colleagues, and by "deep changes" in a teacher's understanding of his or her work, it is unlikely that even the best intended and most theoretically sophisticated pedagogies can thrive.

In the 1930s, a new initiative aimed to establish a uniform system in teaching writing that stressed more "personally colorful accounts." This approach emphasized creative and personal engagement of the student writer in his or her work. Once again, two extremes resulted. Because of the lack of adequate methodology and teaching materials, some schools and teachers were excessively lenient with this requirement. On the other hand, some teachers once again exaggerated the importance of stylistic devices over the limits of pupils' abilities, and underemphasized the content of students' writing. Eventually this approach was criticized for forcing pupils only to engage in creative writing to the detriment of other forms, and by the 1950s a new curriculum came to the forefront that highlighted a link between reading and writing as a way to improve students' communication. A set of model text types became the basis for the structure of teaching writing within the curriculum. According to the 1954 curriculum, students were to read an article, answer the content questions, analyze the language of the article, and reproduce the plot of the text. However, because the model texts served as mere illustrations of stylistic, syntactic, or lexical patterns, the link between reading and writing became merely a formal matter far removed from the communication demands of real life.

This brief history of the teaching of writing in the Czech lands reveals a combination of traditional approaches to teaching rhetoric, the lack of adequate methodological skills of writing teachers to support progressive movements, and the failure to create a structured conception of writing that could be implemented at every level of the educational system. These conditions have endured until the 1990s.

How the Tradition Influences Current Practice

Looking again at my daughter's essay in light of the brief outline of the history of teaching writing, I can understand the meaningless red lines in the margin of the essay in a new way. These marks clearly signal the clash between the demands for children's writing and their preparation; between the ways children have been taught to write and the ways they are

evaluated; between the current requirements for a critically thinking learner and a traditionally oriented teacher. The Czech teacher is now exposed
to a flood of new approaches to teaching, but too often he or she is still
rooted too firmly in a tradition characterized by three key features.

First, the political orientation of the educational system encouraged
the development of children only within the strict borders of socialist
conformity. In this context, critical thinking, independent ideas, and diversity represented danger. Even though the government has changed in
the Czech Republic, the educational bureaucracy is slow to adapt itself
to the new political and cultural realities, and most of those who teach,
administer, and write curricula in the schools are still heavily influenced
by this tradition. The conception of teaching writing was officially based
on the following 10 key educational principles stated in *Didactic of
Rhetoric* (Hubáček, 1989):

1. the principle of links between school and real life;

2. the principle of respect for learners' age diversities;

3. the principle of versatile education;

4. the principle of an integrative approach to teaching writing;

5. the principle of apprehension;

6. the principle of adequate demand;

7. the principle of the structure of curriculum;

8. the principle of teaching by example;

9. the principle of activity;

10. and the principle of permanence of knowledge. (pp. 21–22)

These 10 principles referred to the whole system of education during the
socialist era. Although the principles generally sound progressive, they
were limited by the ideology of the totalitarian regime. The aim of the
first principle, for example, described as preparing students to be able to
express themselves clearly and freely, collided with the requirement of
gradual incorporation of learners into the socialistic society in which critical discussions were oppressed or at least discouraged. The educational
value of the appropriate choice of sample themes presented in textbooks
as it is stated in the second principle was understood as a way to "achieve
ideologically and politically correct attitudes" (Hubáček, 1989, p. 24)
where *correct* meant strictly determined by the authorities. Furthermore,
the principle of respect for learners' age diversities was and still is under-

stood as a fixed model of competencies for each age group rather than individual diversities determined by learners' different intellectual, mental, and physical development.

The second characteristic of the educational system that prevented student writers from expressing their ideas clearly and logically was the lack of the necessary conditions for effective writing instruction. In particular, I would note the lack of methodological experience of the teachers of writing, the lack of teaching materials, and the constant time pressure caused by strict adherence to an overly ambitious curriculum. The teachers in question were always Czech language teachers rather than writing teachers. Their job was to teach correct grammar; sentence analysis, and literature, while writing compositions was reduced to mere explanation. They took a product orientation, not a process orientation, to writing. Only a few books on composition pedagogy were available, and these provided too narrow a theoretical base and did not offer enough methodological strategies. The time deficit and lack of methodology led to a very elementary routine of teaching *about* writing that was restricted to teacher-centered, frontal explanations of some rules and principles of essay writing. Such a simplified and ineffective approach was even supported by the official educational principles in which the deductive approach to teaching writing was suggested, because the inductive approach—in which students themselves derive conclusions and really contribute to the teaching and learning process—was considered "less effective, time-demanding, and economically too expensive" (Hubáček, 1989, p. 46).

The third characteristic of the Czech education tradition that limits the teaching of writing is the manner in which teachers are prepared for their careers. The preparation of Czech language teachers has long been the responsibility of the Pedagogical and Philosophical faculties. The study of the Czech language at Philosophical faculties (the equivalent of North American colleges of arts and sciences) focuses mainly on the preparation of experts in linguistics or literature, while pedagogical training for these students is only a marginal concern. The situation at Pedagogical faculties (the equivalent of North American colleges of education) is different in the sense that special seminars are devoted to methodological preparation for teaching rhetoric, but the field preparation of future teachers is insufficient and superficial. Yet, even if the range of methodological resources is limited to a few books on didactics and methodology mainly for teaching Czech language or occasionally for teaching rhetoric itself, the future Czech language teachers do have a certain command of techniques and strategies to teach writing. This preparation, however, aims mainly at two tasks: analyzing the Czech language curriculum and examining students' sample compositions. Teacher trainers, for example, are asked to read a narrative text written by a fourth-grade student and to analyze the choice of words, rearrange the essay into paragraphs, examine the variety of parts of speech used in the text, and compare the whole essay with other students' products (Brabcová et al., 1984). The analysis of pupils' products is meant to disclose some "imperfections in the process of compiling the products" (Brabcová et al., 1984, p. 81). A very positive aspect of these seminars is the requirement that teacher trainers experience the writing tasks presented in the textbooks and thus understand the aim of a particular activity, its possible pitfalls, and its pedagogical value. Nonetheless, the focus on requirements, rules, and parameters, and the total lack of professional literature does not provide them with sufficient strategies and techniques to achieve these requisites.

Because the precise criteria for assessing writing are generally absent in the practice of teaching writing at elementary and secondary levels as well as universities, the students neither know what is required from their writing performance nor do they comprehend the judgment of their effort. An appropriate assessment should refer to the procedures that provide information about the "nature and extent of the children's learning, its correspondence with aims and objectives of teaching and its relationship with the environments which are designed to facilitate learning" (Satterly, 1989, p. 3). While the aims and objectives are stated explicitly in the curriculum for both elementary and secondary schools, the process of achieving them is based on the traditional, product-oriented approach underlying the model text-analysis-reproduction methodology in the majority of writing classes. This pattern is out of step with much of the recent developments that encourage students to explore their own knowledge, experiment with ideas, and use writing as a means to extend and deepen their thinking. The structured and successive process of teaching writing that would primarily stem from students' own experiences and thinking is totally missing not only in Czech schools but also in academic thinking about teaching writing.

Reasons for Hope in the Current Situation

The year 1989, when the border of Czechoslovakia reopened not only to democracy but also to new ideas in education, brought the opportunity for changes in our schools that had been awaited for ages. After decades of the uniform totalitarian school system, many new types of schools, both private and public, emerged. They offered a variety of alternative educational programs that give enough space for creative teachers to try new approaches. The current educational policy aims at creating a new national curriculum, promoting a gradual and integrated system that would enable lifelong learning, respecting children's individual interests and abilities, and ensuring better conditions for teachers' professional and career development. However progressive these ideas sound, they remain in the shape of suggestions and issues that are still being discussed. Nevertheless, we can find signs of hope in recent changes at the elementary school level, even if a majority of the secondary and tertiary schools continue for the most part to practice traditional approaches.

Elementary Level

We are beginning to see a change in the Czech language curriculum for basic school (grades 1 through 9) in the shift from submission to the doctrine of socialism to more open objectives that allow an integrated, student-oriented approach to the teaching and learning process. Teaching writing in the first stage of the basic school (grades 1 through 5) now involves the practice of brief narration with an emphasis on chronological order, description of simple objects and actions, and composing an informal letter. As students produce and analyze written texts, they should come to understand the basic structure of a piece of writing and be able to compose a condensed outline. Three 45-minute lessons per week are allocated to the teaching of the Czech language, and it is up to a particular teacher to decide how much of this time he or she dedicates to practicing writing. Besides grammar and spelling, literature and rhetoric, a separate component is devoted to teaching writing skills that includes training in writing individual letters, words, and sentences as well as practicing legibility and refining of handwriting.

In the second stage (grades 6 through 9) practice in more involved narration and description continues in a more detailed and structured way and extends to writing personal portraits, simple expositions, and reflections. Finally, the aims of the curriculum highlight the necessity to provide students with opportunities to perform a discussion during which their own experiences, ideas, and attitudes should be expressed and confronted. The aims and objectives of this new writing curriculum suggest a promising basis for students' growing ability in the field of rhetoric;

however, the gap between the common classroom conventions rooted in the long-established teaching tradition and the goals of the new curriculum has not yet been bridged.

Secondary Level

The Czech language curriculum in secondary schools links the basic rhetorical forms practiced at the elementary level and amplifies them in specific writing tasks referring to the field of study of particular schools. As is true of many of the countries participating in the RWCT project, secondary education in the Czech Republic occurs in a variety of institutions, not in a single comprehensive high school as is common in North America. The *gymnasium* provides a classical pre-university secondary education, while other students may attend vocational schools, art schools, music schools, business schools, or any of a number of other high schools that prepare students for specific careers.

Even if the content of the curriculum varies according to the type of secondary school, the basis for teaching writing is almost the same. In the course of 4 years, the writing of narrative and descriptive essays, reports, reflections, and personal letters is included. Furthermore, students are required to produce oral and written discourse, brief expositions, business letters, curriculum vitae, and another professional writing depending on the type of school. The emphasis is put on stylistics, language devices, and structure, the criteria reflected in the activities and tasks presented in the textbooks. They require students to analyze a text mainly in terms of diction and sentences. Students are also expected to compare and evaluate a variety of sample essays and to infer basic features of a particular form of writing. Thus the whole concept of teaching writing in secondary school aims at "leading pupils to analyzing texts and stylistic expressions" (Hubáček, 1994, p. 7) rather than providing them with the opportunity for structured, systematic practicing of writing resulting in genuine communication of their own ideas and experiences. Paradoxically, writing compositions is a compulsory part of assessment, not only during the school year, but also as part of the formal examinations at the end of a student's secondary studies. Students find themselves in the odd position of being judged on an activity they have never really been taught. The general approach to teaching writing in secondary schools narrows to mere composition assignments several times a year with little or no instruction, followed by correction of an in-class written product. The final composition in the last grade, in addition, serves as a necessary prerequisite for the students to take final examinations and influences their ultimate grade.

University Level

The lack of sufficient training in writing culminates at universities where teaching writing is either neglected completely or aims at specific purposes within particular fields of study. Although students are supposed to submit an array of essays, reports, research projects, and other written assignments in order to pass their exams, they almost never receive explicit training in writing or in critical thinking. The first attempts to incorporate writing into the curriculum have been provoked recently by the low level of students' performance during the compilation of their diploma theses, especially at teacher training colleges. Thus, some departments have provided special courses in academic writing that aim exclusively at preparing students for diploma thesis writing. Surprisingly, this trend occurs mainly in foreign language departments, encouraged by an ample source of materials and recent methodologies, while the Czech language departments lag far behind. Generally, instead of being prepared for effective, logical and structured writing, students simply receive writing assignments they are expected to fulfill with little or no guidance.

The Need for Change

Two crucial changes are needed if teachers in the Czech Republic are to cease merely *teaching about writing* and begin helping students themselves *learn to write*. First, we need immediate help for teachers of writing through a series of courses and seminars that would introduce new approaches to writing classrooms. Second, we need a long-term innovation of the whole writing curriculum in the Czech Republic.

Current and future teachers must be prepared in a fully professional manner for their responsibilities as teachers of writing. Clearly, the teacher preparation programs in universities will need to be changed so that new teachers will teach writing in new ways. Preservice teachers need to experience in their own studies the power of writing as a way of learning. They need to write in all their university courses as part of the regular, ongoing work of learning, and they need assignments that call for original thinking on topics of compelling interest. University professors must demonstrate in their responses to student writing that they care about more than grammar and stylistics, so that when their students themselves become teachers, these new teachers will have healthy ideas about the powerful uses of writing in their own lives. Finally, teacher-training programs need to incorporate specialized courses in the teaching of writing so that beginning teachers will be familiar with the theory and practice of writing process pedagogy.

Teachers in the midst of their careers also need opportunities to acquire new pedagogical skills in the teaching of writing. Inservice workshops, summer conferences, professional journals, and other retraining opportunities for teachers can take many forms. The RWCT program offers a small but useful beginning in this work. The goals of RWCT, of course, are more comprehensive than simply writing, but writing nevertheless is an important part of these goals. By gathering teachers from across grade levels and from all subject areas of the curriculum, RWCT can stimulate our thinking about the power of writing as a way of learning, and it can begin to introduce a process methodology to Czech teachers. But we need a much more comprehensive and thorough set of seminars focused specifically on writing to fully professionalize our writing teachers according to accepted practices in other countries. These retraining opportunities should provide teachers at all levels not only with a variety of classroom strategies that would help learners to compose a variety of types of writing, but also with insights that would encourage the *process* of writing as a fundamental basis for teaching rhetoric.

The second change refers to the whole system of curriculum. Teaching rhetoric should become an integrated part of the national curriculum that would proceed from the elementary to the tertiary levels. Writing within this curriculum must be seen as an instrument to develop learners' critical thinking to encourage them to be self-conscious, curious, and independent.

However, in order to give life to these ideas, many obstacles of the Czech traditional school will have to be overcome. So far the Czech educational system has hindered the development of functional literacy. Thus it has not developed the student's ability to inquire, to express his or her ideas and opinions, and to become an independent learner. Writing teachers have boundless opportunities to stimulate students to debate, to ask questions, to formulate opinions, and to work with information. More and more teachers from the elementary school to the university are gradually coming to understand that writing instruction has the potential to play a significant role in transforming old ideas about the relationship between the student and knowledge into productive ideas and habits for today's society.

REFERENCES

Brabcová, R. et al. (1984). *Forms of work in didactic seminars on Czech language and rhetoric for elementary schools.* Prague: Univerzita Karlova.

Èechová, M. (1982). *Theory and practice of teaching Czech language at grammar schools.* Prague: Univerzita Karlova.

Hubáček, J. (1989). *Didactic of rhetoric.* Prague: Státní Pedagogické Nakladatelství.

Hubáček, J. (1994). *Practical stylistics for secondary schools.* Prague: Fortuna.

Satterly, D. (1989). *Assessment in schools* (2nd ed.). Oxford, UK: Basil Blackwell.

CHAPTER TEN

School Libraries as Laboratories for Critical Thinking

Božena Blazková and Patricia L. Bloem

From the very beginnings of the Reading and Writing for Critical Thinking (RWCT) project in the Czech Republic, participants and leaders have looked for ways to extend the program's influence beyond the individual classroom. RWCT participants have presented workshops at conferences of various nationwide school reform associations and have sought to cooperate with other grass-roots progressive movements. A recent attempt to persuade the general population to rally around school reform has developed through efforts of an RWCT participant who edits and airs bimonthly radio programs on education. A third approach, one with great potential to create change in elementary schools, is to reconceptualize the work of school libraries. This chapter first provides a brief history of the school library in the Czech Republic, then describes how one school library is applying the concepts of the RWCT program to promote pedagogical change throughout an entire school.

Clearly the mission of a school library is different than that of a town or city library, although their goals overlap. Both types of libraries should hold plenty of good books suitable for children's reading, but a school library should be linked not only with the practice of reading but also with the *teaching* of reading. A school library must hold a collection that is adapted to requirements of reading instruction and school reading programs. Because most Czech schools do not have professional librarians and because teachers have many demands placed on them, the school libraries for teachers and the school libraries for students are often dormant collections or collections that are drawn from only occasionally. Town and city libraries often have children's departments with interactive programs, programs that bring in authors or inspire children to read new books or to share their creative writing. School libraries, however, rarely have such programs nor have they been tied to sound pedagogical, critical principles, despite their educational setting.

During the years of socialism, the Czech Republic and the Slovak Republic each had one publisher of children's books, Albatros and Mladé Letá, respectively. Children in that era were comfortable reading in both Czech and Slovak—an ability that is beginning to fade with the separation of the two republics—and both publishers were committed to translating a number of foreign texts, particularly from Russian and German. Children grew up reading folktales and fairy tales from Eastern Europe, and as they grew older they read the classics of world literature. After the political changes, many small publishing houses appeared, and many books of religious stories and religious poetry hit the market for the first time in 40 years (Bloem, 1994). Books that previously may have cost 15 crowns soon cost 75 crowns or more, a price beyond the budget of most buyers. The majority of the small presses closed quickly, but Albatros seems to have weathered the storm and continues to provide most of the texts for Czech children. Currently Albatros runs a book program similar to the Scholastic Book Club in the United States, through which children can buy paperbacks; however, many families still do not have the financial resources to participate. Certainly the economic troubles have had a debilitating effect on children's book publishing; however, new fiction for children continues to be published every year. Czech children have books readily available to them, and they benefit from living in a highly literate population with a long tradition of valuing literature.

The History of School Libraries in the Czech Republic

An analysis of the history of Czech school libraries shows that as the country moved to compulsory school attendance, it also issued calls for the organization of school libraries. Decrees in 1871 and 1875 set out library regulations and rules for the selection of books. As early as 1919 a decree advocated "inexpensive and valuable purchase of books of the same author in multiple copies so as to appropriately use them for recommended reading" (Pech, 1927, p. 33). School libraries were, according to the laws set in 1959, an integral part of the so-called unified system of libraries. These school libraries concentrated especially on processing the library collection, contributing to cultural and educational endeavors, and providing information. In 1979, as new school laws were issued, once again school libraries were envisioned by the Ministry of Education of

Czechoslovak Socialist Republic as integral to literacy education in schools.

Librarians from public libraries arranged to provide methodological and professional help in setting up school libraries. Schools were expected to house two libraries, a teacher library and a student library, as separate collections. An optimal proportion of the collection was prescribed at 50% fiction and 50% educational literature for both types of libraries. "The children must familiarize themselves with books at school, especially with the textbook, in all subjects but especially in reading and literature lessons. The school library must become the center of methodological and systematic work with the book" (Petrtýl & Šlampová, 1986, p. 16).

Library science as a field continued to develop gradually during the 1980s. A range of professional reference books was published, meant not only to assist school teachers but to aid librarians of the public libraries as well. A system of lessons for librarians called "Librarians and Bibliographical Preparation of Youth" was created, with the purpose of teaching librarians how to help children use the library. The perceived role for the librarian at that time was to describe for the children the organization of the library, to orient children to use card catalogues and indexes, and to help them find texts and information within the library.

After 1989, after the political and social changes of Eastern Europe and with the beginnings of the changes to the school system, school administrators and educators became interested in the new possibilities that school libraries might play in education. Part of the momentum to reactivate school libraries grew as Czechs learned about other countries' models of education and about the roles that other countries had developed for their school libraries. Czech specialists became informed about UNESCO recommendations for the planning of school libraries and media centers. Cumplová and Kuhnová (1991) state that throughout Europe, "school libraries are school facilities. The vast majority of them concentrate their activities on supporting education within the framework of school teaching. They act as study, information, and reader centers of the school" (p. 5). Journals and professional periodicals during these years frequently published articles about the building of school libraries. The Pedagogical Research Institute organized a series of seminars concentrated on founding school media centers. Gradually, Czech educators realized the need for professionalization of school libraries.

Building on Critical Principles

The Elementary School Lipky in Hradec Králové and The Elementary School of the Peace Cycle Race in Pardubice both developed school libraries after 1989 in response to these pressures and initiatives. The former concentrated on the field of information. The library is fully automated, which means that users can search for books and texts electronically, and a television set and video equipment is available for teacher and student use. Students and teachers in the town of Hradec Králové have the opportunity to work with modern technology and to use this library not only during class time but also in their leisure time. The Elementary School of the Peace Cycle Race, where Božena has worked as a professional librarian for more than 5 years, took a slightly different path. The aim is the same—making the library accessible to children during the school day and using the library within the framework of various disciplines—but there is much more to tell about the Czech experience with this particular school and library, which is one of only a handful of school libraries in the country working to link libraries with classrooms in sound pedagogical ways.

Currently, the whole-day operation of the school library creates a reader climate and an environment that supports children's interests in reading and motivates them to look for information on their own. The students work on assignments and prepare for their classes in the library. They often connect the books they have discovered in the library with various themes they study in class. Each class within the school chooses its own student librarian, whose job it is to meet once a month with the school librarian and then to inform the class about new books and the library activities. The school librarian teaches classes in information science, not as an after-school offering, but rather within the prescribed curriculum under the course name "Learning to Learn." The library organizes literary programs and discussions with the authors of juvenile literature and interesting personalities of the region, as well as literary walks and trips. Several area groups and clubs use the library during their leisure time. With all these activities, the school library tries to create reasons to read, to create joy in reading, and to promote a love for literature. The library frequently hosts programs such as Reading Together for Parents and Children, Thematic Reading Classes, or Series Reading. For the first-grade students and their parents, the library hosts a ceremony and party when the students finish their first alphabet book or reader. Questionnaires on topics such as What My Parents Read, What

Book I Got as a Christmas Present, and The Most Read Book of the Year are very popular. It is evident with these activities that children's interest in books increases with every visit to the library.

A great shift in the activities of the library and in its involvement in the school curriculum came about in 1997 when Božena was the sole librarian selected to participate in the RWCT project. Cooperating with the classroom teachers, she began systematically to induce children to think on their own, to discuss topics together and with her, and to work on a variety of projects and activities. Gradually she introduced new methods and strategies that she learned in the RWCT workshops, not only into the previously organized classes of information science but also into various disciplines and other projects. Students were invited to participate in 2- to 5-hour miniprojects on a variety of topics, to solve problems that require thinking in a variety of disciplines, and to be paired with students from other classes. Slowly the library and school are moving toward a model of interaction that is a type of "student-to-student teaching." As her role shifted to becoming the organizer and coordinator of these activities, Božena has been pleased to see the library fully used by the children and teachers.

With the help of the RWCT Reading Workshop found in *Creating Thoughtful Readers* (Meredith, Steele, & Temple, 1998), Božena has managed to organize regular reading hours for all the classes of the elementary school. At least once a month, she conducts a reading lesson in the library with every child in the school. One of these recent lessons began with a discussion in a circle about what students had read during the holidays, to whom they would recommend their book choices, and why. Some children had not read a single book and explained that they were not interested in reading. Božena purposefully did not enter into the discussion but instead let the good readers explain why reading is not only amusement but also enlightenment. As she suspected, the children—in this case those who had not read during their vacation—were far more susceptible to the arguments and opinions of their schoolmates than to the admonitions of the adults.

For the next monthly discussion, students explored their family reading backgrounds. The children's task was to find out what books their parents had read when they were children. Although some children were not able to glean much helpful information, in a number of other families the children's questions elicited a productive round of discussion and reading, with the parents sharing book titles and experiences and the children wanting to read the books their parents had liked.

In another lesson, students followed Bozena's model of recording responses to texts in a dual-entry diary format. Traditionally Czech readers might take notes on what a text is about or how a story unfolds, but they would not write personal notes about their own observations and responses to word choice, expressions, or the entire text. During the discussions, the children themselves tried to convince each other of the importance of learning to make notes about the stories and texts they read, not only for better remembering of the text but also for deeper understanding. Emphasis was on the students' own experience of reading. The traditional reader diaries began to change into personal records, resulting in children keeping an eye on their own development as readers. In one class, students even tried to write their reactions to the books in the form of a letter to the librarian. The children liked this format because they had a specific audience, and therefore had a real reason for writing. Replying to the individual letters took time, but Bozena felt it worthwhile.

In another successful application of critical thinking pedagogy, the students compared television viewing with book reading using the RWCT framework of Evocation, Realization of Meaning, and Reflection (ERR). As an evocation, Bozena asked each class of students to share the names of their favorite books and then the names of their favorite television shows. She gave them a modern fairy tale by Molavcová (1993), a story about two brothers, Tomáš and Jiří, one who prefers television and one who prefers reading and an outdoor life. After reading the tale, the children discussed the story and completed a discussion web that compared reading to television watching. As a reflection, Božena asked them to freewrite about what they personally prefer and why. Although a few students were eager to find a response that would please Božena, they soon realized that they could be honest about their opinions, as she was honest about her own with them. Most students decided that both activities can be fun and beneficial and were able to state clear supporting reasons. At the end of the session students were more aware of their reading and television viewing habits, and they gradually became more thoughtful about how they sought entertainment.

Reading workshops, those lesson times that involve free reading in the library rooms, became popular in the Pardubice school. There is such a silence at the library during these lessons that teachers or visitors passing by cannot believe that a complete class is inside working diligently. Of course, there are far more activities inspired by the RWCT project than those mentioned in this article. During this period of applying RWCT to the work in the school library, Božena and her fellow teachers throughout the school have grown in their understanding of why it is important for the children to learn to read well, to think critically, and to think independently. Further, Božena has learned how to make the library a site for critical literacy instruction within a school. Only on this solid pedagogical foundation can a good school library program be built. School libraries must teach children to look for information, then choose, process, and use the needed information sensibly. And for that, children need the skills of reading and critical thinking.

Božena's particular experience shows that in the future, primary school libraries must serve simultaneously as reading, study, and information centers. Gradual professionalization of the school libraries will help to create a reader climate and an environment in which the children will have a chance not only to find new information but also to formulate their own opinions. Thus children will learn not only knowledge, but they also will develop and hone their own attitudes, gain necessary skills for living, and learn mutual cooperation and tolerance. At present, the problems of education and upbringing are at the forefront of interest in the Czech Republic, in view of the need to adapt to the European Union standards. Because of these standards, it will be necessary to implement the latest UNESCO Manifesto on school libraries and information centers as soon as possible. Yes, it is important that Czech school libraries become technologically advanced. But just as important and perhaps easily overlooked is the need for these libraries to follow sound pedagogical principles of critical thinking. What makes Božena's library in Parbudice different, then, is her insistence that students learn to hone their critical thinking skills so they can absorb, evaluate, and apply the barrage of new information available through technology. Education in our age must move beyond simply providing current and accurate information. School libraries can play an exciting role in the transformation of children's education by giving them the tools and the thinking skills to put information to use.

REFERENCES

Bloem, P. (1994). Surviving Stalin to be done in by Disney? Children's literature in Slovakia. *The Reading Teacher, 48*(3), 272–274.

Čumplová, L., & Kuhnová, I. (1991). *Školni knihovny v zahranici: Zprač.* Prague: Ustav pro informace ve vzdelavani.

Meredith, K.S., Steele, J.L., & Temple, C.T. (1998). *Creating thoughtful readers* (English version). Newark, DE: International Reading Association.

Molavcová, J. (1993). *Pohadky a pisnicky pro sikovne deti.* Prague: Albatros.

Pech, O. (1927). *Prirucni slovnik pedagogicky.* Prague: Graficka Unie.

Petrtýl, M., & Slampová, J. (1986). *Prirucka pro skolni knihovny: Zakladni smernice a metodicke pokyny pro budovani, spravu, vedeni a cinnost skolnich knihoven.* Prague: Státní pedagogické nakladatelství.

CHAPTER ELEVEN

The Russian Commitment to Theory and the American Orientation to Practice: A Healthy Tension

Carol Beers, James W. Beers, Tatiana Galaktionova, Donna M. Ogle, and Bud Ogle

The Reading and Writing for Critical Thinking (RWCT) project began in Russia in the fall of 1997, with the first team of North Americans visiting Moscow to begin the training of future trainers. During this first seminar, it became readily apparent that the Russian participants wanted to understand more fully the theoretical background for the project. However, the pratice in RWCT is to demonstrate the framework for critical thinking and the classroom strategies first, then analyze the pedagogical and theoretical background later. This approach created healthy tension, with our Russian colleagues questioning why the volunteers preferred not to lecture to them, and the American workshop leaders wondering why the Russian teachers seemed to prefer theory to practice.

The volunteers were surprised by the passion that greeted the discussion of theory in the first and subsequent seminars. It soon became evident that for many Russian educators, the Russian tradition in education is a proud one. Russian educators are proud of their students' scores on national tests and international comparisons. Why should they change their teaching traditions? What could RWCT possibly offer them? This chapter examines the underlying reasons for the tension between theory and practice experienced in the RWCT project in Russia, and it describes the "practical theory" that is the foundation of the program.

The Russian Tradition in Schools

The goal of education in Russia today is very different from what it was several years ago. Today, the goal is to develop individuals. This goal has required a radical change of the whole system of education in Russia. The system had to move away from totalitarian views and become more democratic. The system also had to adjust in order to meet the needs and interests of real students, rather than continue to design instruction for ideal "typical" ones. The last 30 years have been a transition from the rigid style of Soviet education to the more relaxed style of today. Russian teachers volunteered to participate in the RWCT project because they wished to contribute to this process of reform in their nation's schools.

Until the end of the Soviet era in 1991, all schools in the Soviet Union had the same structure with one state program of teaching that was required for everybody. Eight years of school were compulsory, after which students were given three options: continue secondary education for 2 more years at school in preparation for university studies; enroll in a technical school; or enter a teaching college to learn how to be a teacher of young children. The content of education during this era was very ideological and full of strong communist propaganda, especially in literature and history.

The Communist Party also influenced extracurricular activities. There was a special system of political organizations for children. All children in the first through third grades, were considered to be the *octyabryata*. (This name was coined in honor of the Great October Socialist Revolution and meant "the small Octobers"; they also were called "Lenin's grandchildren.") Octyabryata had to wear a special symbol: a badge containing a little red star with the portrait of Lenin as a child in the center. At the end of third grade (between the ages of 9 and 14), children had to become Pioneers, members of the All Union Pioneer organization named after V.I. Lenin. Pioneers also were called "young Leninists." They had to wear a red tie, the symbol of the pioneer organization, and adhere to specific rules, just as the Octyabryata did. The last step was the Communist Youth Union, in Russian the *Comsomol*. Although this was a volunteer organization, a student was looked down on if he or she did not want to join.

The destruction of this system started in the 1980s and was completed by the 1990s. Today, Russian school children have never been Octyabryata or Pioneers. The majority of today's teachers, however, have come from these organizations. Their childhood and youth were connected closely with the ideas and activities of these extracurricular organizations. Thus, many teachers today face the challenge of reimagining both childhood and school as experiences significantly different from what they themselves knew.

Since the beginning of the 1980s, there has been an effort to reform education, although it has been uneven. The 1980s were the years when new approaches were actively developed and implemented. During this period, known as the period of "teachers-innovators," teachers whose style and methods were quite different from the traditional approaches emerged. These teachers were influenced by writers such as Amonashvilly, Shatalov, Shchetinin, Volkov, and Lysenkova, whose writings emphasized the importance of respect and trust between teachers and students.

The beginning of the 1990s was characterized by several changes. Education became more humanized, the number and variety of educational institutions increased, and the content of teacher education was reformed. In 1992, a federal law that gave a legal basis for these changes was approved. As a result, several nongovernmental educational institutions were opened and a large number of innovative programs and methods were developed and introduced into school practice. For the first time, Russian educators had the freedom to teach creatively. These reforms took place at the time when political and general economic crises in the country were getting deeper and deeper.

By the time RWCT first appeared in Russia, this country had extensive experience in developing education reforms and innovations. However, not all the innovations had been researched thoroughly, and educators became increasingly wary of reform programs that lacked a solid theoretical foundation. More significantly, innovations had been rarely used in everyday school practice. This was one of the appeals for Russian teachers as they began the RWCT project: These methods had been used and tested in U.S. classrooms. More significantly, RWCT had been used to teach individual students how to think. Participants recognized this as an important goal for Russian education today.

Russian Teacher Education Programs

Have Russian teacher education programs changed over the years to help Russian teachers adjust to the new education system? The Russian system of teacher education has provided elaborate and differentiated levels of training that vary significantly in content, length, and quality. In fact, many Russian teachers, particularly teachers of young children, have had little or no college training. The levels of training within the teacher education system create an unusual hierarchy within the teaching profession. What is common to many of the varieties of teacher education programs in Russia, however, is that while preservice teachers receive little practical classroom experience, they receive a thorough grounding in educational theory.

Preprofessional classes (for students 15 to 16 years old) are offered in secondary schools. Because so many teenagers express an interest in teaching, secondary schools provide separate classes in educational psychology and teaching. As a rule, these classes establish close contacts with higher education institutions, and many of the students who leave these classes eventually enter these institutions.

Pedagogical academies provide training to students who are interested in becoming teachers of preschool and primary age children. Students generally enter these academies at two points: after finishing eighth grade or after graduating from secondary school (after Grade 10 or 11). Students who enter the academies after eighth grade generally take a 3- or 4-year course of study; students who enter after Grade 10 or 11 study for 2 or 3 additional years. In addition to courses in language, literature, math, social sciences, and science, students take courses in teaching methods. Upon finishing the program, students are qualified to become teachers of children in preschool through Grade 3 or 4.

Pedagogical school, which is the third level, is similar to the pedagogical academy, but it is designed to train 15- to 19-year-olds for teaching in secondary schools. Students in these schools are trained in their content area. These institutes do not provide a broad-based higher education program, but instead provide specialized training beyond the high school level for future teachers.

The pedagogical college, which is designed for students who have completed their secondary program, is a fairly new kind of institution. These 4-year teacher training programs first started to appear in the early 1990s as the lower level of university training. Pedagogical colleges are generally thought to provide better preparation for teachers than the pedagogical academies and pedagogical schools do, because the courses are longer and have more depth and variety. The courses are modeled after Western systems of higher education, with lectures, seminars, and examinations. The education provided by a pedagogical college differs from university training, however, in the balance of theoretical, professional, and practical parts of the curriculum. Pedagogical colleges are more specialized and are thought to provide professional education of lower quality than that provided by the university.

Pedagogical institutes or pedagogical universities provide another type of teacher training. Classes may be offered at these institutions during the day, during the evening, or through correspondence courses. The program usually lasts between 5 and 6 years. At present, a two-level model that offers bachelor's and master's degrees is becoming more popular. Training in these institutions is generally much more varied and can include specialized training in areas such as foreign language, art education, and physical education. Typically, 70% of the course of study is in the students' academic discipline. The rest of the program includes training in psychology, sociology, history of education, school hygiene, and teaching methods.

Although practical experiences are a part of training in all teacher education programs, most of the practical experiences are outside the classroom and unsupervised by the teacher trainers. Students may work in summer camps, in schools, in clubs, as well as in industry to ensure that they know the practical application of their field of knowledge. At the end of their training they may have a student teaching experience. Throughout this training there is an emphasis on teachers learning the content of their teaching and the underlying theories behind it. In this way, it is expected that they will be prepared to impart the knowledge their students need.

Thus, the Russian teachers participating in RWCT were educated in a system that emphasized educational psychology and educational philosophy much more than it did pragmatic classroom methods. Russian teachers are well-versed in educational theory, and program participants were therefore naturally curious to speak with their American counterparts about the theoretical bases of RWCT.

U.S. Teacher Education Programs

Unlike the Russian system, teacher education in the United States occurs at the college and university level, and it rests on three underlying principles. First, U.S. teachers are expected to have a well-grounded foundation in the liberal arts and sciences, theories of learning, and content-specific pedagogy, which results in a liberally educated teacher (Reynolds, 1992); thus, U.S. teachers typically regard themselves as less specialized in their content area than their Russian counterparts. Second, teachers in the United States are increasingly expected to be reflective practitioners who continuously examine not only their understanding of schools, students, and learning, but also the content to be taught and the pedagogical concepts and practices best suited for the diverse student population in today's schools. A third principle supported by researchers and teachers alike is the adage that while "research informs, teachers teach." Even in the midst of high-stakes testing and accountability, these principles guide the content and classroom experiences of novice teachers in teacher education programs throughout the United States.

During the 1960s and 1970s, teacher education in the United States saw a gradual movement away from rigorous academic preparation and toward more emphasis on the teaching process and student learning. There has been, however, a long-standing tradition that supports a strong liberal education foundation at the university level. The emergence of the Holmes Group in the 1980s helped to renew this commitment among private and public liberal arts colleges and universities. Many teacher education programs currently require their teacher candidates to complete an arts and science university major in addition to professional studies in teacher education.

The second principle, reflective practioner, is also an important feature of the professional education of U.S. teachers. To become reflective practitioners, teachers must think about their teaching in terms of objectives, content, assessment, and results. They consider what is appropriate, what is manageable, what is practical, and what will be the consequences of their informed decisions. In the words of Reichert (1990),

> The ability to think about what one does and why—assessing past actions, current situations, and intended outcomes—is vital to intelligent practice that is reflective rather than routine—reflection influences how one grows as a professional by influencing how successfully one is able to learn from one's experiences. (p. 525)

Although it is true that university teacher educators emphasize the theoretical basis for an instructional strategy or approach to student learning, U.S. teachers are more concerned with positive instructional outcomes and how to best achieve those outcomes. They may be intrigued by the theoretical explanation for their students' improved reading comprehension, but they are more interested in practical strategies that promote improved comprehension.

The emphasis on the practical aspect of teacher education is apparent when looking at the teacher education programs of the 1990s of which early and varied classroom experiences in schools have become the cornerstone. Not only are novice teachers spending more time in classrooms as they complete teacher preparation programs, but their cooperating teachers are teaching courses in the programs, and university faculty are teaching and spending more time in the school classrooms. These professional partnerships are intended to elevate the importance of the clinical or practical training that preservice teachers receive in the classroom and validate the theoretical tenets espoused by education professors. The National Council for Accreditation of Teacher Education has recently adopted many of the practical outcomes that result from classroom experiences as indicators of the success of teacher education programs (NCATE, 2000). Thus, although Russian teacher education programs generally de-emphasize practical training in favor of content and theoretical sophistication, U.S. programs increasingly value practical, hands-on experience over the theoretical.

Russian Insights:
Learning to Appreciate Practical Methods

When the U.S. volunteers first presented the critical thinking methodology to the Russians, many participants were skeptical about the lack of emphasis on theory. The Russian tradition is rich in theory. Many of the major influences in Russian teachers' educational practice have been theorists whom teachers studied in their training. In fact, it is rare to meet a Russian teacher who cannot explain in great depth the educational theorists who have influenced teaching and learning in his or her country.

From the start, the first group of Russian participants wanted to find the common areas between RWCT and the Russian educational experience. It soon became evident that the main ideas of RWCT turned out to be consonant with the ideas of the best Russian theorists. Many Russian theorists, for example, have emphasized the need for an "activity approach" for cognitive development, and they stress the need for students to regulate their own actions in order to achieve higher levels of thinking. These theorists' writings, however, have not been translated into practical teaching applications. Therefore, Russian teachers came to regard the ideas in RWCT as concrete strategies they could adapt for use in their classrooms. Russian participants also understood that the logic behind RWCT—the movement from the particular to the general (from the lesson to the analysis)—was not caused by a neglect of theory, but rather was based on sound psychological understanding: Anything new is accepted through personal involvement with the topic in question and through the emotional attractiveness of the material presented.

Russian participants grew interested in other aspects of RWCT as well, especially in its potential to motivate students more actively to read and write for their own purposes. Russian teachers saw in the program an opportunity to begin to reverse the declining interest in reading. In the 1970s, Russia was considered to be a country where people read a lot; in trams, buses, trolleys, and metros, every third passenger was reading a newspaper, a magazine, or a book, and this habit of reading in transport is still very popular in Russia. The words of the famous Russian writer Maxim Gorky used to be very popular: "All the best in myself I owe to books." Today, in Russia as around the world, the situation is different. Children prefer television cartoon shows and teenagers prefer computers. This makes it more and more difficult for teachers to keep students engaged in books. Many students do not like to read or do not want to read. Students are less familiar with serious literature, especially the classics. The active learning methods promoted by RWCT offer classroom approaches to reading that may cause students to want to read more on their own.

The same has been true for writing. Not so long ago the attitude toward writing was very close to Russian attitudes toward real art. In Russian the same word (*pis'mo*) is used to indicate a letter written to somebody as well as the process of writing. In its first meaning, *pis'mo* is gradually becoming extinct because this means of communication is used less and less. Technical progress has destroyed the culture of writing. One can use the telephone or send a laconic e-mail message. The increased attention RWCT brings to the writing process may help students to find deeper satisfaction in writing, and therefore encourage them to write more.

Although Russian educators are concerned about the reading and writing interests and skills of their students, they have had few concrete strategies to develop these skills and interests, which are viewed as critical for the next generation of Russians. RWCT was viewed by project organizers in Russia as an important vehicle for teachers to learn a variety of strategies to develop the thinking abilities of their students.

At this writing, the project in Russia is entering its fourth year of implementation. It has become an integral part of many teachers' professional lives. These teachers use the framework for critical thinking in their lesson planning, and they have tried many of the strategies and modified them as necessary to fit Russian contexts. The universality of the RWCT framework and of the strategies, as well as the availability and efficiency of the ideas offered, has been impressive for many participants. Teachers, parents, and administrators are influenced by the comments they hear from teachers who attend workshops and use the strategies at various levels. Teachers in Novosibirsk, for example, have offered these comments in response to their training:

> After this session, I want to try this new methodology. I do not know why, but I want to live again.

> I've replenished my knowledge of new methods and positive emotions. I want to work again!

> My view has changed on the inside world of children.

> I'll give children more opportunity to talk and to learn by themselves. They can grasp material, discussing information in pairs and groups.

> Children like to predict, to ask questions of each other. Children do not want to leave such lessons; they want more time.

> Most of all, I've been impressed by the changes in students. Children have liked to write. Before only three or four students liked to do this. Now all 20 do it. They have not been afraid to tell their opinion. They like to work in pairs and groups. They want to help each other to understand.

When someone offers teachers effective ways to improve education for students, teachers everywhere respond with enthusiasm. Russian teachers were no different. They were appreciative of the concrete strategies, which provided a framework for organizing lessons that are effective and not complicated. Many of the teachers in the second wave have done their best to learn these methods and use them in their practice. As teachers have tried and used these strategies, other teachers, parents, and school administrators have expressed their desire to learn more about the program.

U.S. Insights:
Articulating a "Practical Theory" for RWCT

Just as time and experience have led the Russian participants to adapt to the differences and to embrace the opportunities offered by RWCT, so too the American volunteers have begun to articulate more often and more fully the theories behind their approach. The experiences in cross-cultural collaboration with Russian educators have challenged the U.S. educators to clarify their statements of theory. Throughout the 4 years, dialogues between Americans and Russians have been lively—full of questions and debate. RWCT participants from Russia came into this project both curious and apprehensive. From the beginning, they raised issues about the theory behind RWCT: Did RWCT have a well-elaborated theoretical basis? Although they found the strategies useful, this question about theory continued as an undercurrent throughout the 4 years of training. Encouraged by their Russian colleagues' questions, the RWCT volunteers have sought to articulate the "practical theory" behind the program.

In many Russian classrooms, as in classrooms across the 24 countries where RWCT operates, an authoritarian teacher dominates, and students too often are expected merely to memorize lecture information. Students stand and recite when called on to answer teacher-posed questions. One participating teacher commented that she had never been asked for her opinion during her entire schooling.

Given this context, the roles of students and teachers require a major paradigm shift if students are to become active thinkers. Careful planning, consistent attention and reflection, plus strong professional support are all required. As RWCT volunteers sought to respond to their Russian counterparts' call for an elaboration of the theoretical base of RWCT, they emphasized four points:

1. Students need confidence in their own voice to articulate their ideas.

2. Students need to respect their peers and consider their reasoning.

3. Students need to understand that texts (and other authorities) contain arguments that have voice, point of view, and evidence.

4. Teachers must be reflective practitioners who constantly evaluate how they teach and make adjustments accordingly.

Students Need Confidence in Their Own Voice to Articulate Their Ideas

In contexts where students have not been encouraged to think for themselves, teachers need to model, as well as encourage and reinforce student thinking and sharing of experience. For many students even finding the words to express their own thoughts in school settings may take effort. Developing confidence in sharing those thoughts requires a secure environment (Gardner, 1991; Pressley, 1987, 1992).

This first step is essential if students are to think critically. When they have confidence that their thoughts and experiences contribute to their understanding of concepts, they can use their own prior knowledge and experience to construct deeper learning. We know learning requires active construction on the part of the learners (Dewey, 1902).

Trusting one's own ideas also means being willing to articulate them and to provide rationales for them. This elaboration on one's point of view or experience lays the groundwork for evaluation of alternative possibilities. Articulating one's own ideas also involves learning to express them in ways that an audience can connect with and understand (Calkins, 1994; Murray, 1985). It also means being willing to modify these ideas once we gain new information. This may sound simple, but for students who have never had such experiences in schools, being asked to share their ideas and opinions can be intimidating. Classrooms need to be safe and supportive for such transformations to occur.

Students Need to Respect Their Peers and Consider Their Reasoning

The second point of discussion recognizes that it is important for students to develop respect for the ideas and experiences of other classmates. Not only do students need to articulate and value their own ideas and experiences, they also need to value the voices of others. In the classroom this means learning to listen to and respect the contributions of classmates (Bruner, 1983). As students listen to their peers share ideas, they begin to realize that each person sees only a portion of all possibilities in interpreting and constructing meaning. In the best situation, the learners become eager to balance their own meaning with that of others and to seek alternatives. They ask, "What did you think about this? Why did you respond like that?" They are not satisfied with a single voice, but realize the richness that comes from shared learning. Understanding and valuing the richness of different voices contributes both to a more open-minded learner and a more humble thinker who realizes the limits of any one perspective (Barell, 1995; Johnson, Johnson, & Holubec, 1994).

The U.S. volunteers experienced a particular area in which this sense of shared meaning was not generally valued—the teaching of literature. During a Great Books discussion, Russian participants became frustrated —they wanted the correct interpretation of the text, not a series of individualized opinions about it. (See Temple, Chapter Three of this volume, for an account of a similar experience in Romania.) Part of this orientation can be traced directly to the system of high-stakes testing in place in Russia. Students are evaluated on knowing *the* correct interpretation of literary works. Literature lessons traditionally conclude with the teacher telling the students the one correct, official interpretation. Only the right answer counts. In fact, during a workshop with teacher educators in St. Petersburg, one woman commented, "I think these thinking strategies can work well in most content areas—except for literature." So we both need to consider the importance of students respecting each other's ideas and of teachers valuing students constructions of meaning as we develop this foundation for critical thinking.

Students Need to Understand That Texts Contain Arguments That Have Voice, Point of View, and Evidence

The third foundation for critical thinking is understanding that texts and lecturers reflect a voice and point of view. With this understanding comes the need to go beneath the surface presentation to ask questions of authoritative voices; to understand the messages more fully and to evaluate their content (Rosenblatt, 1978; Costa, 1985; Beck, Mckeown, Hamilton, & Kucan, 1997). Again, this foundation requires a paradigm shift, because in Soviet life there was generally only one official position tolerated.

We can begin examining text by asking for more information about the authority and experience of authors. Understanding the contexts and purposes for writing contributes to understanding. Comparing different texts on the same topic can help readers understand there may be neither right nor wrong but different points of view. Examination of the arguments and evidence becomes important as learners think more deeply about their own conclusions.

Teachers Must Be Reflective Practitioners Who Constantly Evaluate How They Teach and Make Adjustments Accordingly

A teacher who wants to nurture critical thinking must be a reflective practitioner, and the ultimate success of RWCT in Russia may rest on the ability of Russian teachers to develop these habits of mind. To become reflective practitioners, teachers consider what is appropriate, what is manageable, what is practical, and what the consequences will be of their informed decisions. It is vital that teachers think about what they do and why they do it (Brown, 1991; Goodlad, 1984; Shulman, 1986; Schon,

1987). These reflective practices influence how one grows and changes and prevents stagnation in a classroom; should RWCT strategies become used as a rigid prescription for a thinking classroom, with little change over the next several years, they will accomplish little. The reflective teacher is one who continues to seek ways to teach more effectively. Of course, one becomes reflective only with the support and continual feedback of one's peers. Networks of support and vehicles for the exchange of ideas and experience will aid in the development of reflective practices. (See Chapters Four, Five, and Six of this volume, for more on the theoretical base of teacher reflection.)

Final Thoughts

The discussions between U.S. and Russian colleagues in RWCT have caused us to understand each other more fully and to articulate our own positions more carefully and more fully. After 3 years of mutual work and talk, Russian participants are more tolerant of the "action first, analysis later" approach of RWCT, and many have become convinced that the practical teaching strategies of RWCT serve genuine needs in the Russian context in ways that are compatible with the teachings of Russian educational theorists. Similarly, the U.S. volunteers have worked to spell out the theoretical underpinnings of their practice more fully. In this context, both Americans and Russians have been pushed to examine their own thinking and experiences and to try again to create bridges of understanding among our education professionals. We certainly continue to rethink and revise our own "voices" as part of this collaboration. The task before our group is daunting, considering the enormous changes that are underway in Russia and the vastness of the country. We hope that our initial work together has served to overcome some of the difficulties in the road ahead.

Authors' Note

The authors are grateful for the assistance of Olga Varshaver, our translator, and Sergei I. Zai-Bek, a colleague who provided additional insights.

REFERENCES

Barrell, J. (1995). *Teaching for thoughtfulness: Classroom strategies to enhance intellectual development.* White Plains, NY: Longman.

Beck, I.L., Mckeown, M.G., Hamilton, R.L., & Kucan, L. (1997). *Questioning the author: An approach for enhancing student engagement with text.* Newark, DE: International Reading Association.

Brown, R. (1991). *Schools of thought.* San Francisco: Jossey-Bass.

Bruner, J. (1983). *Child's talk: Learning to use language.* New York: Holt, Rinehart & Winston.

Calkins, L. (1994). *The art of teaching writing* (2nd ed.). Portsmouth, NH: Heinemann.

Costa, A. (1985). Teaching for, of and about thinking. In A. Costa (Ed.), *Developing minds.* Alexandria, VA: Association for Supervision & Curriculum Development.

Dewey, J. (1902). *The child and the curriculum.* Chicago: University of Chicago Press.

Gardner, H. (1991). *The unschooled mind: How children think and how schools should teach.* New York: Basic Books.

Goodlad, J. (1984). *A place called school.* New York : McGraw-Hill.

Holmes Group. (1990). *Tomorrow's schools: A report of the Holmes Group.* East Lansing, MI: Author.

Johnson, D.W., Johnson, R.T., & Holubec, E.J. (1994). *The new circles of learning: Cooperation in the classroom and school.* Alexandria, VA: Association for Supervision & Curriculm Development.

Murray, D. (1985). *A writer teaches writing* (2nd ed.). Boston: Houghton Mifflin.

NCATE. (2000). *NCATE 2000 Standards.* Washington, DC: National Council for Accreditation of Teacher Education.

Pressley, M. et al. (1987). *What is good strategy use and why is it hard to teach? An optimistic appraisal of the challenges associated with strategy instruction.* Paper presented at the annual meeting of the American Educational Research Association, Washington, DC.

Pressley, M. et al. (1992). Encouraging mindful use of prior knowledge: Attempting to construct explanatory answers facilitates learning. *Educational Psychology, 27*(1).

Reynolds, A.C. (1992). What is competent beginning teaching? A review of literature. *Review of Educational Research, 62*(1), 1–35. Washington, DC: American Educational Research Association.

Riechert, A.E. (1990). Teaching teachers to reflect: A consideration of program construction. *Journal of Curriculum Studies, 22*(6), 509–527

Rosenblatt, L. (1978). *The reader, the text, and the poem: The transactional theory of the literary work.* Carbondale, IL: Southern Illinois University Press.

Schon, D. (1987). *Educating the reflective practitioner: Toward a new design for teaching and learning in the professions.* San Francisco: Jossey-Bass.

Shulman, L. (1986). Paradigms and research programs in the study of teaching: A contemporary perspective. In M. Wittrock (Ed.), *Handbook of research on teaching* (3rd ed.). New York: Macmillan.

Lessons for Educational Reform From the RWCT Project

Lessons From Abroad: What North American Educators Can Learn From Central and Eastern European Education

Patricia L. Bloem

> We must all learn many things from you [Americans], from how to educate our offspring and how to elect our representatives, to how to organize our economic life so that it will lead to prosperity and not poverty. But this doesn't have to be merely assistance from the well-educated, the powerful, and the wealthy to those who have nothing to offer in return. We, too, can offer something to you: our experience and the knowledge that has come from it.
>
> Václav Havel, 1989, Address to Joint Session of U.S. Congress

As my fellow RWCT volunteers suggest in other chapters of this book, North American educators have much to learn from the teachers and schools of Central and Eastern Europe and Central Asia. Charles Temple (see Chapter Three of this volume) speaks of high levels of achievement in literacy, mathematics, and science in Eastern European schools. Alison Preece and her coauthors (see Chapter Seven of this volume) describe the deep commitment teachers in Macedonia exhibit to the notion that educating students in critical thinking is essential for the formation of citizens of democratic cultures and open societies. Nearly all of the chapters speak with awe and admiration for the professional competence and personal integrity of our colleagues from the RWCT host countries.

In this chapter, I aim to extend and amplify the lessons I believe educators in North American schools can learn from the experience of their counterparts in Central and Eastern Europe and Central Asia. During my 3 years of involvement in the RWCT program, I have tried to describe the strengths of these teachers and schools to students in U.S. universities, to teachers in local schools in Ohio and Michigan, and to professional colleagues in other U.S. teacher education programs. In this chapter, I offer four lessons that I have learned from my experiences in the Czech Republic that are applicable to the schools and teachers in my region of the United States. Although my fellow volunteers might point to different strengths and different lessons than the ones I offer here, I have tried hard, as President Václav Havel of the Czech Republic urged Americans to do, to listen to the experience and the knowledge Central Europeans have to offer.

These are tough times for U.S. schools. Headlines shock with horrific stories of school children killing other children during the school day, and editorials lament the test scores of the country's youth. In the teacher's lounge, educators discuss their frustration over state-mandated tests and having to teach a test-driven curriculum. Parents and politicians share a dim perception of public education.

How odd, given this context, that 40 North American educators, mostly teachers of teachers, were invited in 1997 to lead workshops and to work closely with classroom teachers throughout nine countries of Central and Eastern Europe and Central Asia through the Reading and Writing for Critical Thinking (RWCT) project. Along with many of my RWCT colleagues, I wondered, given the magnitude of our own troubles, why would we go?

In discussions among ourselves, program volunteers have offered several answers. Most volunteers go because we believe in the importance of critical thinking in forming democratic citizens. The ideas on which the program is founded—ideas from Dewey, Vygotsky, Freinet, Rosenblatt, and Gardner—have wide applicability. Despite the fact that our own school systems have monumental problems and do not universally promote active reading and writing, we believe the powerful methods of critical thinking will help to create independent thinkers no matter where they were born. Thus most program volunteers are actively promoting their use of these methods on both sides of the Atlantic Ocean.

But a second reason for participating gets at the heart of this chapter: We go to this part of the world because we have a terrific amount to learn from the Eastern European teachers and from their efforts to reform their school systems. For those of us who have worked in the Czech Republic, it is especially obvious that these teachers are benefiting from centuries-old traditions that respect learning and the arts. In particular, I argue that we can learn from our Czech colleagues in four areas: First, American teachers should compare and contrast our attitudes toward reform to those of Czech teachers so we can see the limitations of the defensive stance we often take toward our schools. Second, we can learn from the Czech tradition of a focused role for the classroom teacher. Third, American educators can reflect on the traditions of Czechs and other Central and Eastern European cultures of respecting knowledge. Finally, we can learn from their experience of shaping a democracy through education.

Let me make two frank acknowledgments before I develop these ideas. Of course it is true that, just as in the United States, one can witness extremes of good and bad teaching in the Czech system, sometimes in adjacent classrooms. Authoritarian teaching in which careful memorization of facts was the highest order of thinking was part of the milieu out of which our Czech participant teachers have come, and many of them have joined the program because of their desire to stop replicating the kind of education they themselves endured. As in most countries, one can find disheartened and burnt-out teachers, ineffective administrators, ill-equipped classrooms, and chronically inadequate budgets. But theirs is also a system of many accomplishments—one that excels in such experiential learning as sending children to the mountains for nature camp once or twice during the school year; one that ranks highest in the world in math and physics for middle school students; and one that creates a highly literate population.

Further, I want to acknowledge that comparisons between one country's educational system and that of another are at best unreliable and usually unfair and false, because educational systems grow from different histories, different constraints, and different purposes. Thus one country's success may not be replicable in another country, and teachers from around the world may have vastly different ideas of what it means to teach and teach well. Take, for example, the Eastern European way of thinking about theory. One of the often repeated stories shared among RWCT volunteers is of a Russian teacher, engrossed in a lively presentation and discussion of a critical reading strategy, who stood up and exclaimed, "OK. I can see that it works in practice. But will it work in theory?" The North Americans grinned with delight. Too many of us had been familiar with the reverse; after our meticulous working out of theory, a student or colleague rolls his eyes and asks us please to get practical. North American teachers of K–12 are famous—infamous may be a better term—for wanting workshops that tell what to do on Monday morning. Too often North Americans want practical information and give little thought to foundational underpinnings. Our entire system of selecting, training, supporting and rewarding teachers has contributed to this pragmatic mind set, and I do not believe that we can realistically apply practices from another system that would rest on a wholly different set of behaviors and values.

Clearly, attitudes and cultural circumstances between Czech and American teachers vary widely and needs are different. For example, North American teachers need to address diverse populations, while the Czechs, fearful of being devoured as a small nation among giants, need to hang on to what is truly Czech. But much is the same too: Schools in both countries have learned how to make a little money stretch a long way; both must fight aliteracy and the lures of passive television viewing; and both must learn new ways to enlist and involve parents in the cause of literacy and learning. If we can get away from vacuous comparisons, we are in a better position to learn from each other's experiences.

Embracing Positive Attitudes Toward Change

The media on both sides of the Atlantic Ocean have commented on the disillusionment that citizens of the former Soviet bloc feel about the slow pace of reform. Certainly Czech teachers are frustrated that they have not found solid leadership on various levels of government, business, and education. They share the fear that their fledgling democracy may never soar. However, our Czech colleagues express resolve and enthusiasm in their newly acquired freedom to make choices. For example, 10 years ago every secondary school student throughout the country had an independent reading assignment to read from a prescribed canon of required books set out for his or her grade level. Now, teachers are free to follow the list or not, depending on student needs. Likewise, the country's education ministry officials are moving away from their myriad regulations, allowing more professional freedom for classroom teachers. Not so long ago, every grade-level teacher in the country was required to teach the same page of the same textbook on the same day. Now, teachers have a great deal more latitude in deciding what and when and how to teach.

Of course, in the old system the required books were readily available, while today, teachers interested in change must be innovative and resourceful in finding the necessary resources. And, ironically, teachers feel restricted by the lack of decision making experience and by their paucity of teaching strategies. Many long for role models and say, "We only know one way to teach." Many feel little confidence that they know what is best for their students and can create a constructive learning environment for them. Yet when they try to create new patterns for learning in their classrooms and see the galvanizing effect it has on student learning, they are charged up, ready to try again, determined that their students will have a better and different education than they experienced.

Slowly, Czech teachers are learning new ways to work together with their peers. New professional teaching organizations are springing up. One such group, the grass-roots school reform organization Přátelé Angažovaného Učeni (PAU; loosely translated, Friends of Engaged Learning), is an energetic group of people who are pushing for reforms. The teacher as an agent for change is an exciting idea in Central and Eastern Europe. The tone of the October 1998 PAU Conference (for all levels of educators, elementary through university) was positive, encouraging teachers to revise their own teaching, to explore new territory, to influence others in their schools, and to help to craft their own vision to direct the flow of reform.

The contrast between such a group and its North American counterparts is stark. As Patrick Shannon (1990) pointed out, the history of progressive educators—those who promote child-centered pedagogy and who base their thinking on Dewey, Freire, Vygotsky, and Freinet—has always been troubled, but our current moment is especially noxious. He quotes a discouraged teacher documenting her lack of freedom to plan and implement literacy lessons that she feels will best serve her students:

> You know and I know we work in a straitjacket.... In [our district] they call [the reading program] a whole language program. We use the basals four days and then have an out-of-basal day.... They say "innovate," "don't use all the workbook pages," "make decisions," "you're in charge." But then they turn right around and tie our evaluation to basal tests. You can't pass those tests without using the basal.... My students start out behind, and the basal keeps them behind, and they never catch up. It's terrible.... But all we do is more of the same—more basals, more skills, more tests.... The message from them [the administrators] is clear—no matter what they say: "Use your basal; it's your fault if the students don't learn, it's you who [are] failing your students." (pp. 179–180)

The teachers in the area in which I live would not even agree that their administrators pay lip service to the idea that they, the teachers, "are in charge." In some buildings teachers are given a script to follow during reading instruction. A middle school teacher expressed regret at not being able to participate with his eighth graders in an international literature exchange project: "They've inserted so much into my curriculum—like a new career unit—that I can barely teach the one novel I think is most important." Many teachers are appalled but comply when they are told that they must teach to the test. Students throughout Ohio and other U.S. states spend hours of school time preparing to take a series of tests that determine whether or not they are promoted or graduate. Teachers work diligently with students, and hope they will succeed, yet are aware that they are not allowed to make the final decisions. Stated Tierney (1998),

> In the name of educational reform, legislators have returned to a form of educational accountability that relies on objective tests.... This practice is having an alarming impact on the current generations of students in schools and on the professionalism of their teachers—an impact justified more on the basis of legal defensibility and technical efficiency than on learning goals, ethical considerations, or regard for issues of social equity and justice. (p. 20)

Thus many American teachers are struggling to respond in a hostile work environment, not setting the agenda for change but responding to criticisms and to an imposed agenda, not on the offense, but rather, on the defense. The president of the National Reading Conference (Ruddell, 1998) pleaded that scholars and teachers "resist politicians' attempts to define our field," and urgently asked that our voices stop the floodgates of noneducators defining our work for us. She is right to ask, because teachers typically do not jump into the political fray. States one fourth-year teacher, "We teachers agree that we don't like what is happening with certain aspects of our educational society. I hear (my own voice included) all the usual excuses for why we can't do anything about it...but I feel when the time is right, I will be able to state my thoughts in a clear and influencing manner.... I am also thinking that the time for this possibility to occur will not be far off."

However, even as our profession encounters serious public criticism, American educators can be heartened and inspired by the attitudes toward change we have witnessed abroad. Beleaguered we may be, but teachers can find a way to shape our own visions.

Focusing the Teacher's Role on Academics

North Americans need to learn from a commitment to a streamlined role for teachers. Czech teachers teach the academics. Many of them work 5 or

6 hours a day, and that time is confined to what our colleagues refer to as "teaching the lessons." True, elementary school teachers may incorporate art projects into the classes, or they may take the students out to the grass or the parking lot to play an occasional game of ball or jacks, and many teachers eat lunch in the cafeteria with their students. But school is for academic education, and teachers are meant to focus on the lessons.

There are other arrangements for what Americans tend to think of as "the extras," and people other than the academic teachers run those programs. Throughout the Czech Republic as well as in other countries throughout Central Europe, there is an old and well-developed system of arts schools separate from regular public education. Typically, young elementary school children (up to Grade 4) spend about 5 morning hours in school with very little of that time spent on "specials" of art, music, or gym. Parents then have an option of enrolling their child in after-school care—a program of homework, games, field trips, crafts, and physical education—or in a sports program or an arts school.

After-school programs are organized around the classroom unit, and especially in elementary schools, they include most members of a class on most days after school. The students might climb on the trolley and visit a nearby museum, then return to the classroom for a homework session and board games. On warm days they might finish homework first, then walk to a nearby park and play for several hours. These programs are not staffed by the academic teachers but rather by the after-school staff, which includes mostly women hired for the afternoon sessions.

Older students have a 6- or 7-hour school day and an even stronger attendance rate at the special schools. Typically in the Czech Republic, these include sports programs and education in the visual arts, music, or drama, but Hungary is known for its "singing schools" that train children and adolescents with a sophistication similar to the schools for choir boys in England. The arts schools were—before the changes—staffed by professional musicians, visual artists, and theater people, not the regular classroom teachers. Under socialism, the cost to parents for these special programs and schools were negligible, but now these schools are struggling to figure out how to continue. The commitment is strong to maintain them if at all possible. At least to Western eyes, the arts seem to permeate these children's lives, especially urban children who are regularly exposed to museums and galleries and dramatic productions.

Czech schools themselves are about academic education, not everything else. The education establishment in the Czech Republic has created other institutions to handle the "extras," although many Czechs would not categorize sports, music, or art as extras, but rather as other essential skills and endeavors that they want their children to engage in. This delineation of educational tasks allows teachers to focus more clearly on teaching, on the curriculum, and on student achievement. The central task of the classroom teacher, thus, is to concentrate on core academic subjects; he or she is not drawn in a dozen directions. Schools have a focused and manageable mission.

This is quite different in the United States, where schools are asked to do it all. U.S. schools provide not only the 3R's, but also visual arts; choral, band, and orchestral music; drama; a myriad of sports for both sexes; career counseling; driver's education; training in peer mediation; and before- and after-school programs. In fact, we seem to be developing momentum for our schools to take over more aspects of our daily and communal lives, from early morning day care to evening parenting classes, to Saturday school and summer school. Michigan high school principal Bill Chilcutt points out that especially for the poor, American schools have taken on responsibilities formerly held by families, including providing meals, sex education, driver's training, and basic discipline. Former Cleveland, Ohio, principal Venerine Branham uses the word *diluted* when she describes the overall educational mission of schools. Because of all the roles that schools must play, we now expect that teachers are adept at a large variety of skills.

Certainly we can not replicate the Czech system unless there were other institutions to pick up many of these roles. Given our political realities, perhaps schools are the only viable institution to provide these services. But the legacy of the Czech system has two points worth analyzing. One is that the role of the teacher is not stretched so broadly that teachers feel that they are responsible to do it all, not obligated to so many roles. To apply this in the United States might mean that the school as an institution may take on more dimensions, but that the classroom teacher will be able to focus more narrowly on his or her primary function. Second, for the Czechs the academic institutions are not the only source for education in town. Burdened American teachers could take comfort in a truth that the Czechs have woven into the fabric of their society—that schools are just one vehicle for education—that the education offered by school stands in contrast to lessons learned through family and home life, through community life in after-school programs, and in schools of the arts and sport programs.

Valuing Knowledge

We need to learn how to value knowledge. In 1992, when I enrolled my son in a public Czechoslovak third-grade class (before the Czech and Slovak Republics split in 1993), his teacher and I realized that the language barrier would impede much of his learning for at least the first semester. But she was determined that he could do any numerical work any other child could do. She also was merciless in her literature assignments. If the other children were required to memorize and repeat "Lastovičky," a 19th-century Slovak poem considered a national treasure, my son would too, despite the fact that the only thing he could tell me about the words he so carefully repeated was that the poem was about a bird. Although this teacher's attitude may not have been universally Czechoslovak, it was representative of the teachers in that school, who for good or for ill and sometimes both, pushed their students to absorb information. The students, as my son's teacher had decided, needed to memorize those old touchstones, just as their parents had labored over memorizing the same lines. Why? First, the poem was part of their cultural heritage; second, memorizing demanded a discipline that would serve her students well; and third, in her professional judgment, it was a good thing for them to have this knowledge.

A U.S. college teacher, writing in response to an e-mail message on Hungarian education, wrote "I have always found the focus on straight memorization to be appalling. But, interestingly enough, I have found myself rethinking that position. Our stress on critical thinking and creativity has been great—except now I'm getting students who don't know anything and view critical thinking as uneducated reactions! So they can't think critically nor do they know the information. I don't think it bodes well for the future of our country" (L. Seward, personal communication, 1998). American teacher Ralph Fletcher (1999) espouses a teaching practice that he calls "marinating students in literature." By contrast, former Soviet bloc schools have valued the pedagogy of "marinating" students in *knowledge*—in facts, ideas, books, theories, concepts, names, dates, places. Because the easiest way to gain knowledge is by reading, they assign difficult and demanding texts, essays, and philosophical reading rarely found in U.S. schools.

I do not mean to imply in any way that what is laudable is factology, the great emphasis of the educational establishment in the former regime on memorization and recitation of facts. Factology is exactly what has driven the participant teachers from the Czech Republic into the RWCT program, and it is what they want to avoid in their own teaching, even while U.S. politicians seem eager for factology and scientific management of education to take firmer hold in our country. Factology is not the answer for either system. But there has to be a balance between knowledge of the facts, blocks that you can build on, and ability to problem solve and employ reason. Students' minds need to be filled with knowledge as they become critical thinkers. They need not just decontextualized skills but a rich storehouse of materials with which to think.

Clearly my assessment of both systems reflects generalities, but frequently American classrooms sparkle when it comes to problem solving and application of reason and creativity. Americans need to learn from Czech teachers how to build deep funds of knowledge that come from valuing intellectual work, from reading widely and deeply, from respecting information, and from studying and learning with rigor.

Somehow both educational systems need to find a balance, and both can borrow from each other. Conventional wisdom might show that U.S. schools should study how the Czechs have achieved their outstanding rankings in worldwide comparisons of math and science education. A *San Francisco Chronicle* article reports,

> In the Third International Math and Science (TIMS) Study, the worldwide examination that provoked deep controversy in America over U.S. students' abysmal scores, formerly communist countries dominated the upper standings. The Czech Republic, Slovakia, Slovenia, Hungary, and Bulgaria were among the Top 10 participants in the study, finishing neck-and-neck with Asian standouts such as Singapore, South Korea, Hong Kong, and Japan. The United States, France, Germany, and Britain lagged far behind. What makes this performance all the more impressive is a second feature of Czech education: The industrial world's best educational system is also one of its cheapest. Americans spend just under $7,800 per student annually on their public school systems. Czechs spend barely one-third of that amount. (Viviano, 1998, p. A1)

Although these are admirable statistics, there are many reasons to question them. Quantitative international comparisons are often suspect, and as a society, we need to read the results of most quantitative norm-referenced tests with skepticism. When a number of RWCT volunteers and participants discussed the high scores of Czech high school students, a Czech high school math teacher, a brilliant educator, shook her head and said, "Yes, there are a few who achieve great scores. But, oh, how many of our students hate math." Her comment needs to be heard too in the attempt to find the needed balance. Discussions of process versus product or traditional versus progressive education always seem to degenerate into simplistic ways of looking at complex issues. I suspect that the answers for both systems will lie with Dewey (1938), who distrusted ideas of education that formed dichotomies: "The fundamental issue is not of new versus old education nor of progressive against traditional education but a question of what anything whatever must be to be worthy of the name *education*" (p. 90).

Part of the difficulty Americans have in valuing knowledge is valuing the person who has that knowledge. The United States has an anti-intellectual climate, where politicians and generals, athletes and business executives are viewed as heroes. In an old section of Prague, on the other hand, high on a hill overlooking the city, lies a beautiful cemetery with ornate headstones and art nouveau sculpture. The cemetery is the destination of many school field trips, as teachers acquaint their students with the intellectual giants of their culture. Famous Czechs are buried there, people held in great esteem, such as the composers Dvořák and Smetana and the artist Mucha. There, in the most prestigious cemetery of the capital of the Czech Republic, are artists, educators, historians, even a grammarian, but not a single politician or military leader. The Czechs value their intellectual and artistic leaders along with the knowledge they have brought to the world. Do U.S. children even know the names much less sing the praises of the intellectual leaders of the United States?

Linking Teaching to Democracy

Finally, Americans can learn from the way the Czechs tie their talk and action of school reform to the cause of democracy. The Czech RWCT participant teachers recognize that the way we teach our children makes a difference to the kinds of citizens we graduate. Certainly part of the reason it is difficult for Americans to see the big picture is that their population and geographic boundaries are much larger than the Czech Republic. Nonetheless, for the sake of shaping the country's future, we would do well to make the connections between pedagogy and citizenship. What is necessary for sustaining a democracy is a citizenry capable of self-reflection, tolerance, power sharing, critical thinking, and responsibility—all qualities RWCT participant teachers want desperately to be addressed in their schools so that they do not repeat the mistakes of the last 40 years. How they teach and how children learn, they believe, matters to their country and will shape its future.

There is not one pedagogy of democracy, yet there are many styles and ways of teaching that are undemocratic and stand in opposition to what citizens of a democracy need. Every country that wants able adult citizens who vote responsibly needs classrooms of children who learn to read and listen critically, who analyze well, and who can use their critical thinking skills in service of their country. A country that want its citizens to be capable of clear, independent thinking and able to resist manipulation must expose its children to pedagogy that builds these habits of mind.

Formerly a playwright whose absurdist plays were thought to be so dangerous that he was repeatedly jailed, Václav Havel was one of the leading dissidents in communist Czechoslovakia. In 1989, he became president and his photograph was hung in every Czech classroom. His words are powerful beacons for what it means to think about education and democracy:

> We cannot blame the previous rulers for everything, not only because it would be untrue but also because it could blunt the duty each of us faces today, that is the obligation to act independently, freely, reasonably, and quickly.... Freedom and democracy require participation and therefore responsible action from us all. (1997, pp. 4–5)

If the United States is to remain a strong democracy, Americans also need to talk about the connections between our political lives and the ways we educate our children. We need to become articulate about the need for critical thinking, for pedagogical changes, and for the support public education deserves. Public school bashing has become something of a trend, and Rose's *Possible Lives* (1995), McQuillan's *The Literacy Crisis: False Claims, Real Solutions* (1998), and others have shown us how destructive that bashing has been. Perhaps we need to make explicit the connection between how we teach and what kinds of citizens we produce by taking the offensive against those politicians and members of the public who would reduce teaching and learning to rote exercises, who define higher order thinking as passing standardized tests, and who fail to see that it is a school's business to help students to argue with tolerance, to think critically, to form solid judgments, to learn from each other, and to reflect—all tasks that take away time from the state proficiency tests.

Final Thoughts

The RWCT team in the Czech Republic often comments that it is a shame that we cannot shake up the Czech and the U.S. systems of education, and come out with a blend that puts our combined strengths into a new balance. At present the Czechs are learning much more about American values in education than vice versa. In her introduction to a collection of poetry from around the world, Naomi Shihab Nye quoted a letter from a writer in Bangladesh. "We try so hard to know what people are writing in the United States—do people in your country try as hard to know about us?"(1992, p. xii). The question could have been asked just as easily by a Czech, and the answer still would be no.

Just 2 months after becoming president, Havel addressed a joint session of the U.S. Congress, speaking the epigraph that opens this chapter. Several years have passed since then, and the Czechs clearly have learned a great deal about reorganizing their communal, economic, and political lives, and about educating their children in ways that begin to address their need for new citizens. Now it is time to look at what they offer us. Their gifts of experience and the knowledge gained from it are ours to treasure.

REFERENCES

Dewey, J. (1938). *Experience and education.* New York: Collier.

Fletcher, R. (1999). Teaching the craft of writing. *Primary Voices, K–6, 7*(4), 41–43.

Havel, V. (1997). *The art of the impossible: Politics as morality in practice.* New York: Knopf.

McQuillan, J. (1998). *The literacy crisis: False claims, real solutions.* Portsmouth, NH: Heinemann.

Nye, N.S. (1992). Introduction. In N.S. Nye (Ed.), *This same sky: A collection of poems from around the world* (p. xii). New York: Four Winds Press.

Rose, M. (1995). *Possible lives.* Boston: Houghton Mifflin.

Ruddell, M. (1998, Dec. 6). Keynote address, National Reading Conference, Austin, Texas.

Shannon, P. (1990). *The struggle to continue: Progressive reading instruction in the United States.* Portsmouth, NH: Heinemann.

Tierney, R. (1998). Testing for the greater good: Social injustice and the conspiracy of the proficiency standards. *The Council Chronicle, 8*(2), 20.

Viviano, F. (1998, April 21). World's top test scores not enough for Czechs: Top thinkers seem to belong to West. *San Francisco Chronicle*, p. A1.

CHAPTER THIRTEEN

An Experiment in Boldness: Accomplishments and Challenges in the Reading and Writing for Critical Thinking Project

David J. Klooster

If you have built castles in the air, your work need not be lost; that is where they should be. Now put the foundations under them.

from H.D. Thoreau, 1855, *Walden*

Despite all the optimism expressed and all the initial success celebrated in the preceding chapters, can we say that the Reading and Writing for Critical Thinking (RWCT) project is really as good as it appears? Can it be possible that in 3 short years, teachers' pedagogical practices have been transformed, the atmosphere in classrooms has turned into something completely different, obstinate educational systems have begun to change, and valuable lessons have been brought home to illuminate our own school problems? Or have the program participants created a kind of "castle in the air," a fantasy that cannot stand? If the program is something of a chimera, can a foundation be built under it? Or could it be that the optimism is justified and that the successes are real? While we await the results of a recently launched program assessment conducted by an independent external evaluation team (Heyman & Evans, 2000), we can venture some in-progress assessments of what has been accomplished and what remains to be done. This chapter will look back on the past 3 years, and will peer ahead to try to discern what the future might hold for the RWCT program.

But where does our story begin, and where does it end? Did it begin in those extraordinary days in 1989 when the world thrilled to opening borders and falling walls in Central and Eastern Europe? Every morning in the autumn of 1989 it seemed we would turn on the morning news to hear of another miracle: borders open in Hungary, the Berlin Wall dismantled in Germany, a "Velvet Revolution" in Prague, and a more violent one in Bucharest. More miracles followed: The Baltic nations broke away from the Soviet Union and the other republics gained their independence soon thereafter, and before we could catch our breath, maps were redrawn, new countries emerged from old ones, bitter nationalistic rivalries were re-ignited, and former enemies declared new friendships.

Or does the story begin, as it often does in RWCT lore, when the Minister for Education of the Slovak Republic traveled to Iowa in the early 1990s to ask a simple but profound question: How can we teach democracy? (Temple, 1997). His question signaled a new awareness of the roles of schools in Central and Eastern Europe and Central Asia. No longer legitimate as tools of official ideology, schools began actively seeking new roles, new methods, new curricula, and new leaders. With the urgent need for schools to play a new role in society, educators throughout the former Soviet bloc countries opened their minds to new collaborative possibilities with colleagues from the West, as well as from neighboring countries in Europe.

Another beginning of the story can be found in predecessor projects. Steele and Meredith's Orava Project emerged in response to the Slovak Minister of Education's provocative question about how to teach democracy (see Meredith & Steele, 2000). An ambitious and comprehensive teacher development program, funded by the United States Agency for International Development (USAID), the Orava Project demonstrated convincingly that the fundamental beliefs that would later inform RWCT could be effective and adaptable in the schools of a nation that was shedding its communist past and striving for a market economy and a democratic culture. The Orava Project also proved that a program that begins small can expand quickly, widely, and successfully if responsibility for the program is rapidly handed over to new generations of trainers from the host country, and if these new trainers are prepared thoroughly and mentored carefully. Similarly, the Reading for Understanding program in Romania, a pilot program of the International Reading Association and the Open Society Institute, demonstrated that workshops conducted by visiting North American educators can be welcomed by teachers and parents in Eastern Europe as a vehicle for school reform. Both of these programs demonstrated that innovative strategies for teaching reading and writing could make a significant impact in countries engaged in the transition from socialism to democracy. (See also Steele, Chapter One, and Meredith, Chapter Two in this volume, for further discussion of RWCT's origins.)

Certainly the stories told in this volume can be traced to a very concrete beginning in the astounding generosity of George Soros and the Open Society Institute, whose resources of money, expertise, support, and vision made the program possible. We can also mark beginnings in the willingness of the International Reading Association and its leaders to sponsor the project and to encourage its members to volunteer to be workshop leaders. For most of the authors represented in this book, the beginning of the RWCT story took place in the late spring of 1997, when with little information but plenty of adventurousness, they signed on to be volunteers in RWCT and gathered for an initial meeting at Lake Balaton, Hungary (Temple, Meredith, Steele, & Walter, 1997). For many, after a day or two in the company of their host country colleagues, they knew the story would be a fascinating one.

In the dozen chapters that precede this one, the project participants have told their stories. The narratives have been full of concrete detail to give the flavor of the experiences, and they have offered a chorus of voices —teachers, students, workshop leaders, project coordinators—all singing the praises of a coherent framework for teaching and learning, new teaching strategies, new understandings of the power of teaching, and new friendships. All the stories concur that the project is an unusually bold one—ambitious in its scope, profound in its intended impact, courageous in its people. RWCT is indeed an experiment in boldness.

Even though the story of RWCT is far from over, we need to reflect now on what has been accomplished and on the challenges that lie ahead. We need to assess what a program of this magnitude can realistically expect to achieve in the coming years.

At this writing, the RWCT project is beginning its fourth year of operation. Nine countries have completed the originally funded cycle of 3 years of workshops and dissemination and institutionalization activities. Nine more teams in eight countries have completed the first 2 years of the project; an additional three country groups have completed 1 year, and four new countries are poised to join the RWCT network in 2001. Hundreds of workshops have been held in 20 countries, thousands of teachers have attended, and hundreds of thousands of school children have experienced a new kind of teaching in their classrooms. What lessons can be gleaned from this massive undertaking that may benefit other professional development programs in other settings?

The Major Accomplishments of the RWCT Project

Breadth and Depth of Influence

As a participant-observer in RWCT, I am struck first by the significant influence in the classroom life of large numbers of teachers and students. The region of the world in which this program operates is vast, and the population of the first 20 countries to participate in RWCT is enormous—according to UNICEF (1998) there are over 400 million people in this region, with nearly 100 million school-age children. Yet even in the short span of 1997 to 2000, RWCT has succeeded in reaching a significant number of classrooms. Concrete statistics are not yet available to us, but project organizers estimate that in these 3 years, 15,000 to 20,000 teachers have already experienced professional development workshops focused on critical thinking (Temple, 2000). If we take a very conservative figure of just 25 students per teacher (in some countries the average class size is much larger, and secondary and university teachers reach many more students than 25 each year), we can estimate that at least 375,000 to 500,000 students have experienced something new in their lives in the classroom because of RWCT. Because the dissemination mechanisms of the program work to bring increasing numbers of teachers into the program each year, we can expect that the number of participating teachers will continue to grow rapidly in the coming years. Within a year or two, the number of teachers involved will exceed 50,000, and the number of students influenced will pass 1 million.

In each of the 24 RWCT countries (see maps, pp. xiv-xv), the project begins modestly, with 25 to 35 teachers gathering for workshops 4 times per year. After each workshop, participants return to their own classrooms and practice using the strategies they have learned in lessons with their own students. Using the "train-the-trainers" model (Meredith & Steele, 1995) in which initial workshop participants themselves become workshop leaders after 1½ years, these "first generation" participants become trainers of a "second generation." With careful mentoring and guidance, these beginning workshop leaders typically expose between 100 and 200 new teachers to the program in the second year. In turn, a portion of these second generation participants themselves become trainers, spreading critical thinking strategies to as many as 1,000 teachers in the "third generation," and thus the program expands exponentially in a short time. Especially in the smaller countries in the region, such as Lithuania, Macedonia, and Albania, RWCT has proven itself to be able to assemble a critical mass of teachers to make a significant impact on the culture of education in a country in a short period of time. The task in larger countries is, of course, more complicated, but participants remain optimistic that as workshops proliferate, as new textbooks and other publications are written, and as the program works its way into teacher preparation and development institutions, the active learning and critical thinking methods of the program will contribute in meaningful ways to the educational reform efforts in every country involved. Although the smaller countries can be "covered" in three or four generations of the project, the larger countries will need additional time to offer enough workshops for the professional development of an adequate number of teachers.

It is not just the large numbers of teachers and students touched by the program, however, that is impressive. The depth of influence is even more remarkable. As teachers and students report on their experiences through the program, I am struck by their intensity of feeling and depth of commitment. For example, a teacher from Romania writes, "RWCT has been a very rewarding, exciting, dynamic experience—something I have never experienced before in my life." A teacher from Lithuania notes, "I've changed not only my teaching methods but also my understanding of teaching and learning as a result of RWCT." A participant from the Republic of Georgia comments, "I saw teachers changed personally and professionally. I will try to share this program with every colleague in my country." Another notes, "This project changed my teaching role. I feel more positive," while a teacher from Macedonia says, "My success has been the opportunity to interact with professionals in countries in addition to my own and to share common goals and concerns for children. There is a strong thread of hope and positiveness." The project coordinator in Armenia states, "Teachers mention that RWCT has dramatically changed their lives and classrooms. Each workshop is like a celebration of a big event in their lives." Another teacher comments, "I discovered myself as a *teacher* and helped around 200 teachers to discover RWCT."

For the volunteer workshop leaders in the program the impact has also been profound. Beyond the rewards of travel to remote lands and the chance to expand one's circle of professional colleagues, the program affords the opportunity to reexamine fundamental beliefs about teaching. All of us who have had the privilege of volunteering in RWCT have become acquainted with exceptionally gifted educators from abroad who have challenged us to think more deeply and to articulate our values more clearly. In turn, we have been influenced deeply by their ideas, their commitment, and their ingenuity. We have learned a great deal about effective teaching. One U.S. volunteer writes, "The most valued aspect of the program for me has been the impact on my own professional life. As a college teacher my teaching now always includes critical thinking strategies. I am committed to this model even though pressures in the U.S. are towards more accountability." Another writes, "I've made more positive changes in my teaching in the time I've been with RWCT—3 years—than in the first 17 years of my career." (All quotations in the preceding two paragraphs come from a freewriting exercise at the Conference on Transforming Teaching and Learning, Kesthely, Hungary, June 30–July 4, 2000.)

At the conclusion of the first year of the program, teachers in many of the countries were asked to reflect on their experiences, and their extended responses provide an important view of how the RWCT program affects participating teachers. A representative sample of such reflections comes from Latvia, where teachers were asked about the influence on their personal lives, their professional lives, and their students (Kalnina, 1999). Among their responses were these:

> This year has been a revolution in my life. I feel the changes not only in my attitude toward work at school, but also toward life itself. I have become more natural, bolder. I have gained optimism and self-assurance. But the main thing: Now I am ready to listen and accept different viewpoints even though they are radically different from my opinion. With this it is easier for me to find contact with people. This has left positive impacts on my relationships with other people and with my family.

Another writes,

> I am really happy to be one of the participants in this project. I have become more self-assured, more natural. I can find strength to overcome despair. Our common work helps me to be more understanding, more tolerant, more benevolent.

When these teachers were asked to describe the influence of the program on their professional lives, one wrote,

> My teaching methods have changed. The main stress in my work is now on the student, the development of his skills. My professional activities have

become more purposeful, more disciplined, better collected and clearer. I have made the material I teach simpler, closer to everyday life and more human. Thus the relationships between the teacher and the students have changed as well.

Another notes,

I have gained more assurance in my professional ability. A number of ideas and methods I used rather chaotically and intuitively now have joined in a particular system. I have started to love some of the teaching strategies, I do not like some others, but I have this wonderful feeling: I want to do, I can do, I do!

A Compelling Model for Professional Development of Teachers

A second clear accomplishment of the program evident after the first 3 years is the success of the model of professional development RWCT employs. With remarkable uniformity across geographical and cultural divides, the RWCT workshops have been received enthusiastically by participants and evaluated positively by observers. I would point to seven key elements of the model of professional development in RWCT that have led to this success:

1. **A shared sense of mission to meet urgent needs in the region, and a shared understanding that continuous school improvement is necessary everywhere.** Because of the enormity of the social, political, economic, and cultural transformation in the region, the need for school change is clear to observers from within the countries and from without. Although the nature of the changes required may not yet be fully understood, the RWCT program was able to find relatively broad consensus that active learning, independent thinking, tolerant behaviors, and applied knowing were important elements of the required paradigm for learning. Because the educational needs of the region are pressing, educators from diverse backgrounds were highly motivated to cooperate and to work unusually hard for success. Furthermore, almost all participants understood from the beginning that continuous improvement of schools is a high priority in all countries. Rather than viewing the program only as a North American solution to school reform, especially because, as several authors in this volume note, North American schools are far from ideal, RWCT volunteers and partici-

pants understood the program as part of a progressive movement that crosses national boundaries. After an initial getting-acquainted period, North American, European, and Asian educators were able to join together in a quest to help create educational systems better than those that exist anywhere. Our work was cooperative and mutual, because all our countries—and all our students—shared similar needs.

2. **A sustained 3-year program and staff development model that fosters deep understanding of new approaches to teaching and that provides time for new teaching practices to become habitual.** Genuine change in the classroom behaviors and values of a teacher takes a long time. Although traditional inservice education consists of a day or two of workshops with little continuity from one course to the next, RWCT provides a pedagogically coherent and theoretically sound series of professional development workshops extending over a year or more, with ample opportunities along the way for support, reflection, and encouragement. Because the new values and methods are reinforced in multiple ways over the course of the program, teachers have the chance to make critical thinking methods a regular part of their own classroom approach and a deeper part of their students' experience. One reason RWCT has succeeded is because the program provides teachers with the time they need to achieve real change.

3. **A culture of support to uphold teachers who are making demanding transitions.** Research has shown that teachers engaged in the change process need rich networks of support and encouragement (Bloem, Newton, Williams, Peck, & Duling, 1998), including mentoring, regular celebrations of success, honest reflections on difficulty, and the nurture of a team attitude among participants. Through a system of monthly meetings, frequent workshops, classroom visits, reunions, and conferences, RWCT has provided multiple opportunities for teachers to be supported in their work and encouraged to persist in their efforts to change their classrooms. Although traditional teaching can sometimes be a lonely business, allowing few opportunities for teachers to converse with professional colleagues, RWCT has succeeded in part because it has made extensive "shop talk" among teachers one of its regular and treasured activities.

4. **A lean set of administrative structures that allows the program to operate efficiently and does not impede adaptation to local circumstances.** Educators everywhere are familiar with intransigent educational bureaucracies that move at the speed of glaciers and seem to inhibit change whenever possible. So far RWCT has managed to avoid creating excessive layers of administration, and the program has fostered a culture of rapid development and an expectation that the program will adapt to local contexts wherever it goes. Participants from both sides of the Atlantic Ocean are sometimes dazzled by the speed of progress within the program, but the kind of success the program has enjoyed is only possible when participants are empowered to act independently and are not hindered by a conservative bureaucratic system. Of course, when there are few administrators, each one must be superb; there is no place for the incompetent to hide. RWCT was blessed with outstanding project coordinators in our host countries, men and women of genuine talent and boundless energy. Without their creative thinking and hard work, the program could never have prospered.

5. **Inclusion in the workshops of participants from all levels of the educational community, including teachers, university faculty members, pedagogical institute staff, and Ministry of Education officials.** If you put a group of university teachers in a room together and ask them to analyze what is wrong with education, they will quickly agree that the primary and secondary schools are not doing their jobs; if you gather teachers from secondary schools, they will soon concur that the primary schools are at fault. Because RWCT intentionally gathered teachers from every grade level—as well as principals, inservice trainers, and government officials—in its workshops from the start, this kind of finger-pointing and shifting of responsibility to others never developed. Instead, teachers from various levels learned to enjoy the company of educators from across the spectrum of every kind of school and from throughout the educational establishment. They rolled up their sleeves and got to work. Because they could not blame others for what was inadequate, all educators were forced to reflect carefully on the problems their schools faced.

In addition, the varied educators in the workshops were able to work cooperatively on a range of projects. New partnerships emerged in projects such as team teaching, model schools, laboratory schools for colleges of education, conference presentations, and joint publications. Participants formed diverse teams to present workshops to new generations of teachers; often a university professor paired with an elementary school teacher, or a secondary teacher and a principal joined forces to work together. Teachers learned that their similarities were more important than their differences across grade levels, and they joined in their common work with good spirits.

6. **A dissemination model based on the participants' capacities to deliver the program in their own countries.** Another quality of the professional development model embedded in RWCT is the conviction that every teacher in the first generation workshops has the ability to become a leader of the new generations of participants. This transfer of responsibility from visiting foreign colleagues to school teachers within the country itself helped to create a sense of responsibility and ownership. Participants in the first round of the program made a serious 3-year commitment to the program, and as a result they approached their work with an uncommon level of intensity and responsibility. In this model of professional development, no one sits as a passive recipient of others' good ideas. Everyone engages in the process of preparing for the next level of involvement.

7. **Institutionalization of the program into the educational fabric of each country through inservice centers and universities.** For the professional development of teachers to continue over the long term, no system can rely on outside funding and outside experts. Instead, professional development has to become a routine way of organizing the systems of teacher preparation, supervision, and reward. RWCT volunteers and participants began talking early about the ways they could find new institutional "homes" for the program within the pedagogical faculties of universities and other elements of preservice education of teachers, as well as within the administrative structures that oversee the work of teachers. The results of such efforts vary from country to country, depending in large part on the openness of the Ministry of Education and the receptiveness of teachers and administrators within universities. But the need has always been evident that for RWCT to flourish in the long term the program must find sources of institutional support and nurture in the existing components of each nation's educational infrastructure.

Envisioning Schools as an Element of Social Transformation

The most significant accomplishment of the RWCT program, in my view, has been the clear vision it has provided to program participants and host-country educators of the connection between schooling and social transformation. Our colleagues in Central and Eastern Europe and Central Asia had developed in a context in which education served to preserve and extend the ideological and social control of the existing regime. So overt was this agenda of ideological control that many universities employed a Dean of Ideology whose job was to ensure the "purity" of all courses. Our colleagues in Western countries were most accustomed to thinking about education as a process of personal, individual development, more or less divorced from political concerns. All of us who have participated in the program have come to new insights about the role of education in producing *citizens*. We have seen and are investigating anew the relationships schools have to family, community, and workplace. Although we have not made democracy and social transformation the leading point in our workshops, it has become increasingly clear to many of us that relationships and abilities developed within schools are inextricably linked to individuals' behavior as citizens and community members beyond school.

With a keen sense of the extraordinary historic moment in which we live, as governments are transformed from authoritarian socialism to fledging democracies, educators from various countries have joined to investigate the roles of schooling to promote open societies and democratic cultures. As colleagues from East and West, we have felt both unusually privileged and deeply responsible to see change on both an international and a personal scale unprecedented in human history. Although educators may be most familiar with their role as custodians of the past, as accountants for what has already happened in human affairs, the RWCT program has provided its participants with the opportunity to participate in and even to contribute to the changes currently taking place in the world. From this experience is emerging a set of ideas about the relationship of school and society. It will take many years to theorize this relationship fully, but we can begin to name some of the principles involved:

- Democracy is best taught by creating genuinely democratic classroom practices for students to experience and discuss.

- For citizens to acquire the complex set of skills, attitudes, and knowledge to function successfully in a democratic culture, schools must provide abundant opportunities for students to practice democratic behavior.
- Tolerance for the ideas of others and responsibility for one's own ideas are essential democratic virtues that can be nurtured by teachers with appropriate classroom teaching strategies.
- In our current era of the information explosion, schools cannot provide students with all the knowledge they will need, but instead must equip students to become resourceful producers and critics of knowledge so they can become responsible members of their communities.
- Factual knowledge without critical attitudes and abilities is lifeless; critical ability without a foundation in factual knowledge is pointless. To serve democratic culture effectively, schools must nurture both deep learning of facts, ideas, and theories, and the critical attitudes and abilities to work independently with that knowledge.

What Lies Ahead for RWCT in Central and Eastern Europe and Central Asia?

Challenges in Sustainability and Institutionalization

From the beginning, program organizers and participants recognized that the 3-year external funding resources from the Soros network required the program to quickly find its own sources of support and its own institutional homes. After 3 years, to those who know it best the program still feels delicate and at least a bit vulnerable. Despite the valor and dedication of teachers in our host countries, the program is still new, and it faces significant challenges in sustainablity. If indeed RWCT is a "castle in the air," our most pressing task, as Henry David Thoreau suggests, is to "build a foundation under it" so that our work will not be in vain.

The initial rounds of workshops allowed teachers to gather in a modest hotel or conference center for a weekend, and they experienced the luxury of having meals provided, a comfortable workshop room prepared, and transportation costs reimbursed. (We discovered another commonality among the world's teachers: Female teachers everywhere work double shifts—one at school and one at home. To have basic domestic needs attended to by others for 4 weekends during the year was a genuine pleasure for many workshop participants.) For teachers earning a subsistence wage, such treatment as professionals was enormously uplifting. Subsequent rounds of workshops will work with dwindling budgets, and may require a larger contribution from teachers themselves (remember that in some countries, teachers' meager salaries may not even be paid for months at a time). Project coordinators in the host countries have been paid through Open Society funds, but now many are scrambling to secure the funding that will allow them to continue to provide leadership and organizational skills in the program, even as the program is at its most ambitious phase of growth. Such forced independence will ultimately be healthy for the program as it grows away from its external funds and finds its natural, native support, but the transition period is fraught with difficulties for teachers and leaders who are already taxed by heavy workloads in their regular jobs.

In the first group of nine countries (Albania, Romania, Czech Republic, Lithuania, Estonia, Russia, Macedonia, Kazakstan, and Kyrgyzstan), the RWCT project is engaged in the process of finding a satisfactory new home. In some countries, RWCT will be institutionalized through university departments of education or faculties of pedagogy. In other countries, Non-Governmental Organizations (NGOs) are being formed to host the project. In a few, the Ministry of Education has already embraced the project and has pledged its support. Yet throughout the region, economic conditions are strained, and the prospects for significant financial backing for this fledgling program are extremely limited.

Compared to other school reform initiatives, RWCT is an inexpensive program. It does not rely on additional equipment, textbooks, or published resources beyond its eight guidebooks. The teaching methods are designed to fit within existing classroom structures and curricular offerings. The program has an exceptionally lean administrative structure, and it makes responsible use of volunteer help. Nevertheless, even the relatively modest requirements for financial backing will be difficult to procure in the coming years.

Maintaining Program Integrity While Encouraging Freedom and Adaptation

In its first "generations," RWCT has succeeded in large part because its core values and practices have been delivered with remarkable uniformity across cultural and geographical divisions. The initial group of North American volunteers were carefully prepared in the summer of 1997 to provide consistent workshop experiences in all nine first-year countries. As individual differences, new generations of leaders, and cultural variations increasingly influence the delivery of the workshops, the program will need to work diligently to assure that the core value of RWCT remain intact.

In the summer of 2000, a set of standards was disseminated among program participants to describe the desired classroom behaviors and professional activities of RWCT participants (Mathews et al., 2000). The standards spell out the requirements for three stages of certification: as workshop participants, as RWCT teachers, and as RWCT trainers. Combining such assessment techniques as classroom observations, portfolios, and a structured interview, the certification standards seek to assure consistent definitions of RWCT practices, and their authors hope the standards will help prevent a loss of integrity or consistency as the program spreads.

At the same time, a highly valued feature of RWCT is its adaptability to local customs, cultures, and people. The program adapts easily to the personalities of its leaders, to local opportunities and constraints, and to available resources. While project organizers and funders are understandably concerned about maintaining the integrity of this enormous cross-national program, many participants are equally concerned with their ability to make the program fit local circumstance and address local needs. These two valid concerns—integrity and adaptability—need to be held in some sort of productive tension for the program to prosper as a lively international movement.

Rapid Systemic Change—In Some Places

As we look to the future, we can foresee that in some countries—for example Macedonia, Latvia, Lithuania, Estonia, Albania, and Armenia—there exists a real possibility that within a fairly short span of 5 to 8 years, the full educational system will adopt and institutionalize new approaches to teaching and learning, and RWCT will be one important element in this reform. In these countries with a relatively small population (3 to 5 million), a fairly homogenous culture, a clearly recognized and widely shared need to change, and enlightened leaders in the Ministry of Education, large-scale change can happen relatively quickly. This change does not depend so much on the availability of significant economic resources as it does on the ability of educational leaders at every level to motivate teachers to work for new purposes with appropriate classroom methods. Many participants are convinced after 3 years of work in the project that such countrywide reforms in education, though not yet accomplished, can realistically be envisioned.

Of course, in many other countries the RWCT program cannot yet foresee countrywide influence. The strained economic conditions of school life across the region prevent many educators from dreaming big dreams. As is the case in most Western countries as well, entrenched bureaucrats tend to care more about perpetuating their own power than in making genuine improvements in schools. Several countries (especially Russia, but also Kazakstan and Romania, for example) are so large that it will take many years to train a critical mass of teachers to implement a program of the scale of RWCT. In other countries, the political and social life remains so chaotic that the conditions for reflection and action do not yet exist. So while we remain optimistic, we are also realistic that significant and lasting change remains distant for some of our colleagues.

A Network of Support

One reason RWCT so frequently succeeds in its early generations is that it builds in a system of support and encouragement for program pioneers. Teachers feel able to take the risks required to achieve genuine change in their pedagogical practices because they are supported by like-minded colleagues in a system of reflection, problem solving, and celebrating successes. If this kind of support works well at the local level, can it also function internationally?

One promise for the future lies in the growing network of teachers and educational leaders from across more than 24 countries who work together for educational reform on an international level. From 1997 to 2000, the Open Society Institute has sponsored a summer gathering in Hungary of participants from the RWCT program, and these meetings have been marked by optimism, insight, and joy. Although we have barely begun to envision the power of our shared experience and commitment, RWCT participants find a profound sense of awe in one another's company, and this sense of enormous talent gathered around common purposes may someday grow into a force for influence and direct action across international lines. The new professional journal *Thinking Classroom*, published in both English and Russian, will help to support the exchange of ideas across the RWCT network and beyond in coming years.

Conclusion

In the fourth district of Prague in the Czech Republic, a small public school sits in a greenspace among towering apartment blocks. As one enters the nondescript building, the first impression is of vibrant color and an undercurrent of purposeful noise. The walls are lined with students' artwork—tempera paintings, ceramic figures of fish and small animals, paper maché masks. From the open doors of classrooms comes the murmur of many voices—small groups of students engaged in a multitude of tasks. In the fourth-grade classroom of Blanka Stanková, a first-generation RWCT participant, students gather in a circle on a carpet below a wall of windows. They take turns recounting favorite details from their recent field trip to an historical site, and then Blanka sends them back to their bright orange desks to begin revising their narratives of the trip. "Your stories need more vivid details, so that your readers can really see and smell and hear what you experienced," she says. Our interpreter whispers to us, "This is amazing. When I was a student 10 years ago, the only writing we did was to take dictation from the teacher. Every student 'wrote' precisely the same story." After 10 minutes of independent writing, Blanka offers a minilesson on writing good titles for stories, and students immediately apply the lesson as they compose a list of 10 titles from which to choose. Next students work in peer editing groups to look for sharp details and to react to their preliminary titles. Blanka, a soft-spoken woman with a confident demeanor, listens in on various groups, offering encouragement or clarification as needed. The 28 students, mostly dressed in jeans and T-shirts, are clearly well accustomed to this mix of full-group discussion, small-group work, and teacher instruction; they work with evident pleasure and informal ease.

A group of observers circles the room. The principal of the school has been so impressed with Blanka's teaching that she has organized her teaching staff schedules to allow regular peer observation in the classroom. Three of Blanka's fellow teachers have come to observe this writing workshop, and all 15 teachers in the building have experienced all or part of the full RWCT program of workshops. In addition, Blanka has teamed with a second-generation participant, Professor Anna Tomková of Charles University in Prague, to create a new kind of experience for preservice teachers. Five students from the university have come to Blanka's classroom not only to observe but also to tutor individual students and sometimes to lead a lesson. They use dual-entry diaries to aid their observations, and they practice kidwatching and other informal assessments.

In Blanka's classroom we can see a number of the successes of the early years of the RWCT program. A teacher already skillful and accomplished before she joined the program, Blanka now works with confidence and pleasure, using progressive methods of instruction in a coherent system of instructional strategies. The child-centered classroom offers multiple opportunities for all learners to excel and to share with their peers the fruits of their learning. Because the teacher is excited about her new approaches to teaching, she willingly passes her new knowledge along to colleagues. In turn, she is supported in her own continuing development by colleagues and administrators interested in and knowledgeable about her work. In partnership with other educators from her area, she is working to ensure that new teachers will be able to see and to practice new pedagogical approaches even before they enter their own classrooms for the first time.

RWCT began as a teacher-to-teacher exchange, a chance for teachers to work together in close and informal settings to achieve change in individual classrooms. It began with a group of teachers so convinced of the value of their framework for teaching and learning and of their practical strategies to promote critical thinking that they wanted to share their knowledge with colleagues. It turned out not to matter very much that the workshop leaders and program participants came from different countries: Their commitment to change was infectious, and the needs of their students were similar everywhere. As the program has developed over its short life, meaningful relationships and sustainable networks have begun to emerge. These networks of support promote educational reform beyond individual classrooms, even across national boundaries. Certainly the volunteers in the program have taken home valuable lessons about children, schools, and teachers to illuminate their own work. Without question, teachers in the 24 RWCT countries have benefited from the opportunity to reflect in a sustained way about their own practice. Their shared experience provides hope that educational reform may truly become an idea without boundaries.

Author's Note

The author wishes to thank the following people, whose stimulating conversation contributed to the ideas presented here: Evangeline Newton, Kurt Meredith, Jim Wile, Sarah Nixon-Ponder, and Ondřej Hausenblas.

REFERENCES

Bloem, P., Newton, E., Williams, L., Peck, J., & Duling, V.P. (1998). When teachers change alone: Case studies of literacy teachers in a non-supportive school environment. In E.G. Sturtevant, P. Linder, J. Dugan, & W. Linek (Eds.), *Literacy and community: The 20th yearbook of the College Reading Association* (pp. 231–242). Commerce, TX: College Reading Association.

Heyman, C., & Evans, A. (2000, July 2). *Understanding program effectiveness: Planning the fall 2000 RWCT evaluation.* Plenary session address, International Conference on Transforming Teaching and Learning, Keszthely, Hungary.

Kalnina, S. (1999). *Reflections after the first year, June 1, 1999. RWCT report.* Riga, Latvia: Open Society Foundation.

Mathews, S., Crawford, A., Temple, C., Silova, I., Balibana, C., Freimane, I., Preece, A., Smith, S., Hausenblas, O., & Firsov, G. (2000). *Project certification standards and procedures.* New York: Open Society Institute.

Meredith, K., & Steele, J. (1995). *Core teacher leader handbook for leading staff development.* Bratislava, Slovakia: Orava Foundation for Democratic Education.

Meredith, K., & Steele, J. (2000). *Orava Project 1994–1999: Educational collaboration for the 21st century.* Bratislava, Slovakia: Orava Association for Democratic Education.

Temple, C. (1997). Can literacy instruction teach democracy? A report from Slovakia. *The Reading Teacher, 50*(5), 438–440.

Temple, C. (2000, July 1). *Overview of accomplishments.* Plenary session address, International Conference on Transforming Teaching and Learning, Keszthely, Hungary.

Temple, C., Meredith, K.S., Steele, J.L., & Walter, S. (1997). *Report on the Reading and Writing for Critical Thinking Institute.* Cedar Falls, IA: Consortium for Democratic Education, University of Northern Iowa, Department of Education.

Thoreau, H.D. (1855). *Walden; or life in the woods.* New York: Penguin.

UNICEF. (1998). *Education for all.* The MONEE Project regional monitoring report, No. 5. New York: Author.

AUTHOR INDEX

SUBJECT INDEX

Page references followed by *f* indicate figures. References in *italics* indicate a map.

A

B

C

D

DEFINITION MAP, 56

DEMETER, REKA, 40

DEMOCRACY, 38, 177; concept of, 39; linking teaching to, 176–177; participatory, 105–106; teaching, 180, 189

DEMOGRAPHICS, 34

DESIGN: Principle of Unfolding Design, 4–5

DIRECTED READING-THINKING ACTIVITY (DRTA), 40; teaching case, 84–85

DISCIPLINE, 104

DISCOURSE PATTERNS, 123–124

DISCUSSIONS, 161–162

WALT DISNEY EDUCATION, 40–41

DISRUPTIVE STUDENTS, 88–89

DISSEMINATION, 18, 188

DOCUMENTING CRITICAL THINKING LESSONS, 82–93

DOCUMENTING INSTRUCTIONAL PROBLEMS, 84–86

DOMAIN LEARNING: Model of Domain Learning (MDL) viewpoint, 111–116; stages in, 111

DRTA. *See* Directed Reading-Thinking Activity

DUAL-ENTRY DIARY, 40

DUDESKI, JORDAN, 101

DYNAMIC CHANGE PROCESS, 15–16

E

EASTERN EUROPE, *xiv*; lessons for North American educators from, 166–178; schools in, 174. *See also specific countries*

EDUCATION: academic, 171–172; concept of, 39; Czech, 135, 175, 178; Czech language, 138–139; Czechoslovak, 174; Eastern European, 166–178; elementary level, 138–139; Georgian system, 123; Hungarian, 174; interactive, 38–47; in Kazakstan, 65–72; literacy, 38–47; Russian system, 30, 153–155; Soviet, 25–26, 152; and students' participation in society, 39; U.S. system, 155–157, 173; value of, 175–176; Walt Disney, 40–41

EDUCATIONAL REFORM, 28–31; in Estonia, 35; framework for change, 2–21; lessons from RWCT project, 165–196; school change, 3–4; students' reflections on school before and since RWCT, 59, 60*f*; Theresian reformation, 132

EDUCATORS. *See* Teachers

INSERT (Interactive Notating System for Effective Reading and Thinking) method, 12, 13*f*

INSERVICE: experience-based, 10–11; participant preparation for, 16–18

INSERVICE CENTERS AND UNIVERSITIES, 188

INSTITUTIONALIZATION, 18, 188; challenges in, 190–191

INSTRUCTION, 29; documenting problems, 84–86; rhetoric, 132–134; strategies for, 9–10, 90

INTEGRITY, 191–193

INTERACTIVE LITERACY EDUCATION, 38–47

INTERACTIVE NOTATING SYSTEM FOR EFFECTIVE READING AND THINKING (INSERT) METHOD, 12

INTEREST, 111

INTERNATIONAL BORDERS, 78–80

INTERNATIONAL READING ASSOCIATION (IRA), xi, 5, 180–181

INTERPRETIVE COMMUNITY, 43

INVENTIVENESS, 99–100

J

JEHE, SIRI, 56

JONES, DONALD: "As Best She Could," 43

JOURNALS, 52, 55; as coteachers, 57; excerpts, 56–57, 63, 76–77; trainer, 52

K

KALAMEES, KATRIN, 50

KARM, MARI, 55–56

KAZAKSTAN, *xv*, 24–25, 65, 191; educational practices, 65–72; history, 66–68; participation in RWCT project, 46; population, 66; public school policy, 69; "Soviet times," 70–71; systemic change in, 193; teacher reflection, 64–81; terminology, 64*n*

KHAN, GENGHIS, 66

KHRUSHCHEV, NIKITA, 67

KIDWATCHING, 194–195

KNOWLEDGE: marinating students in, 174; Model of Domain Learning (MDL) viewpoint, 111; shared ownership of, 122; Soviet damage to, 26; valuing, 174–176

KOSOVO, *xiv*

KUNANBAEV, ABAI (IBRAHIM), 66

O

P–Q

PUBLIC SCHOOLS. *See* Education; Schools

PUBLISHERS, 144

QUICKWRITES, 52

R

S

STUDENTS' LEARNING: MDL applied to, 114–116; situated motivation theory applied to, 119
STUDENT-TO-STUDENT TEACHING, 147
STYLISTICS, 130
SUMMER GATHERINGS, 193
SUPPORT: for critical thinking, 102–103; culture of, 186; network of, 193
SUSTANABILITY, 190–191
SYSTEMIC CHANGE, 192–193

T

TAJIKISTAN, *xv*
TARTU MUSIC SCHOOL, 59–60
TEACHER CHANGE, 125–126; in Estonia, 50–63; reflection as agent of, 50–63
TEACHER EDUCATION: MDL applied to, 113–114; Russian programs, 153–155; situated motivation theory applied to, 118; U.S. programs, 155–157
"THE TEACHER I WAS...THE TEACHER I'VE BECOME" ESSAY, 52, 58–59
TEACHER TALK, 76–77
TEACHERS: benefits of RWCT for, 182–183; changes in, 45, 49–128; confirmation from, 103–104; criteria for participation in RWCT project, 6; Czech, 169; elementary, 88–89; in Estonia, 82–93; first generation, 182; in Georgia, 113; journals as coteachers, 57; Kazakstani, 72–76; need for, 41–42; preparation for inservice delivery, 16–18; professional development of, 184–188; recognition of value of documenting instructional problems for, 84–86; reflection, 78–80; reflection by unpacking, 76–77; reflections on current situation, 69–72; reflections on experiences as trainers, 61; reflections on teachers they have become, 58–59; reflections on teaching, 70–71; as reflective practitioners, 162–163; relationships with students, 100–102, 184–185; responses to training, 159; risks for, 4; role of, 171–173; Russian, 82–93; salaries, 28–29; second generation, 182; self-evaluation, 162–163; "The Teacher I Was... The Teacher I've Become" essay, 52; third generation, 182–183
TEACHING: benefits of RWCT for, 184–185; changes observed in, 45; choosing strategies for, 90; extending strategies, 43–44; in Georgia, 113; linking to democracy, 176–177; participants' reflection on,